INSIGHT GUIDES

OMAN & THE UAE

APA PUBLICATIONS **L**
Part of the Langenscheidt Publishing Group

INSIGHT GUIDE
Oman & THE UAE

ABOUT THIS BOOK

Editorial

Project Editor
Dorothy Stannard
Editorial Director
Brian Bell

Distribution

UK & Ireland
GeoCenter International UK Ltd
The Viables Centre,
Harrow Way
Basingstoke, Hants,
RG22 4BJ
Fax: (44) 1256-817988

United States
Langenscheidt Publishers, Inc.
46–35 54th Road
Maspeth, NY 11378
Fax: (718) 784-0640

Worldwide
APA Publications GmbH & Co.
Verlag KG Singapore Branch, Singapore
38 Joo Koon Road
Singapore 628990
Tel: (65) 865-1600
Fax: (65) 861-6438

Printing

Insight Print Services (Pte) Ltd
38 Joo Koon Road
Singapore 628990
Tel: (65) 865-1600
Fax: (65) 861-6438

© 1998 APA Publications GmbH & Co.
Verlag KG Singapore Branch, Singapore
All Rights Reserved
First Edition 1998

L ike all Insight
Guides, this book is
a joint effort. It involved
a team of expert writers
and photographers, all
of whom are long-term
residents of Oman or
the UAE or established
authorities on particular
aspects of the region's
history or culture.

Oman and the UAE have been
popular destinations for expatriate
workers for several decades.
Following the oil boom of the
1970s, oilmen, engineers and
service personnel flocked here
from many different countries,
transforming the region almost
overnight.

Now, both countries are
becoming increasingly attractive
to ordinary travellers, who come
for R&R in superb hotels, lazy
days on white-sand beaches,
adventure travel in deserts
and wadis, and some of the
best duty-free shopping in
the world. Most attractive
of all is the distinctive and
exotic culture, which is full of
interesting contradictions. It is
not unusual, for example, to
see falcons on the arms of city
slickers or a Bedu armed to the
teeth browsing in Nizwa's new,
purpose-built *souq*.

How to use this book

The book is carefully structured to
convey an understanding of the
countries and their cultures and to
guide readers through their sights
and attractions:

◆ To understand the region, you
need to know something of its
past. The **Features** section covers

the states' history and
culture in lively,
authoritative essays.
◆ The main **Places**
section provides full
details of all the areas
worth seeing. The chief
places of interest are
coordinated by number
with full-colour maps.

◆ The **Travel Tips** is an easy
reference listings section with
information on travel, hotels,
restaurants, etc. Information may
be located quickly by using the
index printed on the back cover flap
– and the flaps are designed to
serve as bookmarks.

◆ **Photographs** are chosen not only
to illustrate the beauty of the
countries, but also to convey
their diversity and the everyday
activities of their people.

The contributors

The guide was
commissioned and
edited by **Dorothy
Stannard**, a managing
editor in Insight Guides'
London office who had
already commissioned
books on Morocco, Tunisia,
Jordan and Egypt. After working out
content and structure, she set
about finding a team of writers and
photographers who could fulfil the
Insight brief.

Covering most of Oman – the
Batinah Coast, Sur and the Wahiba
Sands, Nizwa and the Interior, and
Dhofar – is **Christine Osborne**, a
photojournalist who began her long
association with Oman in 1975
during the Dhofari War. Osborne
also contributed many of the
images in this guide.

Writing on Muscat, Oman's capital, is the journalist **Tom Athey**, who worked as the editor of *Oman Today* until moving to Dubai to work for Motivate publishing company. Athey also wrote the features on forts and camel racing, and compiled the Travel Tips on Oman. Completing the Oman Places section is the chapter on Musandam written by **Carl Phillips**, an archaeologist at London University who specialises in the region. Phillips also contributed to the chapter on Dhofar, the picture story on frankincense and wrote the essay on archaeology at the front of the guide.

The UAE places chapters were tackled by two UAE residents. **Ann Verbeek**, an art curator and historian before turning her hand to writing and editing, wrote the chapters on Abu Dhabi, Dubai, Ras al Khaimah and Fujairah, while **Matt Jones**, tackled Sharjah (where he lives), Ajman and Umm al Qaiwain as well as the short feature on wadi-bashing. He also shot some of the pictures for these

chapters. Jones, formerly a journalist with *The Gulf Today*, now works in PR for Emirates.

Contributors to the history and features section include **William Facey**, a director of The London Centre of Arab Studies, who wrote The Maritime Heritage and Islam in Southeast Arabia; **Alan Keohane**, a writer and photographer, who wrote The Bedu, Falconry and All that Glisters (jewellery), as well as contributing photographs; **Geoffrey Weston**, for many years the *Times* correspondent in the Middle East, who wrote The UAE From Rags to Riches, The Oil Boom, Tax Free Bonanza and the short profile on Sheikh Zayed; novelist and racing correspondent **Jamie Reid**, who contributed Kings of the Turf; and **Michael Gallagher**, the curator at Oman Natural History Museum, who wrote on Dhofar's birdlife.

The fascinating history of Oman was written by **Sir Donald Hawley**, who has had a long career in the Middle East. From 1958 to 1961 he was H.M. Political Agent in the Trucial States and from 1971 to 1975 British Ambassador to the Sultanate of Oman.

Completing the guide with Travel Tips for the UAE is **Jane Matthew**, whose long experience of living in Abu Dhabi and now Dubai was also mined for Daily Life and Expatriates, essays giving an insider's view of this intriguing region.

Map Legend

—— -- —	International Border
—— • —	Nature Reserve
✈	Airport
🚌	Bus Station
P	Parking
ⓘ	Tourist Information
✉	Post Office
☪	Mosque
	Castle/Ruins
∴	Archaeological Site
∩	Cave
★	Place of Interest

Main places of interest in the guide are numbered (e.g, ❶) to help you locate them easily on the maps. A symbol at the top of every right-hand page tells you where to find the map concerned. Please note: the maps in this guide are not an authority on international boundaries.

Contributors

Stannard

Osborne

Verbeek

Jones

Facey

Hawley

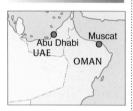

CONTENTS

Maps

Introduction

History

People and Features

Trading
anecdotes,
Dubai

Places

Travel Tips

A DIP INTO ARABIA

In spite of a shared culture, Oman and the UAE offer

quite different attractions for visitors

The most easy-going of the Gulf countries, Oman and the UAE are rewarding destinations for travellers. As increasing numbers of people are finding out, they are worth much more than the standard 24-hour stopover for duty-free shopping on journeys between Europe and the Far East. The two countries complement each another well. While upfront Dubai, Abu Dhabi and Sharjah offer great shopping, bustling waterfronts, dream beaches and sparkling high-rise hotels, Oman, more cautious towards tourism, offers exhilarating scenery, adventure travel and a taste of an older, pre-oil Arabia in its *souqs* and villages. Fujairah and Ras al Khaimah, two of the less well-known emirates, are also known for their scenic beauty.

The first section of this guide is devoted to the history and culture of southeast Arabia, with chapters on formative influences such as seafaring, Islam, and the Bedu, and features on life in the area today. This is followed by a region by region guide to Oman and a state by state guide to the UAE. At the back of the book, Travel Tips provides essential practical information, from visas and passports, business hours and money matters to recommended restaurants and hotels.

PRECEDING PAGES: hennaed hand; Friday *majlis* in Fujairah; beating drums; army band, Dubai; National Day celebrations in Oman. **LEFT:** in the shadow of a watchtower, Oman.

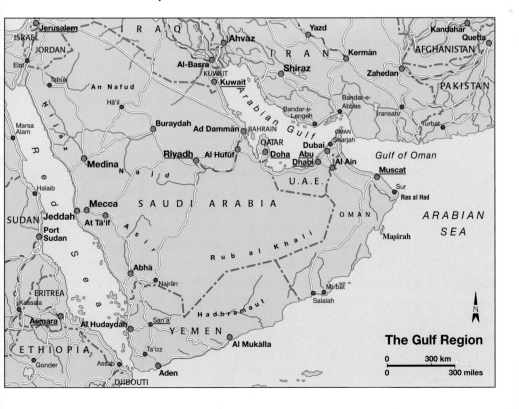

The Gulf Region

0   300 km

0   300 miles

Tabiana
Thapaua Oadi
Pharatha
rona
Rhaili vicus
Abucei
Satula
Coromanis
Sacor sinus
Apphana
Taxias
Obraca
Adari
chrona
Atamos poreus
Licaniees sinus
Gea ciuitas
Aina
Lugana Gersa
Thamydeni
Chersonesi extrema
Sinus
Leaniti
Mallada ciuitas
Athritę
Arre vicus
Digina
Saphtha
Ischam
Salma
Phigia
Ibriona ciuit
Tharo
Lieceni
Magorum sinus
Masemanes
Alata ciuitas
Theimi
Ithar ciuit
Jabri
Zames mons
Bilbana ciuit
Vdeni
Asateni
Ibirtha
Phullon
Salma
Gorda
Marata
Ger.
Magindana ciuit
Atea vicus
Carcos ciuit
Caplina ciuit
Betius fluui
Crea ciuitas
Cabana ciuit
Maichę
Lathripp
Alapeni
Bialanna
Iolisitę
Catara
rei
Anari
Carna
Giratha
Sata
Aeg
Domana
Atia
AR
ABIA
Catanitę
Masthala
L.ur fluuius
Manitę
Olapha
Malan
Marith montes
gitę
Tiagar
Macoraba
Dacharemoizę
Omanitę
Thumata
FOE
Maocosmus metrop.
Smyrnophoros inte
rior regio
Iritę
Labris
Omanum emp.
rium
regia
Carman regia
Jrala
Bliulei
Latera
Cassaniti
Min
Albana
ei
Chargata
gens magna
Laatheha
Amara
Alumeotę
Nagara metropolis
Ioba
ritę
Mamala
vicus
Marasdi
Maraba metropolis
Jula
Adedi pagus
Doreni
Mocritę
Sophanitę
Marmatha
Sabo
Magulaba
Syleum
Mariama
Thumna
Vodona
LI
Ango
Ansar
Sabęi
Achitę
Citheba
Madasara
nitę
monitę
Thabanno
Pudni ciuitas
Manambs
regia
Sabatha me:
tropolis
Gorda
Smyrnophoros regio
exterior
Adi vicus
Thablu
Benum
Miba
Masonitę
Climax
mons
Araganitę
Cachra
Mela Mephi
Pion flu.
Stygis aquę fons
Saruum
metrop.
Embolum vicus
Fretus portus
Thalemmata
Elefori
Sarica
Araga
Napygus
opp.
Sarite
Sapphar
metro
polis
Mieza emporium
Sapharitę
Maphoritę
Arorregia
Rheda
Sachle
Melach
villa
Trulla
Cua
Prionotus mons
Melachi duę
Sesippi portus
Thuris
Lachehor
Hyela
Rhatinę
Macala
Adam duę
Pseudocelis
Sabo regia
Deua
Sochchor
Bana
Dola
Adra
Grstha
ciuitas
Palindromos
extrema
Occelis emporium
Samina ciuitas
Madochi ciuit
Home
Mardache ciuit
ri
Leos vicus
Saba emporii
Acamanitha
vicus
Mela mons
Dola vetus
Diosc
dis in
sula
Arsinoe
Der
Abasama flu
Magnum lit
tus
chi Silon
Maudaith
vicus
Mosylon emporium
promontorium
Agachoclis
Mondi
Cocconati tres
RVBR
Aualites ompo
rium
Aualites sinus
Cobe emps
rium
Elephas mons
Mondi emporiu
Acano ompo:

Decisive Dates

c5000–3000 BC Evidence of coastal and inland settlements. Discovery of Ubaid pottery at coastal sites proves contact with southern Iraq.

c3000 BC Magan, an area roughly corresponding with UAE and northern Oman, supplies the city states of southern Mesopotamia with a range of raw materials, including copper.

c2500–2000 BC Umm an-Nar period, named after excavations on the small island of Umm an-Nar near Abu Dhabi. Period characterised by complex burials, far-reaching trade networks and sophisticated crafts.

AD77 Pliny's *Natural History* mentions the Arabian shore of the Gulf and describes how Arab ships were sewn together.

1st century AD A Greek in the employ of the Roman navy, writes *Periplus of the Erythraean Sea*. This description of trade around the coast of the Indian Ocean describes Omana as Persian.

AD226–640 The Sassanid period. Persian seamen control sea trade.

630 Islam is brought to Oman.

632 Death of the Prophet Mohammed.

751 Oman elects its first Imam, Julanda bin Mas'ud.

8th–9th centuries Arab seafaring and trading are at their height, with voyages as far as China.

The Bat tombs in Oman and the tombs at Hili in Abu Dhabi date from this period.

c2000 BC–1st millennium BC Arab tribes arrive from southwest and central Arabia. They find coastal communities and inland wadis inhabited by people of Persian origin.

1300–300 BC The Iron Age. The *falaj* system develops at the beginning of the first millennium BC.

563 BC Cyrus the Great from Persia conquers Oman, founding the Achaemenid Dynasty.

300 BC The region is part of a trade network involving the whole of the Arabian peninsula. Ad Door at Umm al Qaiwain is an important port. From Sumhuram in Dhofar, southern Oman, frankincense is exported across the seas and over the desert, supplying Greece and Rome.

10th century Sohar in Oman is the hub of maritime trade.

14th century Hormuz, an island off modern-day Iran, opposite the Musandam Peninsula, is at its zenith, completely controlling the mouth of the Gulf.

16th century The Portuguese dominate trade in the Gulf and the Indian Ocean. They capture Muscat in 1507 and then Hormuz.

1624–1738 Ya'ruba Dynasty rules Oman.

1650 Imam Sultan bin Saif expels the Portuguese.

1646 Commercial treaty signed between Oman's Imam and the British East India Company. The Gulf is vital for their passage to India.

1718–28 Civil War in Oman.

1730s Saif bin Sultan II of Oman invites the Persians to help him secure his bid to be Imam.

1742 The Persians establish control of Muscat.

1747 Ahmed bin Said drives the Persians from Oman and is elected Imam. A golden age ensues.Thus begins the Al bu Said Dynasty. Meanwhile the Qawasim of Ras al Khaimah become increasingly powerful and their ports soon dominate the Gulf.

1761 Abu Dhabi is founded.

1820 A British campaign to quash the Qawasim culminates in the razing of Ras al Khaimah and other Qawasim ports, including Sharjah, Umm al Qaiwain, Ajman and Lingah. Thus began the General Treaty of Peace and British involvement in the Emirates.

1830s The pearl trade is at its height.

1833 Dubai's Bani Yas, a sub-tribe of the Bedu Al Bu Falasah, sets up its own principality, ruled by the Al Maktoum family.

1853 The Perpetual Peace is signed. In return for ceasing hostilities at sea, the British guarantee to protect the Trucial States from external attack.

1864 The first maritime telegraph line is laid in the Gulf by the British. Telegraph stations are established on the Musandam Peninsula.

1874 The British East India Company is dissolved.

1892 The Exclusive Agreement is signed with Britain, preventing the rulers of the Trucial Coast from forming agreements with any other foreign government.

1898 Britain's Lord Curzon visits the Gulf in response to increasing interest shown in the region by Russia and Germany.

1920s Following the defeat of Germany in World War I and the collapse of the Ottoman Empire, Britain is at its most influential in the Middle East.

1930s The pearl industry declines following the arrival of the Japanese cultured pearl.

1932 Imperial Airways (later to become British Airways) begins its air service to Sharjah.

1936–1952 The rulers of the Trucial States sign oil concessions with the Iraq Petroleum Company.

1950 Formation of the Trucial Oman Scouts, a defence force led by British officers.

1951 A causeway is built linking the island of Abu Dhabi to the mainland. This is replaced by Al Maqta Bridge in 1968.

1952 Saudis occupy part of Buraimi, but are eventually (1955) driven out by Trucial Oman Scouts. A Trucial States Council is formed, with the aim of solving problems of common interest.

PRECEDING PAGES: Ptolemy's map of Arabia, published in 1584, shows Greek placenames.
ABOVE LEFT: prehistoric rock engravings of camels at Tawi, the Musandam Peninsula.
ABOVE RIGHT: soldier on guard in Dhofar, 1974.

1954–59 Imamate rebellion under Ghalib ibn Ali in Oman. British help restore Said bin Taimur to power.

1959 Oil is discovered in commercial quantities in Abu Dhabi.

1965–1975 Dhofar Rebellion in Oman.

1962 The first bridge is built over Dubai's creek.

1967 Oil is produced in commercial quantities by Oman.

1968 Britain declares its intention to withdraw from the Gulf by 1971.

1970 Accession of Sultan Qaboos bin Said in Oman.

1971 Britain withdraws from the Gulf. The United Arab Emirates is formally inaugurated on 2 December, with Sheikh Zayed of Abu Dhabi as President of the Feder-

ation and Sheikh Rasheed bin Said Al Maktoum as Vice-President and Prime Minister.

1973 OPEC (Organisation of Oil Exporting Countries) quadruple crude oil prices. Oman's first airport, Seeb International, opens.

1979 Another hike in oil prices.

1980 Iran-Iraq War.

1981 The GCC (Gulf Cooperation Council), comprising Saudi Arabia, Kuwait, the UAE, Bahrain, Qatar and Oman, is formed.

1986 Sultan Qaboos University, Oman's first university, opens.

1990 Iraq invades Kuwait. Gulf War ensues.

1991 Oman's Majlis Ash-Shura, a consultative council with 59 elected members, is inaugurated.

1995 Oman celebrates Sultan Qaboos's silver jubilee.

ARCHAEOLOGY

Recent archaeological explorations of Oman and the UAE have revealed a rich and varied ancient history

If there is a general perception that the southeast corner of the Arabian Peninsula has, until recent times, been relatively isolated, nothing could be further from the truth. From as early as 5000 BC, the area played an important part in the development of the ancient civilisations of western Asia.

There are practically no historical documents originating from the UAE and Oman prior to the Islamic period, though there are references to the region by neighbouring peoples and trading partners from as early as *circa* 2330 BC. Unfortunately these are few and far between, so the historical framework used by archaeologists is based primarily on the results of excavations. The names given to different periods in the development of southeast Arabia are usually derived from the names of the excavated sites.

Prehistoric prelude (5000–3000 BC)

Archaeological surveys indicate a constantly changing mosaic of coastal and inland settlements, but many of the earliest sites lie along the shores of the Arabian Gulf and the Gulf of Oman. Until about 16,000 years ago, when sea levels began to rise, the area now occupied by the Gulf would have formed a river valley extending as far as the Straits of Hormuz. The shoreline of the Gulf of Oman would have been distant from its present location and 100–150 metres (330–490 ft) lower than the present-day mean sea level. When the sea level began to rise it attained something like its present level about 8,000 years ago, creating a variety of coastal landscapes, including the sand and mud flats of the Arabian Gulf, the fjord-like coastline of the Musandam Peninsula, the plain of the Batinah and the steep cliffs extending from north of Muscat south past Ras al Hadd. Coastal lagoons, rich in mangroves, also became a significant feature and can still be seen near the

coast of Umm al Qaiwain, at Khor Kalba and at Qurm near Muscat. These varied marine habitats afforded a glut of easily obtained food such as shellfish, fish, turtle and dugong. Mangroves attracted birdlife which could be hunted, and adjacent inland areas supported gazelle and, later on, grazing for sheep, goats and cattle.

The archaeological remains left by these early communities are distinguished by large accumulations of shells that were collected for food and then discarded. Excavation of "shell middens" at Ras al Hamra near Qurm has revealed the ground plan of small groups of circular buildings, indicated by stone foundations or arrangements of post-holes. Other finds show that the inhabitants were adept at making stone tools and shell artefacts, including personal jewellery and functional but nevertheless aesthetically pleasing objects such as large shell hooks.

Such items were often found amongst burials, which form large cemeteries and hint at the social complexity of the fishing communities.

LEFT: Great Hili Tomb near Al Ain (3rd millennium BC).
ABOVE RIGHT: finds from Shimmel, displayed in Ras al Khaimah's museum.

On the Gulf coast similar shell middens are found along the margins of former lagoons, for example at Umm al Qaiwain and the Hamriyah area of Sharjah. Some of the Gulf coast middens have also provided evidence of contact with southern Iraq from 5000–4000 BC, in particular a type of pottery called Ubaid pottery, named after a site in southern Iraq. The pottery was clearly imported at this early date, though whether directly or indirectly has not been confirmed. However, similar finds on the island of Dalma (Abu Dhabi) suggest that the inhabitants were already accomplished sailors by this time.

Coastal midden sites were occupied up to and

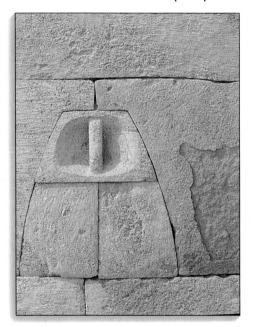

beyond 3000 BC. Prior to this it is probable that the arid conditions of Arabia today were not so harsh and that open grassland was available. Many of the stone tools, including finely crafted arrowheads, found in desert areas probably date from 5000–3000 BC and represent inland hunting and herding communities contemporary with the coastal communities.

The Hafit, Umm an-Nar and Wadi Suq periods (3000–1300 BC)

At around 3000 BC there was a dramatic transformation of the way people lived in southeast Arabia. Contact with southern Iraq, indicated by the presence of Ubaid pottery, ended by around 4 000 BC. Whilst the local communities of southeast Arabia continued to flourish beyond this time, at around 3000 BC there is evidence of renewed contact with southern Mesopotamia. In the late 4th millennium BC there are references in Mesopotamian texts to a place named Dilmun (now Bahrain), and towards the end of the 3rd millennium, *circa* 2330 BC Dilmun is mentioned along with Magan and Meluhha.

Between them, these three places supplied the city states of southern Mesopotamia with a range of raw materials and exotic goods, including timber, stone and, above all, copper. On the basis of the abundance of copper deposits, and archaeological evidence that they were being exploited as early as the 3rd millennium BC, Magan, sometimes referred to in texts as "the Copper Mountain of Magan", is recognised as the area of southeast Arabia which corresponds with the UAE and Oman. Meluhha is generally identified as the Indus Valley.

COPPER MINING

Ancient Magan was an important supplier of stone and copper. Sites in Oman such as Maysar, in the Wadi Samad area near Nizwa, have produced clear evidence for the mining, processing and export of copper on a large scale during the 3rd millennium BC, including anvil and crushing stones, a smelting oven and copper beads and rings, chisels, knives and axes. It has been estimated that up to 4,000 tonnes/tons of copper were produced in the region in the Umm an-Nar period.

Copper was still being mined in the late Middle Ages with travellers to the region reporting on copper mines. However, by the late 19th century copper sheeting was being imported from Bombay.

Both stone and copper are still readily obtained in the UAE and Oman, and though oil and natural gas have dominated the economy for several decades recent attempts to reduce dependence on oil in Oman have seen a regeneration of the ancient copper-mining industry. In 1983 a mine at Lasail, in Wadi al Jizzi near Sohar, was reworked for the first time since antiquity and since then new deposits have been found in Yanqul, north of Ibri, and on the Batinah Coast. An added bonus of the refining process are small but valuable quantities of gold and silver.

Renewed contacts with Mesopotamia from the end of the 4th millennium are an indication of Magan's developing trading relations with surrounding countries, as described some 700 years later in Mesopotamian texts. Evidence includes pottery of Mesopotamian import found in tombs. These tombs are of a type unique to the UAE and Oman at this time, when they became a conspicuous feature of the landscape – large, stone cairns, often placed at the entrance to wadis and in clearly visible groups, or along the ridges or summit of a mountain to form a dramatic skyline. Tombs of this type were first excavated at Jebel Hafit near Al Ain and are

wheat, barley and dates being cultivated. Crops and the herding of sheep, goats and cattle, introduced at an earlier date, as shown by some of the coastal midden sites, led to settlement in inland areas where there was sufficient water for irrigation. A settlement pattern similar to that of more recent times began to emerge and from 2500 BC there is a clear picture of what these early settlements were like.

The period from 2500–2000 BC is referred to as the Umm an-Nar period, named after the small island near Abu Dhabi where excavations by Danish archaeologists first produced evidence for this period. During this period a new

often called "Hafit tombs". Others have a characteristic beehive-shape and are consequently called "beehive tombs". Both the Hafit and beehive tombs date from the end of the 4th millennium to circa 2500 BC.

These tombs indicate the probable distribution of settlement and there is evidence that a farming, oasis-based economy had been introduced by this time. Excavations at the important site of Hili 8, near Al Ain, show that by 3000 BC agriculture was established, with

type of tomb was introduced. Circular and averaging about 9 metres (30 ft) in diameter, it stands above ground and has a smooth exterior wall built of finely worked masonry. Some of the tombs on the island of Umm an-Nar also had relief carvings on the outer wall, depicting wild animals such as gazelles and snakes as well as domesticated animals like cattle. There are also depictions of camels, which were probably domesticated by this time.

Excavation has shown that the tombs were used for multiple burials with a range of grave goods, including pottery (some imported from Mesopotamia, Iran or the Indus), stone vessels, bronze weapons, shell rings and shell and stone

LEFT: sealed entrance to a smooth Umm an-Nar-style tomb at Hili, Al Ain.
ABOVE: beehive tombs (2500 BC), near Al Ain.

beads. The most spectacular Umm an-Nar tomb excavated so far is displayed in Hili Archaeological Park, near Al Ain (*see page 217*). It has carvings on the outer wall of humans as well as animals.

The excavations at Hili 8, near Hili Archaeological Park, show that settlements from this period included large defensive towers. It is probable that similar towers were also built from the beginning of the 3rd millennium, and thus represent an established local tradition. The towers were probably surrounded by smaller buildings made from mud bricks and date palm wood. At Hili, Bat and Wadi Bahla such towers are distributed over a large area. They probably defined and defended the area of habitation and cultivation.

> ### ANCIENT EXPORTS
>
> Distinctive stone vessels were distributed to places in southern Iraq, Bahrain, Iran and the Indus Valley.

From the beginning of the 3rd millennium local pottery had been produced, and during the Umm an-Nar period pottery and other craft industries flourished. Distinctive stone vessels were manufactured and widely distributed, not only locally, but also to places in southern Iraq, Bahrain, Iran and the Indus. Likewise, imported items continued to arrive in southeast Arabia and the resulting distribution of exported and imported goods reflects the network of trading relations described in the Mesopotamian texts of the later 3rd millennium.

At the end of the 3rd millennium Magan ceased to be mentioned in Mesopotamian texts and Dilmun appears to have had a monopoly over the supply of goods to Mesopotamia. However, the range of exports remained much the same, with a large demand for copper, and since Dilmun had no copper sources of its own Magan probably remained the main supplier.

Recent excavations suggest that many of the 3rd millennium settlements continued to be occupied during the 2nd millennium. However, there are radical changes in the architecture of tombs and the range of pottery and other objects produced.

At the beginning of the 2nd millennium at least two types of tomb are characteristic. The first is circular, 3–4 metres (10–13 ft) in diameter, with a central, below ground, stone-lined burial chamber. Such tombs were first excavated in Wadi Suq, at the east end of Wadi al Jizzi which links the inland area of Al Ain with Sohar on the Gulf of Oman. Subsequently Wadi

Suq was adopted to describe the period from around 2000 to *circa* 1300 BC.

The second type of tomb characteristic of the early Wadi Suq period was first recorded at Shimmel, near Ras al Khaimah. The Shimmel-type tombs are rectangular, a few metres wide but several metres long, and stand above ground. Grave goods included new types of pottery and stone vessels introduced at the start of the Wadi Suq period.

Imported items continue to show on-going trading links with surrounding countries, and

coastal settlements, particularly Ras al Jins near Ras al Hadd in Oman, which appears to have flourished during the Umm an-Nar and Wadi Suq periods, provide evidence for the highly developed maritime trade of this period.

In the past it was thought that the Wadi Suq period came to an end around 1700 BC and was followed by a "Dark Age" until the Iron Age at the beginning of the 1st millennium BC. This theory resulted from the lack of Wadi Suq period settlements showing a prolonged period of occupation. More recently, however, excavations, notably at Tell Abraq on the Gulf coast, have shown that the Wadi Suq period persisted until the start of the Iron Age (*circa* 1300 BC).

The Iron Age (*circa* 1300–300 BC)

In the Iron Age period there was an increase in the number and variety of settlements, which may have been due to the development of the *falaj* system of irrigation (*see page 156*). Coastal middens continued to be occupied, villages evolved along the courses of wadis in mountainous areas, and there is evidence for larger villages of mud-brick houses, as excavated at Rumeilah and Hili 2 near Al Ain. There is also evidence of fortified hill-top settlements, such as at Lizq in Wadi Samad, Oman.

As in previous periods, changes are evident in the pottery and soft stone vessels manufac-

Dhofar became important for the supply of frankincense and whilst most of this was transported north through western Arabia southeast Arabia did not become marginalised. By the 1st century AD maritime trade was conducted around the entire Arabian Peninsula.

One of the main sites of the period is Mileiha, south of Dhaid. Occupation here dates from the end of the Iron Age when a large area became occupied for the next 700 years. From the earliest phases of occupation there are amphorae from Rhodes, alabaster vessels from the Yemen, and other imported goods. The town had a necropolis of monumental tombs. From the later

tured. The discovery of distinctive vessels in neighbouring countries such as Bahrain indicates that maritime trade had become an important part of the regional economy.

The post-Iron Age Period

From *circa* 300 BC, in the period following the death of Alexander the Great, the UAE and Oman were part of a network of trade that involved the whole of the Arabian Peninsula and linked the countries of the Mediterranean with those of the Indian Ocean. Yemen and

phases of occupation are traces of a fort, graves with sacrificed camels and horses, and evidence that the town was minting its own coinage.

Contemporary with this phase of occupation (the first centuries AD) is Ad Door near Umm al Qaiwain, which was probably the port for inland Mileiha. Coins of the type minted at Mileiha have been found there as well as similar graves with sacrificed camels, pottery from the eastern Mediterranean, and items from neighbouring parts of Arabia, Iraq and Iran.

In Wadi Samad there is evidence of occupation of the same date as Mileiha and Ad Door and a wide range of items, some similar to finds at Mileiha and Ad Door, have been excavated.

LEFT: Tower Tomb, Eastern Hajar.
ABOVE: Ad Door, post-Iron Age site.

Muskat Harbour

from the Fisher-men's Rock

THE MARITIME HERITAGE

*The UAE and Oman share an illustrious seafaring history. As early as the 8th
century, trade vessels from the Gulf were sailing all the way to China*

Dubai can come as a surprise to first-time visitors. Its modern buildings are imposing but are not distinctively Arabian. One hardly hears Arabic spoken in public (75 percent of the population is expatriate) and the goods for sale seem to come from everywhere except Arabia. It all seems so cosmopolitan.

Yet, paradoxically, these very qualities are what make it typical of Gulf ports throughout history. Walk along the quaysides of the creeks at Dubai and Sharjah and you will be transported back in time, to an earlier kind of cosmopolitanism. Wooden dhows from Iran, Pakistan and India, as well as from other Gulf ports, line the quays up to five deep, while sons of Sindbad unload cargoes ranging from fridges, televisions and building materials to fabrics, spices and aromatics.

The pattern of trade

A casual glance at a map will show that the Arabian Peninsula stands between the Indian Ocean and the Mediterranean, and that this land mass is penetrated by two long seas, the Gulf of Arabia (also known as the Persian Gulf) and the Red Sea, channels for the westward flow of Indian Ocean goods to the centres of civilisation in the Near East and Mediterranean.

Alexandria's foundation and prosperity in the 4th century BC owed everything to the Red Sea trade from Africa and the Indian Ocean. With the coming of Islam in the 7th century AD, both the Gulf and Red Sea were crucial to the eastern trade of the Islamic world. But it is perhaps the Gulf which has the most glorious commercial history of the two, and Oman commands the Straits of Hormuz, which joins it to the Indian Ocean. As the centuries wore on, many commodities were passed on to Europe, first through the medium of Genoa and then Venice.

But not all the Indian Ocean trade was long-

distance. Much of it was within the Indian Ocean itself. Over the millennia, this trading activity brought about a tremendous mixing of peoples around the coasts of the entire ocean and a lot of cultural as well as commercial exchange. The coves at Muscat and Muttrah, and the beach at Sohar, have witnessed the com-

ings and goings of Mesopotamians, Persians, Arabs, Indians, Africans, Greeks, Jews, Turks, Italians, Portuguese and northern Europeans.

The antiquity of the sea route

By the time of the Greek and Roman empires, trade from Ethiopia, southwest Arabia and India into the Near East and Mediterranean was in full swing, much of it by camel caravan along the land routes of the Arabian Peninsula. Gradually this trade transferred from the land routes to the Red Sea, as seafarers from Egypt, with Mediterranean ships, began to master the monsoon routes. By *circa* 100 BC these interlopers had discovered that in their strongly built, square-

---

PRECEDING PAGES: *Muscat Harbour*, from "16 Views of Places in the Persian Gulf 1809–10" by R. Temple.
LEFT: a *ghanjah*, used for cargo off Dubai in 1950.
ABOVE RIGHT: Arab passenger boat in the 13th century.

rigged ships they could sail direct from Aden to India using the southwest monsoon, something which the Indian Ocean ships with their stitched construction were too fragile to do.

A vigorous trade developed, with merchants reaching India and China, and paying for luxury goods with Roman coin. This eventually caused a serious drain of precious metals in the Roman Empire, leading to devaluation and a slump in trade in the 3rd century BC.

When the sea trade revived, during Sassanid rule of Persia in the 5th century, it was in the hands of Persian seamen. They controlled trade between Ceylon and the Gulf, to the detriment

African explorer Ibn Battuta who had first-hand experience of them.

Hull planks were stitched together edge-to-edge with coconut twine, and the ribs were fitted later – the exact opposite of European boats. Gaps were caulked with a mixture of coir and fish oil being rammed into them. Except in larger vessels even a partial deck or a cabin was a luxury. Ships were still pointed at both ends, and used steering oars, one on each side. The square sail had evolved into something more triangular, enabling ships to sail close to the wind though not to tack in a modern sense.

The boat was essentially a cargo-carrying tub

of the Red Sea. It was this tradition that the Arabs took over after the spread of Islam in the 7th century. The first named Arab to make the voyage to China was an Omani in AD 750.

Medieval ships

The average Arabian seaman in pre-modern times spent his days and nights exposed to the elements, in conditions of hardship and hard work. First of all, he would have made a voyage in a smallish vessel, the planks of which were not nailed but stitched together, a mode of ship-building that came as a constant surprise to Europeans and Arabs from the Mediterranean, such as Marco Polo and the North

which needed constant maintenance. Crew and passengers accommodated themselves as best they could on top of the cargo, and ablutions were carried out in a precarious box slung out

THE ARABIAN NIGHTS

The coming of Islam, and the removal of the Muslim capital from Damascus to Baghdad in AD 751, ushered in a Golden Age of Gulf trade. This period of Arab trade with China is associated with the glittering court of the Caliph Harun al Rashid at Baghdad. The sailors and merchants inspired the stories of Sindbad the Sailor and the Arabian Nights, told at Harun's court.

over the side of the boat. The main advantage of such a craft was that it was flexible in heavy surf, and therefore less likely than more robustly built ships to be smashed while coming inshore. These fragile craft could be quite large, some carrying up to 400 men.

At the height of Gulf trade, in the 9th century, Gulf and Omani seamen were sailing all the way to China in such ships, and there was a huge colony of Arab merchants at Canton. By sailing all the way like this Arab merchants could cut out the middle man and make massive profits.

HIGH REWARDS

In a single successful voyage a merchant could make his fortune for life.

early December and make the round trip to China in 18 months, returning with the end of the northeast monsoon in April or May. Ships sailing to India and East Africa also made use of the northeast monsoon season. The breezes of the southwest monsoon in April to May were handy on the return from East Africa, blowing the ships back to the Omani coast.

By the 13th century the stern rudder was invented, but not the tiller: it was operated by a system of ropes, which allowed the rudder to be unshipped easily when the boat was beached.

Gulf merchants' tales of the 8th–10th centuries describe hair-raising shipwrecks and adventures, and enormous mercantile risks. The loss of a single cargo could ruin a group of merchants and even contribute to the decline of a port. The rewards of a single successful voyage were correspondingly prodigious: a merchant could make his fortune for life. They would set out from the Omani coast in late November or

ABOVE LEFT: *A View of Muttrah from the East* by R. Temple 1809–10.
ABOVE: *European Trading Galleons in Muttrah's Harbour,* an oil painting attributed to the Dutch painter Jan Peeters (1642–80).

By now Arab merchants were no longer sailing direct to China. Instead, the Chinese were sailing to the Malabar coast and the Palk Strait between Ceylon and India, where goods were transhipped to Indian and Arab vessels. By the 13th century large junks could be seen in Malabar ports, and the 14th century saw the extraordinary Ming Voyages, when the Chinese in fleets of vast junks sailed around the shores of the Indian Ocean, reaching East Africa and the Omani coast at Dhofar.

These voyages stopped abruptly in the 1430s and the Chinese left the Indian ports. By the time of the European discovery of the East in 1498 their voyages were a distant memory.

The great ports

Medieval merchants set out from the great Islamic port of Basra on the Shatt al Arab in Iraq. But the large ships required to make the China run could not anchor off Basra, and so ports further down the Gulf became important points of transshipment – first Siraf in Persia, and then Sohar on the Omani coast.

Sohar flourished. It was at the point where trade from Aden and East Africa met the trade coming and going to India and China. Sohar was, as the 10th-cen-cat, with its natural harbour, had supplanted Sohar and Qalhat on the Omani coast.

Cargoes combined high-value commodities with bulk goods, because all ships need ballast. From Iraq these bulk goods were mainly dates, while the Arabian ports of the Gulf and Oman supplied dates, leather and dried fish. From East Africa the bulk goods were timber; from India, rice, dried foods, teak and other ship-building timber; and from China, copper cash, other metals and sugar.

PRECIOUS CARGOES

The glamour and profit were in high-value goods, which increased in value with every merchant and port they passed through.

tury Arab geographer Muqaddasi observed, "the hallway to China, the storehouse of the East and Iraq, and the stay of the Yemen... There is no city bigger than this on the China Sea. It is a populous and beautiful spot, where wealth and fruits are in abundance... There are wonderful markets all along the coast. Houses are high and built of teak wood and mud bricks, and there is a canal of fresh water."

Eventually Qais Island supplanted Siraf and Sohar, and by the 14th century Qais was ousted by the island of Hormuz. With its satellite ports at Qalhat in eastern Oman and Julfar near present-day Ras al Khaimah, Hormuz completely controlled the mouth of the Gulf. By 1500 Mus-

But the glamour and profit were in the high-value goods, which increased in value with every merchant and port they passed through. Oman and the Arabian shore of the Gulf provided horses, frankincense and pearls. From India and Ceylon came gemstones, glass, iron-ware, swords, cotton cloth, spices and aromatics such as sandalwood and incense. China's silk, porcelain, lacquerwork, metalwork and other manufactures were in big demand. In exchange, the Islamic lands sent glassware, carpets, muslin, brocade, perfumes, incense, weapons and armour – but also money too.

Perhaps the most valuable raw commodities came from East Africa: gold, slaves, ivory, rhino horn and leopard skins. Of all the seafaring Arabs, it was the Omanis who dominated the rich East African trade, introducing its hugely prized products into the economies of the Islamic Near East.

Portuguese power

It was into East Africa, in 1498, that the first Western threat to local control of maritime trade since Greco-Roman times arrived: the Portuguese. Under Vasco da Gama the Portuguese rounded the Cape of Good Hope into the Indian Ocean in 1498, and proceeded to dominate the international trade of the Gulf and Indian Ocean

realised the strategic importance of Aden, Hormuz and Malacca in the trade.

Hormuz, whose inhabitants were a mixture of Arabs and Persians, commanded the Musandam Strait, and in spite of being a waterless island had grown immensely wealthy by raising customs dues on all cargoes passing up the Gulf.

The Portuguese took Hormuz after their capture of Muscat in 1507. While they diverted some of the trade from the Far East around the Cape of Good Hope, they profited from the rest by levying customs dues on the Gulf route just as the Hormuzis had done before them. They built a line of forts along the Omani, African and

EUROPEAN INFLUENCES

The incursion of the Portuguese and the proliferation of Portuguese ships off the western coasts of the Indian Ocean introduced profound changes to Arab shipbuilding, including nailed instead of stitched construction, transom sterns, tiller-operated rudders, and raised and often decorated poop decks. But shipbuilding in the Gulf continued to be carried out in the time-honoured way, entirely by eye.

By the early 1800s British ships were being built in the yards of Bombay, and local rulers such as the Sultan of Muscat owned European-style vessels. This resulted in greater European influences in Arab boatyards and a mixing of local and European styles.

When metal ships eventually took over long-distance trade, the old styles survived in smaller local craft. The last stitched boat in Oman was built in Dhofar as late as the 1970s.

for over a century. Portuguese trade was a royal monopoly carried forward by gunpowder and force of arms, and the small Portuguese fleets had an impact on the people of the Indian Ocean shores out of all proportion to their numbers. They came in search of Indian spices and the spice islands of Indonesia, and of other luxury goods which the Venetian monopoly had made so costly in Europe. Their greatest colonial visionary, Affonso D'Albuquerque, quickly

LEFT: Portuguese carracks.
ABOVE: Vasco da Gama's voyage around the Cape of Good Hope in 1498 changed the face of seafaring in the Gulf.

Indian coasts and farther east, with Goa as their capital. Muscat, Sohar and Hormuz were key to their control of the Gulf. The twin Portuguese forts dominating Muscat's old harbour were built at this time.

The Omani Empire

The Portuguese saw off Ottoman Turkish attacks in the 16th century, but others were to come early in the 17th century from Persia, Holland, England and Oman. Unlike the Portuguese, the other European nations arrived as merchant companies wishing to trade in peace.

During the 1630s and 1640s a renascent Omani Imamate succeeded in ejecting the Portuguese from Muscat and their coastal forts. The Omanis captured Portuguese ships, and went on to establish a maritime empire. Their ships and seamen, who often included European renegades, were an equal match for those of the Portuguese, English, Dutch and French. By the end of the 17th century they had taken control of a stretch of the East African coast down to Zanzibar and Mombasa, expelling the Portuguese. Oman became a power on parts of the Persian coast, and even at times up the Gulf as far as Bahrain.

PASSAGE TO INDIA

The Gulf was increasingly vital to communications between London and the East India Company's possessions in India.

It brought them into conflict with the imams of Muscat and Omani maritime ambitions.

By 1780 the Qawasim were firmly established on the Persian side of the southern Gulf too. Very soon they began to threaten Muscat's control of the trade from India and East Africa into the Gulf.

By now the British East India Company was set to become involved. The Gulf was becoming more and more vital to communications between London and the Company's growing possessions in India. When

In the mid-18th century Oman fell victim to civil war and a revived Persia under Nadir Shah, who took Muscat in 1742. But after 1744 the reunited Omanis drove out the Persians. Omani fortunes began to revive again, just as a rival sea power, the Qawasim of Sharjah and Ras al Khaimah, rose up in the southern Gulf.

The Qasimi "pirates", 1722–1820

The Qawasim of Ras al Khaimah seized Lingah on the Persian shore following the death of Nadir Shah in 1747. The rise of their ports at Sharjah and at Ras al Khaimah, which had replaced ancient Julfar just to the north, where they built up their fleets, was remarkably rapid.

Napoleon's occupation of Egypt in 1798 blocked the Red Sea route one British response was to enter into treaty relations with the Imam of Muscat, a move which inevitably placed them in opposition to the Qawasim. At the same time, the British blamed the Qawasim for the piracy that then plagued the Gulf and led a series of seaborne campaigns against the so-called "Pirate Coast". These climaxed in 1820 in the destruction of the Qasimi fleets and the first of the Maritime Truces.

British officials almost certainly exaggerated the Qawasim's involvement in piracy, but their campaign against them was determined. In 1806 the British attacked Ras al Khaimah. In 1809

Ras al Khaimah, Lingah, Luft and Shinas were burnt and ships destroyed, and Ras al Khaimah was bombarded again in 1816. Finally between 1819 and 1820, a large naval and military operation was mounted which razed Ras al Khaimah. Its ships were destroyed along with those of Sharjah, Umm al Qaiwain, Ajman, Lingah and other Qasimi ports.

The Maritime Peace, 1820–53

It was only after this expedition that maritime peace became a real prospect, and Britain's continuous and official involvement began in what are now the Emirates. The destruction of Qasimi

real emergence as the chief trading port on the southern Gulf was due to the migration there in 1833 of the Al bu Falasah, a clan of the Bani Yas from Abu Dhabi. Its leading family Al Maktoum set about turning themselves into the merchant princes of the Gulf Coast, a position they have held ever since.

One long-term result of the peace was an expanding pearl trade. An ancient Gulf industry, pearling was recorded by Greek and Roman writers and probably traces its origin to the late Stone Age. Pearls are not found in abundance in Omani waters outside the Gulf, but the shallow southern Gulf off the Trucial Coast was rich

ports and ships was followed by a "General Treaty of Peace with the Arab Tribes" in 1820. Britain's primary aim was to pacify the seas and so secure its route to India.

The decline of the Qawasim was hastened by the growth of Abu Dhabi and Dubai as competitors on the pearl banks. Abu Dhabi had emerged only in the late 18th century and its sheikh had signed the General Treaty of Peace in 1820. Dubai too was included, but Dubai's

LEFT: fanciful depiction of a pirate raid.
ABOVE: a pearling boat heading into Dubai in 1949, by which time the pearl trade was in decline thanks to the Japanese cultured pearl.

PEARLING

By 1900 Abu Dhabi's had become the largest of the sheikhdoms' pearling fleets, numbering some 410 boats, about one-third of the total. In all, more than 22,000 men were employed on the pearl banks – a very considerable proportion of the population at that time. The life of the pearl diver was grindingly hard. Diving took place in the hot summer months and boats were out at sea for up to four months at a time. The men would dive on empty stomachs (to avoid getting cramp) to depths of over 20 metres (65 ft). They were vulnerable to attacks by jellyfish and sharks.

in pearl oysters and the warm sea shallow enough to make diving feasible.

In 1835, the rulers of Sharjah, Dubai, Ajman and Abu Dhabi signed an inviolable truce under British pressure, outlawing acts of war at sea during the pearling season. Made year-round for 10 years in 1843, it became the Perpetual Treaty in 1853.

Perpetual Peace

With the Perpetual Treaty of Peace of 1853, the rulers of the Gulf Coast agreed to cease hostilities at sea, and in return the British undertook to protect them against external attack. The British were determined not to become involved in disputes on land. However, as the 1860s wore into the 1870s, the line between peace at sea and peace on land became more and more difficult to discern.

By then the Gulf's importance as a channel for imperial communications had greatly increased. In 1862 the British started a fortnightly steamer service from Bombay to Muscat and some of the Gulf ports. Equally significantly, in 1864 they laid the first submarine telegraph cable in the Gulf, running from Karachi to Bushire and Fao via the Musandam Peninsula in Oman.

LAST VESTIGES OF A WAY OF LIFE

A good example of Arabian seafaring success was Sur in eastern Oman. Here Omani tribesmen turned themselves into great shipbuilders using timber imported from India and East Africa. They were supremely placed to control the trade to East Africa, and did so during the latter part of the 19th century, following in the tradition of the great medieval Hormuzi port of Qalhat nearby.

It is at Sur today that one can see the last traditional boatyard in Oman (*see page 171*), although the work is now carried out by Indian craftsmen. Elsewhere you can look almost in vain for vestiges of the great maritime heritage of the region, but just occasionally, on a long sandy beach or in a secluded cove, one comes across a rotting hulk of an abandoned *badan* or *baqqarah*. Look carefully and you may see that part of its hull still shows some stitching.

In the 1970s the last big *ghanjah*, a ship with more than a touch of the Portuguese galleon about it, still lay beached in Muttrah harbour, but it is long gone now. Another lay below the tideline at Sur. These few relics, all of them built by hand and eye, without the help of drawings or specifications, are the last evidence of a 5,000-year tradition of seafaring.

Oman's decline

British support to Muscat continued throughout the 19th century and into the 20th. Sultan Said (ruled 1807–56), maintained a fleet of warships and merchantmen which included European ships, and even sent one of them to New York and London in 1840 and 1842.

By the time he died in 1856 the Omani maritime realm extended once again from enclaves on the Persian coast to large stretches of the East African coast. Although hampered by Britain's anti-slaving policy, Sultan Said developed the economy of Zanzibar, which became almost a second Omani capital. After his death, the which were lucrative sources of income for merchants and rulers in Muscat, Sur and Dubai.

Oman then began a long period of economic decline which lasted right up until the 1960s, and its role in the international sea trade of the Indian Ocean all but vanished.

Great power rivalry

After 1869, rivalry among the Great Powers began to threaten Britain's position in the Gulf. The Ottomans occupied Al Hasa and Qatar in 1871, and claimed eight Trucial Coast settlements, and in 1887 a resurgent Persia took over some Qasimi territory on the Persian shore. This

Omani Empire was split between his two sons, Thuwaini and Majid, into Oman and Zanzibar.

This split was damaging to Oman economically. Other blows to its maritime prosperity followed in quick succession. Steamships were bad enough, but the Suez Canal was opened in 1869, making the Red Sea much more important than the Gulf. In addition, the British had set about suppressing the slave and arms trades,

LEFT: life on Dubai's creek before the bridges were built across it.
ABOVE: old boum, Dubai. These vessels were used as late as the 1970s for gold smuggling to Bombay, an activity that brought renewed maritime prosperity.

prompted Britain to obtain from the sheikhs of the Trucial Coast a written assurance not to correspond or agree with any other government, or to allow agents of other governments to reside in their territories.

By the early 1890s both France and Germany were trying to establish a presence in the region. In March 1892, therefore, Britain developed the 1887 assurance into an Exclusive Agreement, the basis of her relations with the Trucial States until 1971. Nonetheless in the 1890s Russia also joined the race to seek a foothold in the Gulf.

By the end of World War I all these threats had evaporated, and Britain found itself in a position of unprecedented power in the Gulf.

الْكِتَابَ وَجَعَلْنَاهُ هُدًى لِبَنِى

إِسْرَآءِيلَ أَلَّا تَتَّخِذُوا مِن دُونِى

وَكِيلًا ذُرِّيَّةَ مَنْ حَمَلْنَا

مَعَ نُوحٍ إِنَّهُ كَانَ عَبْدًا شَكُورًا

وَقَضَيْنَا إِلَى بَنِى إِسْرَآءِيلَ فِى

الْكِتَابِ لَتُفْسِدُنَّ فِى الْأَرْضِ مَرَّتَيْنِ وَ

ISLAM IN SOUTHEAST ARABIA

*Islam shapes the principles of government as well as private lives. And in Oman a
particular brand of Islam, Ibadism, has played a crucial role in the country's history*

It is tempting to regard oil-rich Arabian rulers, coming as they do from an authoritarian and paternalist tribal background, as dynastic despots mainly out for themselves and their families. But in common with some other Arabian rulers, Sheikh Zayed is frequently heard to express the view that "oil is useless if it is not exploited for the welfare of the citizen", or that "the main function of our wealth should be the greatest happiness for the greatest number of people" – sentiments which Sultan Qaboos would wholeheartedly endorse.

This principle sounds utilitarian, unexpectedly so in its Arabian context. For Muslims, however, who know little of the social philosophy of the 19th-century British expounder of utilitarianism, Jeremy Bentham, it simply encapsulates the Islamic basis of the comprehensive social welfare policies which the Arabian oil states espouse.

Islam revealed

Islam was revealed to the Prophet Mohammed, a native of Mecca in western Arabia, in a series of revelations beginning in AD 610 and continuing until his death in AD 632. Muslims believe that God vouchsafed these utterances, of which the Qur'an is held to be a verbatim record, as the final and perfected revelation of Islam.

Islam, as the religion of Allah, is believed to have existed unchanged for all time, and to have been the religion of the patriarch Abraham. Subsequent prophets, such as Moses and Jesus, are revered but regarded as not having been in complete possession of the divine Message. Muslims do not believe that Allah is distinct from the God of the Bible and the Torah.

Islam, meaning "submission", permeates all aspects of the believer's public and private lives, laying down rules for everyday conduct and

social relationships. Distinctions between religion, morality, legal affairs and politics do not exist, for they are judged to be subsumed under God's indivisible law. The faithful express their belief without self-consciousness wherever they happen to be, whether at home, in the street or in the mosque, in the five daily prayers.

THE FIVE PILLARS OF ISLAM

The Five Pillars of Islam are public acts which make all Muslims known to each other and create a palpable feeling of solidarity in their faith. These acts are:

- the declaration of faith
- the five daily prayers
- payment of the alms tax (*zakat*)
- fasting during daylight hours during the holy month of Ramadan
- the pilgrimage to Mecca (the *haj*) once in a lifetime.

The obligation to fulfil the *haj* is only applicable if one has the means to make the journey.

PRECEDING PAGES: Islamic ideal depicted in tiles on a fountain at the Clocktower in Muscat, Oman.
LEFT: page from an illuminated Qur'an, Abu Dhabi Cultural Foundation.
ABOVE RIGHT: minaret, Bahla, Oman.

The Arab tribes

To find the origins of this mentality, it is necessary to probe back before the Islamic era (calculated from the year AD 622). Perhaps as early as the middle of the 1st millennium BC, Arab tribes arrived from southwest and central Arabia. The newcomers found the inland oases and mountain wadis already peopled by settled farming communities of Persian origin which were not tribally organised but had a highly centralised, feudal kind of organisation which had enabled them to build the enormous *falaj* systems (*see page 156*).

The incoming Arabs at first fought these people and established control over some areas. As time passed by, however, and especially following the coming of Islam in the 7th century AD, the two peoples began to merge: the Arabs settled and became farmers, while the old settlers were absorbed into the tribal structure of Arab society.

The coming of Islam

Islam arrived in Oman in AD 630 – an historically attested event which formed part of the early spread of the new religion within Arabia during the lifetime of the Prophet Mohammed. The Prophet sent emissaries from Medina, as he did to all the tribes and settlements of Arabia, calling them to Islam. The one he sent to Oman was the general 'Amr bin al-'As, later in the 640s to be the Muslim conqueror of Egypt.

Though 'Amr targeted the flourishing Persian port and capital of Sohar on the Omani coast it was the Arab tribal ruling family, the Julanda, and not the Persian governor, who accepted his message. For the Arabs the call to Islam was the call to eject the ruling Persian colonisers of Oman out of the province of Mazun – the Batinah coastal plain of Oman.

On the death of the Prophet in AD 632 much of Arabia apostatised from the new religion, including many Omani converts. However, the Julanda stood firm, supported by three armies sent from Medina by the Caliph Abu Bakr. There followed a great battle at the Arab port of Dibba, in the north, which proved a decisive victory for the Muslims, and Islam quickly took hold among Oman's tribespeople.

Ibadism in Oman

The Islamic conquest of the empire of the Sassanid Persians in Iran and further east drew many tribesmen from Oman to the great Muslim foundation at Basra, the springboard for the campaigns. Here they were drawn into the political and ideological conflicts which nearly succeeded in bringing down the Omayyad Caliphate, creating enormous disorder in the early Islamic state and producing the rebel *Khawarij* or "Outsiders" movement. Oman's distinctive brand of Islam, Ibadism, began as part of this doctrinal struggle.

Tribesmen returning to Oman over the next two centuries introduced Ibadism into the tribal areas of Oman. In common with other movements which today would be called fundamen-

talist, it was their aim to restore the pure Islamic state according to the teaching of the Prophet, before it had been corrupted by the third Caliph 'Uthman. As in much of the Islamic world, Islam introduced a new and fervent intellectual debate into people's lives, centring on God's law and the organisation of society. This was especially true of Ibadism in Oman, and it was to produce an extensive Omani literature, particularly rich in law and history.

Though there were several other centres of Ibadism in early Islam, notably in Yemen and Hadhramaut, today Inner Oman is the chief survivor, and the Omani national character is indelibly coloured by it.

True Ibadism is distinguished from orthodox Sunni Islam at the political level, in two ways. First, the hereditary principle is anathema. Ibadis believe their ruler should be elected by an electoral college of good and learned men and proposed to the community. This Imam can be drawn from any family, for the first condition an aspiring Imam must fulfil is that of piety and learning. Second, Ibadis do not believe it is necessary to have an Imam at all times. During periods of political upheaval the Imamate can lapse and go into a state of secrecy, abeyance or latency known as *kitman*. This has occurred in Oman's history, sometimes for centuries.

This kind of consultative system works well when everyone is in agreement, but immediately falls apart when they are not. Only rarely, therefore, has the Imamate succeeded in genuinely uniting the tribes of Inner Oman. More usually the Imamate has been the political prize sought by rival tribal groupings.

While the Imamate sometimes succeeded in harnessing and harmonising tribalism, it never eradicated it: the Imam was simply a kind of supra-tribal leader, his office modelled on that of a tribal chief. Nor has Ibadism been able to tolerate pluralism in its midst – it has remained essentially inward-looking, surviving in its inac-

Of all doctrines of sovereignty, this is a rather minimal one and one likely to appeal to a tribal mentality. In common with other Muslim attempts to reflect the rule of God upon earth, the ideal of the good ruler included the condition that allegiance to him should be withdrawn if, when God's law was transgressed, he showed no sign of repentance. There was no standing army under central command to enforce sovereignty, and no elaborate bodyguard: militias were raised by the Imam calling up tribal levies.

LEFT: prayer is performed wherever the worshipper happens to be at the time.
ABOVE: Friday prayers in Sharjah.

IMAMATE RULE

There have been two exceptional periods of Imamate rule in Oman, when Imams have managed to overcome the limitations of the Ibadi system by the force of their personalities and their political acumen. When an Imam's power has been such that he can transcend tribalism and exercise control over the coastal ports, then a golden age of prosperity, learning trade, and architectural achievments has generally ensued. This is what the Imams of the First Imamate in the 9th century, based at Nizwa, and the Ya'ruba Imams of the 17th century, operating from Rustaq, achieved.

cessible mountain retreat. With the xenophobia typical of many devout religious movements, it shrank from contact with foreigners and other creeds, which involvement on Oman's outward-looking coastline inevitably brought. The result has been that until the modernisation of recent decades Oman's history has tended to repeat itself in a well-worn cycle.

The cycle begins with the country united under a strong Imamate. With coast and interior united, wealth increases. As prosperity increases, and in some later instances the Imam himself indulges in commerce, encouraging contact with foreigners, the religious ideal

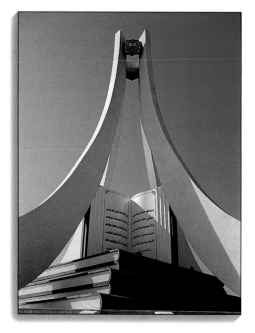

weakens. The Imamate then becomes the prerogative of a single tribal group, and degenerates into secular, tribal power. Pietists are aroused, and civil war ensues, normally resolved by one or both of the sides calling in an outside power, usually with catastrophic results for Oman's autonomy. The resulting disorders await the arrival of a strong new Imam who can unite the people.

Oil wealth has broken the cycle and reconciled Omanis to being united under an enlightened and benevolent Al bu Said ruler. In the modern era, the ruling family has founded its legitimacy not just on piety, but on the sharing of prosperity too.

Sunni Islam on the Gulf coast

Ibadism remained a phenomenon of the fastnesses of the Omani interior. Along the Gulf coast and in northern Oman things were different again. Here the Arab tribespeople were orthodox Sunnis, as were the closely related seafaring Arabs in the ports and villages on the Persian coast of the southern Gulf. There was much mixing with Shiite Persians, and it was a mixture of Arabs and Persians who populated Hormuz in the late Middle Ages and made Julfar, near present-day Ras al Khaimah, prosperous. In the 18th century settlement along the coast of the Emirates took on something like its present configuration as the Qasimi clan turned Sharjah and Ras al Khaimah into flourishing ports, and the Bani Yas made Abu Dhabi their chief settlement.

The people of the coast of Oman and the Emirates have thus been exposed to a great deal of foreign influence, whether as seafarers along the coasts of India and East Africa, or at home where foreign trading communities have grown up. This has led them to tolerate differences, but without abandoning their own traditions and beliefs.

The way in which the legal system has evolved in the Emirates is a good example of this. Before the onset of modernisation, the judicial system relied on the traditional *qadi* to judge cases of law and order, based on his interpretation of the Shari'ah. This included the settlement of disputes arising out of the conduct of business and commerce. However, the ruler exercised the ultimate powers of discretion.

The discovery of oil and the establishment of Federation in 1971 brought an influx of foreign workers and changed the structure of society in the Emirates. The population, indigenous and numbering only around 180,000 in 1968, grew within a few years into a much larger multicultural society.

This necessitated the modernisation of the country's judicial system. New laws were framed to assist the smooth functioning of a pluralistic society while at the same time protecting the interests of the local people. The result is that statutes now not only enforce the criminal justice system based on the Shari'ah, but also

ABOVE LEFT: religious reminder on a roundabout near Muscat. Such monuments are common in the region.
ABOVE RIGHT: shoes must be removed before prayer.

Federal civil and criminal codes, and regulate economic and commercial practice.

In a landmark decision by the Federal Supreme Court in 1993, it was laid down that punishments prescribed under Islamic Law and handed down by Shari'ah courts, could no longer be applied to non-Muslims, who would from then on be dealt with under the civil and criminal codes. In Oman too, which sets great store by the Shari'ah as the law of Oman, there is an additional body of law to deal with administrative, civil and commercial practice.

Despite their new wealth, there is an engaging openness and lack of pretentiousness about Oman and the Emirates and their people. This has much to do with their exposure to the outside world, their seafaring history, and the egalitarianism of their tribal background. They provide business opportunities and employment for millions of foreigners with a good grace. Both countries welcome responsible tourism, and the Emirates host numerous international events, particularly sports, such as Dubai's world-famous horse racing season, tennis and golf tournaments. They quite naturally cling to their traditions and beliefs, but are confident enough in them to keep an open door to the outside world.

SHARI'AH LAW

Shari'ah law, or Islamic law, is derived from the Qur'an and the Sunnah (Way of the Prophet, based on actions and utterances of the Prophet in his lifetime which have been passed down the generations). It deals with every aspect of social behaviour and sets out rules for the conduct of life, including some specific rules and penalties for certain types of criminal acts, as well as for civil liability between individuals. As time has gone by, the body of law has developed through consensus of jurists and through reasoning, the chief concern being that any new formulation should be at least consistent with the Shari'ah.

Some of the more severe sentences under the Shari'ah include amputation for theft and stoning for sexual offences. In the case of adultery, stoning to death may be inflicted only in cases where there are four male witnesses and the accused admits guilt.

Such punishments can be inflicted only with the approval of the ruler of the emirate where the case is brought. A death sentence by firing squad or hanging is the usual penalty for murder and rape, both very rare in Oman and the UAE. In the case of murder a death sentence may be commuted if the family of the victim grants a personal pardon.

OMAN'S GREAT DYNASTIES

The Ya'ruba dynasty succeeded in uniting Oman and turning it into a place of learning and elegance. The Al bu Said turned it into an imperial power

Throughout the greater part of its history since the arrival of Islam, Oman was ruled by Imams, the first of whom, Julanda bin Mas'ud, was elected in AD 751. Some were stronger than others and held dominion over large areas of the country. Others were not able to exercise such central control. Nevertheless there was a fairly constant line of Imams, who followed the Ibadi precept of Islam (*see page 42–3*) from AD 751–1154 when there followed a series of Meliks or Kings of the Nabhan. The Imamate was then resumed but it reached its zenith with the Ya'ruba Dynasty which ruled Oman from 1624–1738, and began and ended in tragedy.

The Ya'ruba Dynasty

According to Omani chroniclers the first Imam of the Ya'ruba Dynasty, Nasir bin Murshid, made the "sun of salvation" shine on the long-afflicted people of Oman. His reputation rested on unifying the country and capturing Sur and Quriyat from the Portuguese and weakening their hold on the Omani coast.

On Nasir's death in 1649 his cousin Sultan bin Saif was elected Imam and it was he who ousted the Portuguese from Muscat, where they had been entrenched since the arrival of Affonso D'Albuquerque in 1507. He continued the unification of the country and built the great round fort at Nizwa (*see page 157*) At this time Oman had considerable seapower, which was used to attack the Portuguese in India.

Sultan's son Bil'arub succeeded him in 1688 though the new Imam's brother, Saif bin Sultan, eventually becoming stronger, was elected Imam and succeeded his brother. Saif had a large fleet, including one ship of 74 guns and one of 60. During his reign the Omanis succeeded in considerably weakening Portuguese

---

PRECEDING PAGES: National Day celebrations, Oman.
LEFT: the Sultanate's emblem of two crossed swords with a *khanjar* and belt.
ABOVE RIGHT: Oman's current Sultan Qaboos belongs to the Al bu Said dynasty, in power since 1747.

power in East Africa, where they had been strong since 1503, and also on the island of Salsette off Bombay. When Saif died in 1711 his son Sultan bin Saif II became Imam and was another strong ruler.

The unification of the country under these five rulers led not only to the revitalisation of

Salsette off Bombay and military prowess but also to commercial prosperity, the encouragement of learning, and buildings of strength, beauty and elegance such as the magnificent castle at Jabrin (*see page 161*), built by Bil'arub. The first trading agreements without the British were made during the Ya'ruba period, in 1646 and 1659.

On Sultan's death in 1718, the unity which Oman had known for nearly a century came to an end and civil war ensued. Fighting over the succession led to tribal animosity and the whole of Oman became embroiled in desultory warfare between the two traditional factions of the Ghafiri and the Hinawi. In the late 1730s Saif bin Sultan II – one of the rival claimants to the Imamate, the other being Muhanna bin Sultan – invited the Persians under Nadir Shah to intervene on his behalf, a decision he came to regret as the Persians refused to give up their conquest.

The two rival Imams had died by 1745 and no Ya'rubi claimant came forward. Meanwhile Ahmed bin Said, who held the fort at Sohar, continued to fight the Persians, becoming both a hero and the elected Imam. In 1747 he succeeded in driving the Persians out.

The Al bu Said

Thus began the Al bu Said Dynasty, which has held the Imamate or Sultanate ever since. It is the oldest dynasty still ruling in the region.

Ahmed himself was a man of outstanding courage, vigour, enterprise, generosity and personality. These qualities were sorely needed at the time. At home he was a good administrator of a fairly strong centralised government and he had a liberal reputation. He had in his retinue scholars, Islamic judges and notables. His bodyguard consisted of some 1,000 freemen, 1,000 Zanzibaris and 100 Nubian slaves. Abroad he led an expedition against the Persians at the request of the people of Basrah in southern Iraq, and the Mogul Emperor Sha Alam sent an embassy to make a treaty to assist Ahmed against his enemies and to establish in Muscat a resident mission in what came to be known as the "Nabob's house".

Ahmed died in 1783 and his grandson Hamad became the *de facto* ruler, though his father, Said, had been elected Imam. On Hamad's death in 1788, Sultan – another son of Imam Ahmed bin Said – took the reins of government, though Said remained nominally Imam. Sultan was brave and of noble countenance and both the British and the French, whose interests were in conflict in the east as well as in Europe, treated him and addressed him as if he were the Imam. He was, however, killed at Lingeh in southern Persia in 1804 by the Qawasim of Ras al Khaimah who were at war with the Omanis over trade.

Said bin Sultan succeeded his father, Sultan, and reigned for 52 years until 1856. Although some of the nobles who held the great castles were often in rebellion and there were incursions by the Wahhabis from what is now Saudi Arabia, his internal authority was in no real doubt. Europeans who met him were impressed by his commanding figure, his courtly, dignified and affable manner and his kindness both to his own people and to foreign visitors.

Said's influence in the Arabian Seas was considerable. Like his father he sought to control the trade passing through the Strait of Hormuz and to this end he retained control of places on the north of the Gulf which had been acquired by Sultan. These were Hormuz, Qishm and Henjam islands together with Gwadur on the coast of Makran, which remained a part of Oman until 1958, and Chahbar.

It was, however, in Africa that he made his deepest impression and from 1829 his heart and

main interests lay there. This was to have profound results later for the sultanate. He sought alliances with local queens in Madagascar and Mozambique and controlled the main Arab settlements on the east coast of Africa, making Zanzibar his second capital and transferring the Omani state archives there. He was very much the "Sailor Sayyid" and had 20 ships of his own for private trade – which he delighted in commanding himself – and paid much attention to the Omani navy. He presented King William IV of England with a fine warship, later called the Liverpool and received in return a handsome yacht, *The Prince Regent*. He also presented King William and Queen Victoria with fine

Arab stallions and mares. Britain and Oman had been in treaty alliance since 1800, but Said also negotiated a Treaty of Amity and Commerce with the USA in 1834.

He gave fresh life to interests in East Africa, particularly by introducing cloves as a cash crop in Zanzibar and establishing rice plantations. Many European travellers have left accounts of him and Burton, Speke, Livingstone, Grant and Stanley all had good reason to thank the Al bu Said rulers of Zanzibar for assistance in their

SAYYID THE SAILOR

Said bin Sultan was very much the "Sailor Sayyid". He had 20 ships of his own for private trade - which he delighted in commanding.

the ruler in Muscat to adjust the inequality in the inheritance, as Zanzibar was at this time by far the richer part. From then on the two parts remained separate, though governed by members of the same family until 1964, when Zanzibar was incorporated into Tanzania.

Thereafter the fortunes of Oman as a maritime power declined, accelerated by the introduction of steamers by the British India Steam Navigation Company in 1862. This put the Omanis at a disadvantage

African explorations. He had 36 children, but a problem arose between two of his sons after his death in 1856 on a voyage to Zanzibar. Thuwaini in Muscat claimed the whole Sultanate but Majid in Zanzibar also claimed it.

The matter was referred to Lord Canning, the Viceroy and Governor-General of India – though the Sultanate had always been regarded as an independent state. With British pragmatism Lord Canning decided that Majid should rule Zanzibar and pay 40,000 crowns a year to

FAR LEFT: portrait of Sayyid Said bin Sultan Al bu Said.
ABOVE LEFT: Feisal bin Turki.
ABOVE RIGHT: Taimur bin Feisal.

since their ships ceased to be competitive in the carrying trade.

Thuwaini was killed by his son Salim in 1866. A struggle for control of the Sultanate ensued between Azzan bin Qais, based in Rustaq, who headed the tribes of the Interior, and Turki, who had been Governor of Sohar and was another son of Said bin Sultan. Turki won the day in a battle in Wadi Dhank in 1870 and was recognised by the British. This event has present-day significance, as the Basic Law of the State issued in 1996 specifies that the Sultan of Oman "shall be a male descendant of Sayyid Turki bin Said bin Sultan", who is also "a legitimate son of Omani Muslim parents."

Turki was sultan until 1888, although he had to cope with rivalries. He was then succeeded by his son, Feisal, who took over at the age of 23 and ruled until his death in 1913. Taimur bin Feisal followed him until 1932, when he abdicated in favour of his son Said bin Taimur.

During these reigns the Interior of the country was not always at one with the sultans and their jurisdiction on the coast. The strong sheikhs of the Harth tribe in the Sharqiyah posed a particular problem and

HABIT OF A LIFETIME

It was Said's tragedy that even when oil revenues began to accrue in 1967 he was unable to abandon the habit of careful husbandry.

Imam Mohammed bin Abdulla al Kharusi died and the new Imam Ghalib, with his brother Talib, tried to establish central Oman as a separate principality. This matter was not settled on the ground until 1959 and even then the problem was of such a proportion that "The Question of Oman" came up every year at the General Assembly of the United Nations until 1971.

Sultan Said bin Taimur took over a country which was still in debt, the economic situation being exacerbated by the gen-

the very name of the country, Muscat and Oman, reflected this dichotomy.

In 1913 the tribes of the Interior elected Salim bin Rashid al Kaharusi as Imam. Eventually accommodation was reached with an agreement – sometimes called (erroneously) "The Treaty of Seeb" – under which Taimur bin Feisal agreed not to interfere in the affairs of the Interior, not to impose taxation in excess of 5 percent and to allow the tribes of the Interior to enter Muscat and the coastal towns in safety and freedom. This administrative modus vivendi – although in a sense it re-emphasised the historical differences between coast and Interior – worked satisfactorily until 1954, when the

eral depression of the late 1920s and early 1930s. By his own sustained and patient efforts he largely restored the situation. His stewardship ensured that when Sultan Qaboos took over in 1970 the state's finances were in a relatively flourishing state. A man of great charm and ability, it was his tragedy that even when oil revenues began to accrue to Oman after 1967 he was unable to abandon the habit of economy and careful husbandry which had been imposed on him earlier by hard necessity.

In 1967 a local rebellion of the Dhofar Liberation Front in the south of the country grew into something more serious, when it received support from the People's Democractic Republic of Yemen and communist countries. The intentions of the main revolutionary body were made clear in their name: "The People's Front for the Liberation of Oman and the Arabian Gulf". The situation reached such a point that Said was displaced by his son Qaboos on 23 July 1970.

The reign of Sultan Qaboos

Sultan Qaboos, the 12th member of the Al bu Said Dynasty, was 31 on his accession and he proclaimed his faith in the future by announcing that his country would be known as "The Sultanate of Oman" instead of "Muscat and Oman". He also said in his first speech that

ber of Arab states, leading to "Imamate Offices" in Cairo, Damascus, Riyadh and Beirut.

Apart from the Omanis associated with the Imamate and those in rebellion in Dhofar, there were many other Omanis in opposition to Sultan Said, and young men, despairing about the limited educational facilities offered by the only three schools in the country, had sought education abroad – especially in Egypt and the Soviet Union. Thus at home the young Sultan found a country severely affected by the brain drain as well as lacking the infrastructure and services of a modern state. Abroad he yet had to acquire new friends. Only Britain and India were repre-

under a new flag people would no longer distinguish between the coast and the Interior and the southern province of Dhofar. Oman was to be one single country. The auguries were, however, not auspicious. Sultan Said had made no effort to seek international recognition, though his country was and had always been regarded as independent. He remained happy under the penumbra of the British, making it easier for the Imam Ghalib to establish relations with a number

LEFT: Oman's flag: white represents peace and prosperity, red for the struggle to liberate and unify Oman, and green for Islam.
ABOVE: Police Cadet Training School, Muscat.

A WORLD OF DIFFERENCE

When Sultan Qaboos came to power in 1970 Oman had become an inward-looking backwater that lagged centuries behind the modern world. There were only three schools in the whole country (in Muscat, Muttrah and Salalah), no newspapers, radio or television, no civil service and only one hospital (with just 23 beds). The average life expectancy of an Omani was 47. Muscat still closed its gates at night, and, apart from the road to the little airport at Bait al Falaj, there were only two graded roads in the whole country– from Muscat to Sohar and from Muscat to Fahud.

sented diplomatically in Muscat, each with a Consul-General.

There was a shortage of Omanis with the training to bring Oman into the modern world. But the Sultan and the Omanis themselves were undaunted and with the help of Britain and others began the onerous tasks ahead. Ministers were appointed and the governments structured to enable Oman to become a modern state using the gradually increasing oil revenues. The objects were to establish internal peace and security; to frustrate attacks inspired from abroad; to attract back talented but disaffected Omanis; and to gain international recognition.

and rebels were able to see for themselves that a new era had indeed begun. The growing physical signs of development brought an increasing number of rebels over to the government side. Thus, as a result of a hard military campaign – fought with the help of Britain, Iran and Jordan in particular – combined with civil measures, the Sultan was able, on 1 December 1975, to announce the end of the war.

A nation transformed

After that the government, which became increasingly sophisticated, was able to concentrate more closely on development and laying

Goodwill missions were despatched to Arab countries. In 1971 applications were lodged to join the Arab League and the UN and both were successful, showing that the international community accepted that genuine change had taken place. "The Question of Oman" was removed from the agenda of the UN.

However, the main challenge to Oman's future in 1971 lay in Dhofar. Although Sultan Qaboos had offered a general amnesty immediately on his accession, the initial effect on the rebels was minimal. Between 1972 and 1975, however, the military balance began to shift in the Sultan's favour, especially as the "hearts and minds" campaign began to carry conviction,

down a countrywide infrastructure. Thus a country without any basic services outside Muscat itself has been transformed since 1970 into a land with a fine road system, public electricity and water even in remote villages, and schools and hospitals spread all over the country.

One of the Sultan's first acts was to encourage general education, and schools in makeshift tents were immediately opened in many places. From this small beginning the Omani educational system has reached standards unimaginable earlier. At its apex is the Sultan Qaboos University, which opened to students in 1986 and there are now seven faculties (Science, Agriculture, Medicine, Engineering, Arts, Commerce and Economics, and Education and Islamic Sciences). The Medical School's degrees are recognised in Britain, the US and Western countries generally, and Omani hospitals are recognised by the Royal Colleges in Britain and by similar bodies elsewhere.

The educational system now embraces some 965 schools and state education, which is free, is provided at the primary, preparatory and secondary levels. There are also teacher training institutions for all levels. The scale of provision necessary may be judged from the fact that the

A LONGER LIFE

The average life expectancy of Omanis in 1970 was just 47. It has since risen to 68.

1970 was 47 whereas it is now 68. The Royal Hospital in Muscat has 630 beds and is magnificently staffed and equipped, and health provision reaches down to the village level with excellent referral hospitals in every region.

Sultan Qaboos has encouraged music of all sorts since his accession, when there was virtually no-one in Oman who could blow a note. Now Oman has very fine military bands, which have even taken the Edinburgh Tattoo by storm. The bands include bagpipers – a form of bagpipe having long been

average number of children in an Omani family is now 7.4.

This statistic also underlines the scale of the necessary commitment to public health. There has been a dramatic change in the general health of the Omani people since 1970 – so much so that, whereas in 1970 the common complaints were associated with the Third World, it is now the diseases of the First World which are concerning doctors. The average life expectancy in

FAR LEFT: schoolchildren were among the first to benefit from the influx of riches.
ABOVE: female students at Sultan Qaboos University, which opened in 1986.

known in the Gulf area. There is also a Royal Oman Symphony Orchestra, which frequently plays with well-known soloists.

None of these developments would have been possible had it not been for a healthy economy and this depends primarily, despite attempts at diversification, on oil and gas. Plans for the export of Liquefied Natural Gas (LNG), of which Oman has considerable reserves, will add an important element from 1999.

What the future holds
The Omanis have an economic vision of Oman 2020 and manage their development through a series of Five Year Plans. Emphasis is placed on

encouraging a competitive private sector and diversification. Agriculture and fisheries are important but industrialisation is also envisaged and already a variety of factories is making an impact on Oman's economy and social life.

The country's geographical location on the Indian Ocean and the south side of the Strait of Hormuz gives it an importance beyond its size and wealth. For this as well as historical reasons the Omani Armed Forces have benefited from a large proportion of the Omani budget. The Sultan's own training at Sandhurst in England gave him both knowledge and a deep interest in military matters. The Forces now consist of an

In Foreign Affairs there has been an extraordinary change since 1970. After admission to the Arab League and United Nations, Omani Foreign policy – which was very much that of the Sultan personally – was to reinforce its age-long connections with India and Pakistan and to develop relations with other Arab and neighbouring and friendly states, notably with the moderate states of Egypt and Jordan.

By the 1990s Oman had diplomatic relations with 124 countries. Oman's foreign policy has been empirical and pragmatic and is based on good neighbourliness, non-alignment and the encouragement of co-operation between the

Army of infantry brigades, each with four battalions, together with armoured, artillery, parachute, reconnaissance and training troops; a special commando unit; and tribal militia, in addition to the Royal Guard. The Royal Navy of Oman has eight fast patrol boats – necessary for Oman's long coastline of 1,700 km (1,000 miles) and four Province Class fast-attack craft armed with Excocet missiles. The Royal Air Force of Oman – the men of which, like the other Armed Forces, are Omanis who have been educated and trained to handle the most sophisticated weapons – are equipped inter alia with Hawk, F3, Jaguar and Hunter aircraft supported by an integrated air defence.

Gulf states and particularly those of the AGCC (Arabian Gulf Co-operation Council). Oman's pragmatic policies often appeared in the past to run counter to the political wisdom of the day but have been subsequently applauded as far-sighted. In the exercise of this policy Oman has maintained a dialogue with Iran, their large neighbour to the north, throughout the Iran-Iraq war and up to the present.

Early in Sultan Qaboos's reign, Oman revived its interest in East Africa and many Zanzibaris and Kenyans of Omani origin were welcomed to Oman, and subsequently played important parts in its development.

Participation of the people in government has

grown steadily. People were always able to appear before the walis, the governors of regions, and participate in their *majlis* (councils), but they are now able to share in more modern institutions. In 1981 a state Consultative Council was formed consisting of 55 members including government officials. In 1991 it was replaced by the Majlis Ash'Shura consisting of 59 members selected from citizens nominated by the people of each *wilaya*, or governorate. There are no official members and the Majlis Ash'Shura is much more directly

WOMEN FIRST

Oman was the first Arab country to have women police officers.

but the armed forces and in government. They are also represented in the Majlis Ash'Shura.

Generally the Omanis retain the courtesy and charm for which they were famous in the past. They still justify the words of the 19th-century traveller, J.S. Buckingham: "The people seemed to me to be the cleanest, neatest, best dressed, and most gentlemanly of all them Arabs...and inspired a feeling of confidence, goodwill and respect."

Thus, from somewhat unpromising beginnings, Oman has been transformed into a mod-

involved than the earlier assembly in considering and questioning the process of government. The Basic Law promulgated in November 1996 not only deals with the royal succession, but also political, economic and social principles, public rights and duties, the organs of government and the judiciary.

Oman was the first Arab country to have women police officers and women now hold high rank not only in the Royal Oman Police,

LEFT: Sultan Qaboos at the three-day Gulf Co-operation Council held in Oman in 1995.
ABOVE: street decoration at Sultan Qaboos's silver jubilee held in 1995.

ern country, strong and respected by its neighbours with defined and agreed frontiers, all the earlier boundary disputes having been settled amicably – most significantly with Yemen.

Sultan Qaboos's achievement in building Oman into a modern nation state will inter alia be illustrated by the many beautiful buildings which have been erected – mosques, government buildings, palaces and private houses. Many are based on the traditional buildings which the government has done much to restore all over the country. They testify to the general harmony which has been created in a state once riven with faction.

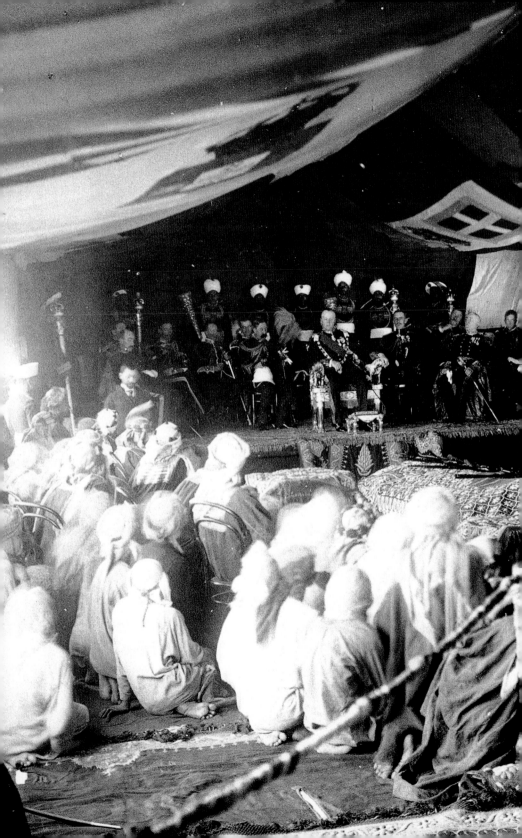

THE UAE FROM RAGS TO RICHES

How the discovery of oil and an urgent need for security persuaded seven
of the Trucial sheikhdoms to put aside local rivalries and form a federation

After more than a quarter of a century of existence, the United Arab Emirates has proved to be the Arab world's most successful attempt at unity despite widespread scepticism at its formation in 1971. Attempts by Egypt under Gamal Abdel Nasser and later by Libya under Muammar Gaddafi to merge with other states were short-lived, and the squabbles surrounding such moves made the emotive concept of "the Arab nation" something of a laughing stock among commentators outside the region. The UAE was one of the most unlikely bids for unity but has shown itself to be the exception to the rule.

Old roots

The well- known rags to riches story of the Gulf states of Arabia created by the oil boom of the 1970s and 1980s caused many commentators to look upon the peoples of the region as upstarts. The UAE is quite new as a state – and its inhabitants are rather proud to be *nouveaux riches* – but these once largely maritime peoples can trace their roots back to prehistoric times. Excavations at Umm an-Nar (now in the shadow of an oil refinery), an island off Abu Dhabi, and elsewhere show that in these early times the Gulf Arabs were under two influences – those of Mesopotamia and of the Indus civilisation in India (*see pages 22–24*).

The coastal dwellers were the first to deal with European travellers, but inland the Bedu (*see page 93*) continued their timeless nomadic existence or settled in places where they could grow a few crops, such as dates, or graze small numbers of livestock. The latter in particular achieved their sense of belonging not in terms of the districts or fixed borders within which they conducted their spartan lives but through

---

PRECEDING PAGES: Britain's Lord Curzon visits the sheikhs from Abu Dhabi, Sharjah, Dubai, Ajman and Umm al Qaiwain in 1903.
LEFT: UAE President Sheikh Zayed bin Sultan Al Nahyan celebrates the end of Ramadan, 1962.
ABOVE RIGHT: aerial view of Abu Dhabi town 1962.

their tribal allegiances to a local sheikh. Long before the rise of Islam in the 7th century, the land that is now the UAE and the other Gulf states of eastern Arabia – Kuwait, Bahrain, Qatar, Saudi Arabia and Oman – had a tightly structured Arab society that was divided into tribes, sub-tribes and clans.

Key tribes

The Bani Yas , who had become a powerful federation of clans, were described as "land-faring Bedouin", wandering great distances in search of grazing for their camels and then returning to their date gardens around the Liwa oases on the edge of the Empty Quarter, the vast unbroken sand desert immortalised by the explorer Wilfred Thesiger in *Arabian Sands* .

As long as anyone can remember, the leader of the Bani Yas has always come from the sheikhs of the Al bu Falasah sub-tribe. One of them, called Nahyan, was the ancestor of the present ruling family of Abu Dhabi. As pearls became increasingly popular in India and then among European women in the 19th century, the Bani Yas gravitated towards the rich pearl banks of the Trucial Coast.

The town of Abu Dhabi was founded as early as 1761 after a good supply of water had been found there. In Dubai, fresh water flowed abundantly into aquifers from the Hajar Mountains, and a settlement that grew up there was a dependency of Abu Dhabi. In 1833, Dubai's Bani Yas set up its own principality, which has been ruled by the Al Maktoum family ever since.

By 1900 the pearling industry was enjoying such a boom that not enough men could be found to man the 1,200 boats engaged in the

tional consortium. But oil exploration only really began in earnest after World War II.

The decline of the British Empire after the war, especially the granting of independence to India in 1947, helped to speed changes in the Gulf. The British presence in the region was to linger a few more years. With British help the Trucial Oman Scouts (a defence force) was set up in 1951, while the following year a Trucial States Council was formed to bring a kind of unity to the coastal region through twice-yearly discussions on common problems and interests. The rulers of what became the United Arab Emirates had not met all together since 1905.

trade. Control passed irrevocably to the sheikhs who ruled the coastal areas, and this power was further reinforced when the British made it clear they were only interested in the coastal areas and effectively endorsed only their rulers.

The pearl boom collapsed in the 1930s with the arrival of the Japanese cultured pearl. The ensuing depression caused some pearl boatmen to burn their boats in desperation for fuel. But the search for a new fuel had begun.

Oil concessions

Between 1936 and 1952 the rulers of the seven Trucial States signed oil concession agreements with the Iraq Petroleum Company, an interna-

The British withdraw

The big bombshell came when Britain's cash-strapped Labour Government decided that big savings must be made in defence. In February 1967 the Prime Minister, Harold Wilson, announced that Britain's military presence east of Suez was to be scrapped by the end of 1971. It spelt the end of British protection in the Gulf and was in breach of written agreements between Britain and the Trucial States, as well as the unwritten Arab law of trust and friendship. The British decision led directly to the formation of the UAE and speeded the process of modernisation in the region, which had already been accelerated by the discovery of massive oil deposits. But the emirates were ill-prepared for sudden independence and had few qualified people, particularly in the spheres of defence and foreign affairs, which the British had long taken care of.

The UAE is formed

Shortly after the British decision to withdraw from the Gulf, the rulers of Abu Dhabi and Dubai announced that they would form a federation and reached an agreement over off-shore oil rights. The speed of their action helped to settle frontiers, even though the UAE is now

ABUNDANCE OF RICHES

In a few years Abu Dhabi's resources were to carry the emirate's income to the highest in the world.

between any opposing views. Sheikh Zayed bin Sultan Al Nahyan, Abu Dhabi's ruler, repeatedly said that the resources of Abu Dhabi – which in a few years were to carry the emirate's income to the highest in the world –were "at the service of all the emirates".

Dubai and Abu Dhabi invited the other Trucial States – Sharjah, Ajman, Umm al Qaiwain, Ras al Khaimah and Fujairah – to join them in the federation, together with Qatar and Bahrain. There was clearly a strong mutual desire for security, modified by a wish

a patchwork of subdivisions making up the seven emirates that form the federation – a process that had never been formalised before because of the changing tribal allegiances.

Abu Dhabi, well aware by 1970 that it was the richest oil emirate, was especially anxious to reach an overall agreement on a federation and clearly demarcated borders because of the mounting importance of oil revenues and the oil rights that would be granted once land divisions had been agreed. From the outset it adopted a policy aimed at finding a middle ground

ABOVE LEFT: Abu Dhabi in 1954.
ABOVE: the Ruler's Palace, Abu Dhabi, also in 1954.

for a degree of independence in each emirate, as the departure of the British drew near.

By June 1971, Bahrain had decided it was secure enough on its own and announced in August it would not join the federation, while Qatar followed suit less than three weeks later. Six of the remaining sheikhdoms had reached agreement on a federal constitution by July, and the UAE formally came into being on 2 December. In Ras al Khaimah, Ruler Sheikh Saqr bin Mohammed al Qasimi – hoping that he would find oil on Qatar's scale – held out for another two months before swallowing his pride at the prospect of massive largesse from Abu Dhabi and joined the federation too. Sheikh Zayed of Abu

Dhabi became President of the Federation, with Sheikh Rashid bin Saeed Al Maktoum, Ruler of Dubai, as Vice-President and Prime Minister.

Security was a major motivation for forming the UAE, and such concern was justified in view of the massive oil deposits that had been discovered in the region since the 1930s. The possibility of a threat from the Soviet Union (particularly after the invasion of Afghanistan and its support for the Marxist regime in South Yemen) always existed in the

SAFETY FIRST

Security was a major motivation for forming the UAE, and such concern was justified in view of the massive oil deposits that had been discovered since the 1930s.

Qatar and Oman) seized the chance to set up their own organisation – the Arabian Gulf Co-operation Council. It was conceived on the lines of the European Economic Community but with defence interests hidden under the surface. The AGCC formally came into being in 1981.

Iraq's invasion of Kuwait in 1990 sharpened the focus on a number of needs. Above all, it was instantly recognised that the threat from Baghdad was a threat to all six GCC countries. It was launched on the flimsy pre-

minds of the Gulf leaders and of the Western politicians whose countries came to depend on the Gulf's oil.

Closer to home new threats emerged. On the eve of the British military withdrawal from the Gulf and formation of the UAE, Iran occupied the islands of Abu Musa and the Tunbs, claimed by Sharjah and Ras al Khaimah respectively. That dispute has never been resolved.

The volatility of the region was underlined by the Iran-Iraq War, which broke out in 1980, as well as the Arab-Israeli conflict. With the strategic giants of the Gulf – Iran and Iraq – busy fighting each other, the six oil-rich Gulf monarchies (Saudi Arabia, Kuwait, the UAE, Bahrain,

text that Kuwait and the UAE had allegedly exceeded their oil export quotas set under the Organisation of the Oil Exporting Countries (OPEC) agreement. By a stroke of good fortune for the people of the UAE, Kuwait was the nearer country to Iraq and thus was the first in what might have been a series of domino-style collapses, including the UAE, in the face of Saddam Hussein's army, if the international community had not acted swiftly to check him. One thing that the Iraqi move did make clear was that the UAE and its people had never been more important in their entire history.

ABOVE: levelling the desert for agriculture.

Father of the UAE

Ever since the United Arab Emirates was formed in 1971 it has been led by one man, Sheikh Zayed bin Sultan Al Nahyan, but he is much more than head of state. Not only is he the father figure of the nation but he also spans two eras – the one of near-starvation and the current one of astonishing wealth.

Born in 1918 in the picturesque Al Hisn Fort in Al Ain, where he grew up, Sheikh Zayed has never lost his love for his birthplace, where he became Governor in 1946. The explorer Wilfred Thesiger met him in the 1940s and described him in his classic book *Arabian Sands* as "a powerfully built man of about 30 with a brown beard. He had a strong intelligent face, with steady observant eyes, and his manner was quiet but masterful. He was dressed very simply, in a beige coloured shirt of Omani cloth and a waistcoat which he wore unbuttoned...He wore a dagger and cartridge belt; his rifle lay on the sand beside him.

"He had a great reputation among the Bedu," Thesiger went on. "They liked him for his easy informal ways and his friendliness, and they respected his force of character, his shrewdness and his physical strength. They said admiringly, 'Zayed is a Bedu. He knows about camels, can ride like one of us, can shoot and knows how to fight.'"

Zayed's hands are still calloused from the days when he used to dig, move stones and plant trees while working on restoration of the ancient *falaj* system of canals needed to irrigate the date groves of the Buraimi oasis near Al Ain.

It was in 1966 that his brother Shakhbut, who had ruled the emirate since 1928, abdicated, and Zayed replaced him. The first oil exports had begun only four years before and two years later the British Government was to announce its withdrawal from the Gulf, so that Abu Dhabi and the other Trucial States would have to manage all their own affairs.

The new ruler thus took over in stirring times and quickly joined forces with the late Sheikh Rashid bin Said Al-Maktoum of Dubai in laying the foundation stones of a new federal state. The two were elected President and Vice-President respectively (*see page 64*).

President Zayed's considerable skill in achieving lasting harmony between the traditionally rival inter-ests of the UAE's seven emirates, each with its own ruler, is now well-established – particularly in the face of a chorus of scepticism at the outset from commentators who claimed it would never work. There is no doubt that Abu Dhabi's soaring wealth helped. Zayed has always been quick to help the poorer emirates financially and to spend money on vast public works throughout the country, including a welfare state that is second to none worldwide.

One of the most impressive sights for any visitor to the UAE is the landscaping and planting in a country that is still 70 percent desert. The dream of the poor Bedu to make the desert bloom has come true in Abu Dhabi, as nowhere else. "Greening" the

desert was a vision that was always dear to Sheikh Zayed's heart. Outdoor plants and trees are given away free on demand to all UAE householders.

Abu Dhabi city now boasts some two dozen parks and nearly 1,500 hectares (3,700 acres) of grass. They are watered by electronically controlled sprinkler systems and decorated with spectacular fountains. Zayed's beloved Al Ain has some 40 parks and is connected to Abu Dhabi City, 160 km (100 miles) away, by a six-lane highway divided by a constantly watered grassed reservation, planted with palm trees, bougainvillea, oleanders and other flowering plants, while a thick belt of trees on either side keeps the desert at bay. It is a far cry from the sandy track that was all that connected the two places in his youth.

ABOVE RIGHT: Sheikh Zayed bin Sultan Al Nahyan, the leading light in the transformation of the UAE.

FOOTPRINTS IN THE SAND

Oman and the UAE are on the rim of the Empty Quarter, a vast wilderness of dunes impenetrable to any but a few Bedu until as late as the 1930s

CARSTEN NIEBUHR

Arabia has attracted some of the world's best-known explorers, from Charles Montague Doughty to Richard Burton. Names associated with Oman and the UAE in particular include Ibn Battuta, Marco Polo, the 18th-century Danish explorer Carsten Niebuhr (left), whom William Gifford Palgrave called "the intelligence and courage that first opened Arabia to Europe" and, in the 20th century, Bertram Thomas, Wilfred Thesiger and Sir Ranulph Fiennes, who attempted to find the lost city of Ubar (*see page 192*) as recently as 1991. In addition to such well-known names there were British political agents and Western officials in the employ of the sheikhs who by the very nature of the territory – tribal and inaccessible – were often the first foreigners to set foot in a place.

△**PERCY COX**
When Percy Cox, British Agent in Muscat from 1899–1904, visited Tanuf, he was told that no rain had fallen since the last British agent to visit had taken photographs there 25 years before. The sheikh demanded compensation for the crops that had perished as a result.

WILFRED THESIGER

The explorer most fondly remembered in Oman and the UAE today is undoubtedly Wilfred Thesiger, whose two great crossings of the Rub al Khali (Empty Quarter) are documented in his book *Arabian Sands*. Thesiger seized the opportunity to cross the Great Sands when he was offered a job in the region by the Anti-Locust Research Centre. To make himself less conspicuous in hostile country he pretended to be a Bedu from Syria, a disguise that could explain his strange looks and accent. His disguise was generally successful, and often only his closest Bedu companions knew the truth. The one thing that gave him away, they said, were his unusually large feet. They advised him never to leave footprints in the sand.

▷ **DRESSED FOR THE PART**
Thesiger in Bedu dress

THE FIRST TO CROSS THE SANDS

Though Wilfred Thesiger 's crossings of the Rub al Khali are probably the most famous, the first Western person to cross the Great Sands was Bertram Thomas in 1931, who trekked from Salalah to Doha in 55 days. He was followed later that year by Harry St John Philby, who took a more difficult route through Saudi Arabia.

Thomas described his journey in his book *Arabia Felix*. He said of the Sands, "a vast ocean of billowing sands, here tilted into sudden frowning heights, and there falling into gentle valleys...without a scrap of verdure in view. Dunes of all sizes, unsymmetrical in relation to one another, but with the exquisite roundness of a girl's breasts, rise tier upon tier like a mighty mountain system."

He also talked of the "roaring of the sands" which, he said, resembled a ship's foghorn.

Thomas was in Oman as Financial Adviser and Wazir to the Sultan of Muscat and Oman, a post he took up in 1924 after serving as Political Officer in Iraq. Through his position he gained the respect of unpredictable tribal leaders who usually scorned, even murdered, infidels.

This proved invaluable on his journey through the Sands. Thomas claimed the Rub al Khali "obsesses every white man whose life is cast in Arabia".

◁ **MARCO POLO**
Another famous visitor to the region was Marco Polo (1254–1324). He visited Dhofar – "a great and noble and fine city" and then sailed up the Omani coast to Qalhat.

◁ **IBN BATTUTA**
The 11th-century North African geographer Ibn Battuta visited southeast Arabia when he was just 21. His original six-month *Haj* extended to a 24-year trip taking him as far as China.

△ **CROSSING THE RUB AL KHALI**
This map shows Thomas's journey in 1930–31 (orange) and Thesiger's crossings in 1946–47 (green) and 1947–48 (purple).

منصة حفر في المناطق البحرية

THE OIL BOOM

The speed and scale of change brought by the discovery of oil in the Arabian Gulf was unprecedented in world history.

If you had travelled to Abu Dhabi by air in 1959, you would have found there was no regular air service and, if you had managed to find a charter plane, you would have touched down on a bumpy airstrip on Abu Dhabi Island – or you might have had to land at Britain's Royal Air Force base in Sharjah, which accepted a few commercial flights. Once on the ground, you would have had a bumpy ride by Landrover over the sand dunes until you reached a single line of palm trees, a white-washed fort and a cluster of buildings that marked Abu Dhabi town. Hens, goats, donkeys and camels wandered then between the houses and their fences of woven palm leaves.Two other white buildings dominated the sea front – the police headquarters and the oil company, and the odd fishing boat might have been drawn up on the beach.

It was in that year that oil was first discovered in commercial quantities in Abu Dhabi – in the offshore Umm Shaif field. The following year it was found on shore in the Murban field. Two more years were to pass before the first oil exports left Abu Dhabi via Das Island. Dubai first exported oil only in 1969, but Dubai had long been the bustling centre of the entrepot trade for the entire Gulf region, centred on its famous creek. Abu Dhabi, although much bigger in territorial terms, was the poor unsophisticated rival down the coast – a relationship that was to be revolutionised almost overnight.

In reserve

Today, the UAE's proven hydrocarbon reserves amount to 98 billion barrels of oil – enough to last well into the 22nd century at present extraction rates – and 6.13 trillion cubic metres (210.43 trillion cubic ft) of gas, estimated to be enough for at least 350 years. The oil reserves alone represent 10 percent of the world's total, the third largest after those of Saudi Arabia and

Iraq, while gas reserves (4 percent of the world's total) are the fourth largest after those of Russia, Iran and Qatar. This wealth is staggering for such a small country with a population of only 2.3 million. The speed and scale of change it was to bring in its wake has never been approached in world history and would

certainly have been totally incomprehensible to the poor fishermen and pearl divers of Abu Dhabi in the 1950s. This was the archetypal rags to riches story.

Of these massive reserves, no less than 92 billion barrels of oil are to be found in Abu Dhabi, with 4 billion in Dubai, 1.5 billion in Sharjah, 0.5 billion in Ras al Khaimah, but none so far in the other three emirates. Abu Dhabi's reserves are forecast to be enough for another 130 years, Dubai's for 25–30 years, while the other fields in Sharjah and Ras Al-Khaimah will be exhausted much earlier. These figures give a fairly accurate impression of the relative prosperity and economic power of the seven emi-

PRECEDING PAGES: petroleum exhibition in Abu Dhabi.
LEFT: drill poised to drop into the seabed.
ABOVE RIGHT: offshore oil rig.

rates, although Dubai depends more than the others on its trade and entrepreneurial skills.

Prospectors toiled for 39 years in the Sultanate of Oman before discovering commercial quantities of oil in 1964, and exports followed three years later. Although the Sultanate has also enjoyed the fruits of modern development, the effects were delayed a few years until Qaboos bin Said acceded in 1970.

Oman is less well endowed with oil and gas

SPEND, SPEND, SPEND

When the oil money first flowed out to the people, shoppers would go out and buy 15 loaves of bread at a time – not because they needed so many but because they had never been able to afford to buy so much in their lives.

was the oil-price shock of 1973, when the 13 countries of the Organisation of the Petroleum Exporting Countries (OPEC), of which the UAE is a prominent member, quadrupled crude oil prices and then increased them massively again in 1979. From around $5 for a standard barrel of crude oil in 1972, oil reached a peak of $34 in 1979.

In Abu Dhabi in particular, money is no object. When the oil money first flowed out to the people, as

than other Gulf countries. Its known reserves of 5 billion barrels of oil are likely to be exhausted in less than 20 year, although gas reserves are rather healthier at 2.7 trillion cubic metres.

Although the UAE is in most ways a model of a free-market economy, oil and gas reserves and production – as in the other Gulf states – stay firmly in state hands, each emirate controlling its own. Without the poorer emirates in the UAE to look after, Abu Dhabi would, it has been argued, be able to claim the highest per capita income in the world if it were an independent state on its own.

Discovering so much oil and gas by the 1960s was not alone the key to all this prosperity. It

it did quite quickly, shoppers would go out and buy 15 loaves of bread at a time – not because they needed so many but because they had never been able to afford to buy so much in their lives. Looking back, the locals now smile sheepishly at what had seemed at the time outrageous extravagance. Cynical Western expatriates today may remark that, in the richest Gulf states, belt-tightening for the average local means thinking twice about replacing the Rolls Royce when the ash trays are full or sighing at the unaccustomed prospect of turning down the air-conditioning in their luxurious homes when they leave for one of their many globe-trotting vacations.

The two oil shocks benefited all the countries around the Gulf, which, through a geological freak of nature, contain more than half of the world's oil reserves, 45 percent concentrated in the hands of Saudi Arabia, the UAE, Kuwait and Qatar. Iran and Iraq have vastly bigger populations than the six monarchies of Arabia and so the new oil money did not go so far there. Less well endowed Bahrain – the first country in the region to export oil (in 1934), which is now almost exhausted – and Oman are not OPEC members.

WELL ENDOWED

Through a geological freak of nature, the countries around the Arabian Gulf are known to contain more than half of the world's oil reserves.

world's most lavish hotels, set on immaculate private sandy beaches along a superb winding corniche. Luxury is the norm. Dubai's creek offers more of the same, while some of the wealth has spilled over into the much poorer emirates. In Oman, trade was limited to dates, limes and animal skins in the pre-oil 1960s, but in tourism Oman is now second only to the UAE.

Most Europeans who came to the UAE during the oil boom recall gigantic dusty construction sites in Abu Dhabi and Dubai, as

The 1970s and 1980s saw businessmen, particularly from the West, rushing to the Gulf like bees to a honey pot. Many made a lot of money. The UAE, for its size, absorbed a lot of them and like its neighbouring states at first paid gullibly through the nose for modern development, before its sharp trading instincts reasserted themselves.

Changing landscapes
Abu Dhabi's capital today is an extraordinary modern city of tower blocks, some of the

---

FAR LEFT: Abu Dhabi's first refinery at Umm an-Nar.
ABOVE: Sharjah oil workers pose for the camera.

REAPING THE BENEFITS

Not least among the investments was social security, all of it free to locals (though not to expatriates, whose companies footed the bill). Citizens enjoyed the last word in schools and universities, while new hospitals resembled 5-star hotels with the finest medical personnel and the best equipment that money can buy. Any cases that required overseas treatment were granted it at government expense. There was no need for taxes, and essential utilities such as water, electricity and, of course oil, were so heavily subsidised that their consumer prices were derisory.

this once barren desert territory turned itself into a modern state. Even those who returned after an absence of a decade were astonished at the scale of change. Now that all major construction work has been finished, there is a gentle, unhurried atmosphere, as most of the frantically competitive Western businessmen have gone home. Tourists are not needed in Abu Dhabi, but its people are proud of what they have achieved, so why not show it off to paying guests ?

Too quick too soon

The problems of rapid development were experienced by all the countries of the Gulf, and in

enough. In 1971 the city of Jeddah had a budget of less than £850,000. Six years later it had leapt to £225 million. The Mayor had streets of compacted sand simply covered with asphalt so that people could see money was being spent, but it lasted only a matter of weeks and in places the blistering heat caused the roads to expand into waves that rose 2 metres (6 ft) into the air.

And in Qatar, where in living memory people had been starving, the government gave everyone a free house and the money to furnish it and buy a luxury car. They also had the right to a government job at a handsome salary: if there was no job available, the salary was still guar-

often more acutely than in the UAE and Oman. Saudi Arabia, richest of all the Gulf states by far, with more than a quarter of global reserves of oil and the world's biggest oil fields, on shore and off shore, saw even more astonishing changes. By the mid-1970s , the port of Jeddah, through which nearly all Saudi imports passed, was such a bottleneck that ships were queueing outside for six months to unload their merchandise. Cement bags were being winched to the shore by helicopter in desperate bids to beat the shipping queue but then changed hands for 30 times the price they had fetched only months before. Oil revenue accumulated so fast that government departments could not spend it fast

NATURAL GAS

The UAE has led attempts to recover the enormous quantities of natural gas extracted automatically with oil but previously wasted by flaring. It now recovers virtually all of it, with 92 percent coming from Abu Dhabi, 5 percent from Sharjah, 2 percent from Dubai and 1 percent from Ras al Khaimah. The UAE is the world's seventh largest exporter of natural gas with very bright prospects for future exports. Oman, too, has considerable reserves. From 1999 a massive new development by LNG (Liquefied Natural Gas) will pipe gas from central Oman to Sur for export, increasing revenues by 20 percent.

anteed. Many Qataris took up the right to lease their car back to the Government and then earned a further salary for driving it on official duties. As one ageing driver put the situation laconically, "God decided it was our turn".

Kuwait invested a lot of its oil revenues wisely, and by law 10 percent had to be put into the Fund for Future Generations. After the second oil price shock of 1979, it was calculated that the Kuwaitis could all sell off their valuable piece of real estate called Kuwait, invest the proceeds and

GREEN DREAMS

Greening the desert came to be regarded not just as a dream but as a practical need.

schools, the government buildings, airports and defence establishments had been put into place. The foreign businessmen who went home after the oil boom subsided were led by the big construction companies and the purveyors of goods and services that could soon be provided by the Gulf Arabs themselves. Once the modern infrastructure was in place, the local builders could take over.

Wealth bred all kinds of fears for security. Up and down the Gulf there was an uneasy feeling that one day the Western and other developed

then retire to the south of France on an income of not less than £50,000 a year – every man, woman and child. Kuwait became the first nation of independent means in history. National pride stopped this happening, but some doubtless regretted it had not been done when Iraq invaded Kuwait in 1990.

The chance to take stock

As money was the last commodity that was in short supply, it did not take many years before all the highways and houses, the hospitals and

ABOVE LEFT: natural gas at Jebel Ali port, Dubai.
ABOVE: natural gas plant, Dubai.

countries that imported so much oil from the Gulf might hit back in the face of oil price rises by refusing to supply the Gulf states with food, and so food security, as much as military protection (on which huge sums were already being spent), became a new sphere of investment.

Despite the inhospitable climate and the lack of water, massive resources were devoted to agriculture, and greening the desert came to be regarded not just as a dream but as a very practical need. Incredibly, Saudi Arabia became the world's sixth largest producer of wheat, far more than the population could consume, while Dubai was able to export surplus strawberries to Europe in the winter months.

Forward planning

Despite the unprecedented cornucopia, the shrewdness of the Gulf Arabs quickly showed behind their spending sprees. Even the Saudis, whose oil could last until the end of the 21st century, planned for the days when the oil runs out or is superceded by some as yet unknown source of energy. Diversification away from oil was planned as soon as the bonanza began.

Extracting the oil was so easy and cheap that the prospect of very low-cost energy to fuel local industry soon became a reality. Steel and petrochemical industries sprang up, eventually reaching world-class, as well as cement works,

construction firms and food processing. Then came furniture and pharmaceutical factories. Imports of many commodities were cut dramatically. Exports have grown steadily.

The headlong rush to spend was bound to ease up eventually. In 1982, the Kuwaiti Government, one of the most cautious in the region, put its foot down, doubling the local price of petrol (the first rise in 12 years) and raising diesel prices 700 percent. Filling up the tank of your Cadillac for $3 was no longer on. The days of wanton profligacy were over.

A global oil glut was already building up, caused partly by new sources of non-OPEC oil from regions like the North Sea, Mexico and China. Prices on the open market began to fall, and the following spring the official price of oil fell – for the first time since the boom – by $7 to $27 a barrel. Two years later prices collapsed, at one stage edging below $10 a barrel and in subsequent years have mostly hovered at around $15–20 a barrel, while quotas agreed between OPEC members became necessary.

But by then massive financial reserves had been built up in the Gulf monarchies, and although they suffered relative recessions, there was a reluctance to make unpopular economies although some cutbacks were made. Budget deficits became the norm, although not in the UAE, but there was no question of bankruptcy. The Gulf economies had simply settled down to the kind of level that Western countries were used to, which meant borrowing on the international markets.

The Gulf War

Iraq's invasion of Kuwait in 1990 was the only occasion when Western governments have been seriously involved in the Gulf politically and militarily since the start of the oil boom. It proved that the West would keep their promises and defend the status quo in the Gulf to safeguard the supplies of oil on which they depend.

In OPEC negotiations, Kuwait, the UAE and Qatar have not necessarily sided with the Saudis, although the four have rarely been in direct conflict. They compete against each other but cannot afford to differ over oil policies as much as they can with other members of OPEC.

Sooner or later the countries with smaller oil reserves will run out, and oil in the Gulf will be the preserve of Saudi Arabia, Iraq, the UAE and Kuwait, but new oil discoveries continue to push that scenario further into the future. Will that mean an oil shortage and another oil price shock? The experts, who have often been wildly wrong, say this would harm oil producers as well as importers. But expanding production is costly and time-consuming. If the Gulf Arabs act too soon they will be left with white elephants – too late, and there will be another oil price explosion that will damage their investments overseas. Whatever the answer, the UAE Government is determined that the last barrel of oil ever sold will come from their country.

ABOVE LEFT: buying at source.
ABOVE RIGHT: sooner or later the sun will set on oil.

DAILY LIFE

In spite of the massive changes that have taken place in Oman and the UAE,
everyday life is still very traditional in many respects

The UAE and Oman are frequently misunderstood by outsiders. People imagine them to be traditional Muslim countries with many restrictions for everyone. In fact, both countries succeed in mixing modern life with established social traditions. They combine a delight in their culture and heritage with a sense of their place in the modern world.

Another common misconception is that women in the UAE and Oman are compelled to lead very restricted lives, barred from working outside the home or driving. In fact, in the cities women are increasingly strong in the workplace and although home is central to their lives, education and work are also important.

Family values

Life tends to revolve around the family home, in cities and rural areas alike. Family life is important for both men and women, though the roles of the sexes are different. Broadly, it is the men who go out to work and finance the home, and the wives and other women of the family that organise and run the house and children. However, there are plenty of exceptions to this stereotype. Many richer women own and run businesses, in some cases performing roles that shield them from the public. And less well-off women often work for large institutions such as banks and public utilities, doing office work and dealing directly with customers. Some work at women-only branches.

That said, expectations for girls are fairly well established – to grow up, marry and have children, although nowadays many are well educated and have often travelled abroad. As a result, many young women will work prior to marriage, and even continue working afterwards, although this is mainly in the cities where there tend to be larger family units of relatives to look after the children.

PRECEDING PAGES: making *halwa*; enjoying a smoke.
LEFT: the army band plays on, Dubai.
ABOVE RIGHT: Oman's first pay-phones were introduced in 1980.

Eighty percent of girls have an arranged marriage with a partner from a suitable family known to her own family. Often a girl will marry a first cousin or person from the same tribe. Girls marry young, usually shortly after puberty, and Muslim women always marry a Muslim, although the same is not true of men.

Muslim men socialise regularly outside their homes, unlike the women, who mainly socialise in one another's houses. Men are not usually involved in the daily routines of childcare, but families do go out together as groups. Increasingly fathers are seen in public in domestic family scenes, playing with their children in the park, shopping with their wives, or going out to dinner as a family.

Bride to be

Marriage is a major point in a girl's life and this important event is governed by strict traditions. First, the girl's family receives a marriage proposal from the groom's family, who will then visit the girl's family. If all goes well, formal arrangements begin. According to custom, the male members of the two families meet to discuss the bride money and set the date for the wedding. The agreed sum of money and jewellery given to the bride remains her own throughout marriage, so that in the event of a divorce she has this to fall back on.

Once the marriage licence has been arranged and recorded in the courts, preparations are made for the preliminary and wedding-night celebrations, usually

ANOINTED

The evening before her wedding the bride will be massaged all over with perfumed oil and will hold her "henna night".

The bride is kept in seclusion for three days before her wedding day (it used to be seven days). During this time she is pampered by a beautician, engaged for the duration, and surrounded by her mother and closest female family. The evening before her wedding she will be massaged all over with perfumed oil and will hold her henna night (*laylat al henna*). For this the bride wears a traditional gold-embroidered green dress and elaborate gold jewellery, often part of her wedding gift. She sits on traditional

held at the bride's house. Invitations are issued verbally between the women, while the men announce the occasion at the mosque. These days printed invitation cards may be sent out.

On the day of the wedding the bride's house is lit up with hundreds of lights strung around trees and the house walls. Huge, colourful tents are erected for the guests and tables are laid with many different dishes. Food is served in separate areas for the men and women, and it is usual for guests to take away parcels of food to give to friends and relatives unable to attend the festivities. To cope with this mass catering, a special kitchen is usually constructed within the wedding area.

cushions – *te-keyya* – and henna is applied to her feet and hands in intricate patterns.

The henna, a powder made from the leaves of an Egyptian tree, is mixed into a paste with water and then squeezed through a cone of paper like icing and left on the hands and feet to dry overnight. When the dried crust drops off the next morning it leaves a lacy stain on the skin which lasts for several weeks. The best henna artists can command large payments.

Entertainment is an important component of any wedding. At city weddings, which now tend to be modern affairs in large hotels, the highlight is usually a singer and a band. In rural areas dancing is an important part of the festivities. In the popular "hair dance" (*ayala*) girls swing their long hair as they dance in a circle. Singing often accompanies the dancing and loud clapping keeps the rhythm going. This can go on for hours and the effect is noisy and exciting.

Men are allowed to marry a non-Muslim, although in many cases their wife will convert to Islam at some time during their marriage. Islam allows a Muslim man to have up to four wives, providing he can afford to treat them equally, but polygamy is not a widespread phenomenon today. In general

BABY CARE

A newborn baby's eyes are lined with *kohl* to cleanse and protect them from infection.

The blessing of children

Married women are expected to bear children, and the birth of a child of either sex is considered a very happy occasion. These days most women give birth in modern hospitals, a development that has slashed the previously high mortality rate. Despite the clinical surroundings, the atmosphere is festive with many visitors, all bearing presents and offering special foods for the new mother and baby. Huge bouquets of flowers line hospital corridors, and all the new mums on a

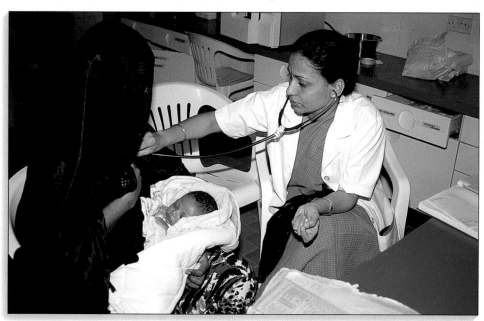

it occurs only when a first wife is unable to bear children, or is a non-Muslim.

Divorce is relatively uncommon, and is usually instigated by the husband in the event that his wife is sterile or has not borne a son. Women can also divorce a man, although this is seldom done as the stigma of divorce is greater for a woman. A divorced woman will normally return to live with her family, taking with her the money she took into the marriage as her means of support.

ABOVE LEFT: cooking for a wedding feast, Oman.
ABOVE: mother and baby are checked out at a maternity unit in Salalah, Oman.

ward are congratulated by all the visitors, even though they have probably never met before.

As with marriage, the birth of a child is attended by many traditions. The mother is given specially prepared food and drink, including camel and goat's milk, and the baby's eyes are lined with *kohl,* believed to cleanse and protect the eyes from infection.

The way of death

In Islam mourning is not an important part of death. The deceased will be washed and anointed with perfumed oils and then wrapped in a white cloth and borne on a simple bier to the cemetery. The body is always buried (on its side facing Mecca) and if possible burial should take place on the day the death occurred. Forty days after death, the close relatives will hold a feast to mark the ascent to heaven, believed to occur after this 40-day period.

National dress

All over the Gulf region, one of the most striking features for the visitor is the very noticeable national dress of both men and women. Virtually everyone wears it, and in Oman national dress is mandatory for anyone working in public services. In the Gulf areas men wear a *dishdash*, a white or pastel-coloured ankle-length robe, with a headdress (*ghutra*), held in place by black ropes (*iqal*). On formal occasions, men sometimes wear an over-garment, a gauzy black or brown robe (*bisht*) edged in woven gold thread. In Oman men favour headdresses wrapped like turbans without the black ropes used in the Gulf. One of the most distinctive accessories worn by Omani men on special occasions is the *khanjar* (silver dagger) tucked into the belt.

Women cover their heads and bodies with a voluminous black overdress (*abbaya*). Underneath this they wear a black head scarf to cover their hair. These garments often hide brightly coloured dresses which are long-sleeved with very beautiful necklines and elaborate wrist to elbow decoration, sometimes sewn with crystal beading and sequins. Wealthier women may wear French designer clothes under their plain black *abbaya*.

The *abbaya* may also be edged in beads or sequins and the under scarf is sometimes also very beautifully decorated. The result is that a sense of style is not lost by these black robes. Make-up, too, is important, and used to increase allure.

The traditional face mask (*burqa*) worn in Oman and the UAE is a light and simple structure semi covering the face, with a thin strip across the forehead and over the nose, leaving the eyes and cheek areas free. The mask stops under the nose, covering the top lip but leaving the chin free. It is made from black cotton material, the front covered with a golden, purple or red dye with a blueish sheen. There are several designs and women may wear a gold one for special occasions.

The mask is worn by many married women, though not by all women in public. Instead the

headdress may be drawn across the face as a veil. To wear the *burqa* or not is a matter of personal choice, and can be dependent on the situation. City women often wear this mask in very public places such as supermarkets and shopping malls, yet may not wear it when driving their cars. In Dubai many women do not wear it in the streets at all. In Oman and in the more conservative, rural areas of the UAE it is still common.

The social round

Social visiting is an important part of daily life and a favourite form of relaxation. Men and

THE COFFEE CEREMONY

Every visitor to a UAE or Omani home will be offered coffee or tea as a symbol of hospitality. The traditional Gulf coffee – *kahwa* – is made from green coffee beans, is very strong and sometimes flavoured with cardamom or saffron. Poured from a distinctive coffee pot, it is served in tiny cups without handles, which are refilled several times until a guest indicates that he has had enough by shaking the cup from side to side. Three cups is considered the polite number to drink, indicating pleasure at the coffee, but not drinking to excess. The social custom of drinking coffee is also important in business.

women usually socialise separately, with men visiting one another in the *majlis,* the public part of the home, to sit together, drink coffee, talk and exchange news, and eat sweetmeats. The entrance to the *majlis* is always separate from the main door into the domestic sections of the house, where the women frequently hold their own, all-female social gatherings for family members and neighbours.

It is customary for all guests to remove their shoes when entering the sitting areas of a home – a measure originally adopted for reasons of

UP IN SMOKE

The appearance of the incense burner marks the end of a social occasion.

offered *seh*, a preserve made from mashed ripened dates.

At female gatherings similar customs are followed, but with the additional offering of perfumes, a selection of which will be passed around on a tray. Each women will unstopper the bottle of the scent she prefers and anoint her face and clothes. Afterwards the incense burner is filled and passed around, so that each guest can fan scented smoke onto her face. Men may also use incense. These ceremonies signify the end of the occasion.

hygiene when streets were considerably dustier than they are today but now simply a matter of polite behaviour.

Food is a key ingredient of any social meeting. Coffee or tea is always offered as a symbol of hospitality even during quite brief encounters, as are dates and sweetmeats. In Oman one might be offered *dibis*, a date syrup derived from pressed dates, mixed with *tahineh* and spread on bread. In the UAE it is common to be

ABOVE LEFT: studying for the future at Sultan Qaboos University, Muscat.
ABOVE: young men watch the world go by on a corner in Ajman.

High days and holidays

Other important social occasions are the main religious festivals. The *majlis* is particularly important during these holidays or during the nights of the month of Ramadan. This is the month (a moveable period governed by the Hejira calendar) when Muslims fast during daylight hours. After sunset, there is a busy round of dinners and meetings.

After Ramadan has ended, the holiday celebrations of Eid take place, when gifts are exchanged and important meetings take place in both the business and social worlds. This is an important time for tribal leaders and businessmen to visit and reinforce ties.

Education and work

Employment of nationals in the local workforce, filling jobs previously occupied by immigrant expatriates, is increasing in both Oman and the UAE. Many young nationals are now well educated, and qualified to fill jobs in industry, banking and other main sectors of the economy. More and more international companies are starting training schemes for these young men and women, enabling them rather than the vast army of expats to run the country.

THE HOODED CLAW

It is not unusual to witness falcons being carried into city offices, where they are placed, hooded, on perches next to their owner's desk.

Education is the key to the future of both countries. Women have grasped this fact with great success, and are forging ahead in education and employment. Their results at university are impressive, and they are fast becoming a skilled force to be reckoned with. Middle or higher income women are often sent abroad to be educated, although with the growth of first-class universities in the region this is no longer necessary.

Even in rural Oman women are being encouraged to attend local women's centres where, among other things such as learning about birth spacing and family health matters, they can receive training in needlework. The aim of this programme is for Omani women to be able to replace expatriate tailors in rural areas over the next few years. Such centres include a creche.

Sporting passions

Within the UAE and Oman there is much for the young national to do in the way of leisure activities. There are many cinemas, bowling alleys and indoor sports, but thanks to a good climate for much of the year outdoor sports are popular. Many nationals are passionate followers of their football teams in the national leagues.

But traditional sports are still enjoyed, including horse racing, camel racing, and falconry. Horse racing, particularly in the UAE has become a world class event (*see pages 115–119*). Camel racing is an old traditional sport, though the modern owner usually follows his camel in a four-wheel drive around the inside of the track, while the spectators in the box watch the action on enormous television screens from the comfort of an armchair. The ancient sport of falconry continues and it is not unknown to see falcons being carried into city offices, where they are placed, hooded, on perches next to their owner's desk.

Other forms of game hunting are not widespread although many of the rich pursue the sport abroad. Modern substitutes are clay pigeon shooting and rifle clubs. Water sports are also extremely popular thanks to the combination of superb beaches and climate. Traditional dhow races are held annually, as well world-class power boat racing in which UAE competitors have excelled. Water skiing, jet skiing and windsurfing are popular. Sand-surfing is another variation on a theme.

Woman tend to visit parks and beaches, some of these are built specifically for women and children.

These factors and the ever-changing attitudes of society as the possibilities and needs of modern life are absorbed, create an exciting and interesting place to live. Each generation makes its own small changes to a culture living in a traditional way.

ABOVE LEFT: view to a kill, statues of falcons beside a window at Dubai's World Trade Centre.
RIGHT: surfing the dunes.

THE BEDU

The life of the Bedu used to be one of thirst and hunger, and of great journeys to find water. The lack of such hardships today is testing the strength of their culture

The Bedu of Oman and the Emirates are among the oldest tribal peoples of the world. Tracing their ancestry from a mythical hero called Kahtan in the Yemen, these southern Arabian tribesmen are sometimes referred to as the "Pure Arabs". Kahtan has been identified with Yoktan, listed in the Old Testament as a descendant of Shem, a son of Noah, making these tribes of older, purer Arab stock than the younger northern tribes that trace their ancestry from Ishmael. Of these southern tribes the Bait Kathir and Rashid are the most famous, having been Wilfred Thesiger's companions on his exploration of the Empty Quarter in the second half of the 1940s. Other tribes in the region include the Harasis, Al Wahiba, Ajman and Jenuba. Bedu is the Arabic word for nomadic tribespeople. The singular is *Badawi*, but as this word is little known in the West, Bedu is used throughout this book. The more common Western version, *Bedouin,* is a strange double plural which does not exist in Arabic.

For modern Westerners concepts of tribal descent and purity of blood lines may appear somewhat irrelevant. In Arabia, family ties and tribal identity are the building blocks of society, modern as well as traditional. A citizen of any Arabian Gulf state is identified by a personal name, then as the child of a father and grandfather, and then by their clan and tribal name.

This sense of being from a line of descent, of belonging to a family grouping that extends through a clan and a tribe to a wider society is fundamental to Bedu life and is probably the single most important influence within the relatively young states of the Arabian Peninsula.

Adapt or die

The Bedu evolved as nomadic herdsmen, living off the products of their animals, drinking their milk, weaving their hair, making leather from

PRECEDING PAGES: men making *halwa*, a sticky sweet made with honey and sometimes almonds.
LEFT: Bait Kathir Bedu in Rub al Khali, Oman.
ABOVE RIGHT: Harasis Bedu girl.

their skins and eating their flesh. Their lifestyle was the supreme adaptation of man to the hostile environment of some of the hottest, driest areas on earth. The land is too sterile for them to stay long in any one place. The vegetation is too thin and grows too slowly. Instead the Bedu have learnt to move, following the limited rains,

grazing their animals on small patches of grass wherever they can be found. It was not an easy life but it was survival. T.E. Lawrence wrote that "the Bedouin ways were hard even for those brought up in them", that they were "a death in life". If one asks the Bedu today what life was like in the old days, their tales are of constant thirst and hunger, of great journeys to bring water from wells or to look for areas that had received some rain.

Whenever one thinks of the Bedu one imagines them with their camels and their goat hair tents. The *bait sharar* ("house of hair") is synonymous with the Bedu. The reality is slightly different. There are tribes who have never lived in tents and those who have traditionally only used tents during winter when a shelter from the cold, wind and occasional rain has been a necessity. In Oman it is only the tribes of the Empty Quarter, the Bait Kathir and Rashid that have used tents. Previously the tribes of the stony plains, where trees are more plentiful, built their camps around the shade of these natural shelters, often covering them with blankets or cloth to improve them. Other tribes, especially on the coast, used palm fronds to build easily assembled and dismantled shelters called *barasti*. These are still a common sight around the Wahiba Sands in Oman and along the coasts of

the Arabian Gulf. More recently the Bedu have started to use metal grills to form temporary shelters. These are common among the Bedu on the Jiddat al Harasis in Oman, where they resemble metal bedsteads up-ended and joined together to form small cabins.

Tent life

But the goat-hair tent remains a potent symbol of the nomadic way of life. It is easily pitched and taken down – customarily the work of women, although usually helped by men. The main division within is between the men's section and the women's side where the family's possessions are stored and food is prepared. The

sides are usually separated by a decorated woven curtain. In a large tent a third division may be used for storage or cooking. The divisions effectively create a public and private space, all male visitors being entertained in the men's section. It is here that the coffee and tea utensils and fire are placed. Essential for entertaining, the coffee hearth comprises a fire on which the coffee beans are roasted using a ladle and stirring rod, plus coffee pots of various sizes, and bags of wool or animal skin containing the coffee, tea and sugar. Added to this is a mortar either of brass or wood, the kettle and tea utensils. Other articles might include a camel saddle and, once guests have arrived, rugs and cushions for them to sit on.

The kindness of strangers

Hospitality is an essential part of Bedu life. All passers-by are welcomed by a set exchange of greetings and the asking of news, to which the reply is always that there is no news or only good news. Guests are then refreshed with tiny cups of coffee and glasses of sweet black tea of which it is polite to drink three cups before refusing more by wobbling the empty glass.

In a land where people are few and far between and there is little to sustain life, hospitality becomes a means of survival. In the past any traveller seeing a tent would immediately travel towards it, sure of receiving a friendly welcome. In exchange for his news he would be greeted with tea and coffee and be invited to share a meal. According to custom, he would be assured of food and shelter for a period of three and a third days. It was, and still is today, a system of mutual support. In the desert, today's guest may well be tomorrow's host. In the absence of men, women and even small children are also bound by this code of generosity. It is not unusual to be invited into a camp by a young boy who will make coffee with great dignity, following the Bedu code with care and concentration, knowing that in the absence of his father, the family's honour is in his hands.

Hospitality is part of a strict code of honour

NO NEWS, GOOD NEWS

Passers-by are welcomed by a set exchange of greetings and the asking of news, to which the reply is always that there is no news or only good news.

and protection in a world fraught with danger. Visitors knew that they would not only receive food and shelter, but also the protection of their host for the duration of their stay and for another three days after – this being the time it takes for all traces of his host's food to pass through his body. The code tying the host to his guest is called the bond of salt. Even if a visitor carried only the salt of his host in his stomach, he could call on his protection.

In fact a traveller need not even reach the tent but simply

it can only be lost through shameful conduct women are a protected part of Bedu society, and the tribes' women are kept well away from the opportunity to bring shame on the the family.

In the past when a family's fortunes were uncertain, governed by acts of nature and the fortunes of inter-tribal raiding, the Bedu developed a fatalism whereby everything lay in God's hands. The only things a person could be sure to control were his dignity and honour. This meant that even if circumstances left a man

HONOUR MATTERS

Honour is held not just by the individual but by the family and tribe as a whole. It is passed on from genera-tion to generation. It can be lost as well as won.

receive a response to his greeting of "*As-salaam aleykum*" (peace be with you) for this code to operate. With the reply "*Waleykum as salaam*" (with you be peace) came the protection of the speaker and all his or her kinfolk, even if the words were spoken by a child.

The code of honour called *sharaf* is extremely strict, honour not just being held by the indi-vidual but by the family and tribe as a whole. It is passed on from generation to generation, and lost as well as won. *Ird*, the honour of a woman, plays an important role in the family *sharaf*. As

ABOVE LEFT: girl in the Wahiba Sands, Oman.
ABOVE: making rope and camel harnesses.

destitute he could still be proud in more wealthy company, knowing that he would be judged pri-marily on his reputation and conduct.

Camels, a crucial commodity

Up until the adoption of motor vehicles, the entire lifestyle of the Bedu relied on the camel. It was the beast of burden by which they moved their tents and possessions as well as the mode of personal transport. The camel is still a source of milk, meat and wool. The wool, prized for its strength and warmth, is used to make cloaks and equipment such as udder bags, as well as the detailing on the tent curtain.

Under hot summer conditions the Bedu try to

water their camels every day or two days, but in winter the period can be weekly or, if the grazing is good, the herds will not be watered at all. If need be, the camel can show incredible stamina. H.R.P. Dickson, a British political agent in Kuwait between 1929 and 1936, and author of *The Arab Of The Desert*, reported how one Bedu shiekh, in about 1925, rode a camel between Riyadh and Nasriyah, in Iraq, in eight days, covering a distance of about 1,287 km (800 miles). On Wilfred Thesiger's first crossing of the Empty Quarter in the winter of 1946–7, his party travelled for two weeks across the sands without finding a well where it could water its animals.

Different tribes have developed their own thoroughbred strains that are valued for particular characteristics. Thus the Omanis breed tall, long-legged camels famous for their speed and stamina. Camel racing has become the main way in which the Bedu can show off their skills as breeders and trainers. Race meetings in both Oman and the UAE attract enormous crowds with winning camels being exchanged for vast sums of money in much the same way as race horses in the West.

All camels in the Middle East and Arabia are domesticated and the work of herding, breeding and milking them is traditionally the task of men. Each camel will be branded with the mark, called a *wasm*, of its owner and tribe, on its neck, shoulder or hind-quarters. However even a man with over 100 animals will commonly know his own camels individually and will usually have given names to each of them.

Camels are kept by the Bedu primarily as a source of milk. Thus the majority of animals are female. The Bedu will rarely kill an adult camel, unless it is obviously sick and dying. However, they will slaughter the occasional calf, especially a male. The only time that adult camels are normally killed for food is in order to feast a large number of guests such as for a marriage or to honour a visiting shiekh.

The Bedu's diet consists primarily of camel milk drunk cold or hot or boiled with bread (a mix called *threat* by the Bait Kathir in Oman), or cooked with rice. Meat is an occasional luxury and more often than not is goat's meat bought in the market. Along the coasts fresh and salted fish is an important staple for people and animals, and sun-dried sardines are a traditional supplementary feed for camels.

The role of Bedu women

Whatever the impression of women in Muslim society in general, Bedu women enjoy a great deal of freedom and play an important role. In such a harsh environment, and with the heavy demands of a nomadic existence, it would be impossible for the family to survive without the women taking their share of responsibility. What segregation exists is not a reflection of lack of status. Women's separation from strangers and the use of veils is due more to a sense of modesty and the protective concern of the menfolk. It is a custom more akin to a code of chivalry than a regime of repression.

THE WAY THE BEDU RIDE

Camel saddles vary between southern Arabia and the north. In Oman and the UAE the frame of the saddle (*shedad*) is no more than an anchor that sits over the hump and holds in place a cushioned strap that runs over the camel's hindquarters. The rider then sits or kneels behind the hump, supported by the cushioned pad of the strap. This requires a great sense of balance which the Bedu like to display by standing up on their camels. Instead of bits, a loop halter is placed around the animal's muzzle or a rope is simply attached to a ring through its nostrils.

As children, brothers and sisters are taught to have a special sense of closeness. A young boy is encouraged to see himself as his sister's protector, to bring presents to his female siblings. He is their chaperone in public and champion of their honour. A Bedu male would not tolerate any person harming his sister's reputation, verbally or otherwise, and until his sister is married he will act as a surrogate husband. Even after her marriage he is responsible for the protection of her honour (more so than her hus-

> ## WOMEN'S WORK
>
> Where families have no sons, the daughters will often be found herding all the animals, entertaining guests and driving the family vehicles.

camel herds. Where families have no sons, the daughters will often be found herding all the animals, entertaining guests and driving the family vehicles.

Under normal circumstances, the segregation of the sexes so obvious to the stranger hardly exists. When staying with families, foreign visitors may be surprised by how quickly barriers are broken down. After a few days, Bedu women often start to relax as they see their men accept a visitor. They may even dispense

band) as her reputation is that of his family's, thus her honour is his honour.

Similarly young girls are their brothers closest confidantes and are encouraged to contribute to their brother's comfort and public image. Sisters will sew and weave their brothers' clothes and camel trappings, as well as cook their favourite foods for them. From a very early age a girl takes an active part in the daily work of the family. She will herd the sheep or goats if they have any, and a teenage unmarried girl will typically be left to pasture one of the family's

with wearing their face masks if the guest comes to be regarded as an honorary member of the family.

Dress code

The costumes for both men and women are similar in basic outline among all Bedu and practically common to all Arabs. Both sexes wear a long garment that covers the body from the base of the neck to the ankles, with long sleeves, that adheres to the Islamic demand for modesty. However details of cut, material and colour are variable particularly among women. This basic dress, called a *dishdashah* or *dishdash*, is traditionally made of cotton, but can also be made

ABOVE LEFT: Al Wahiba Bedu astride his camel.
ABOVE: Bait Kathir with his *khanjar* in his belt.

from silk, wool or commonly from nylon or a cotton mix. Traditionally the cut of a Bedu woman's dress was larger and looser than her settled sister. The sleeves were longer with trailing cuffs. When working the women would often roll up the sleeves to the shoulder and tuck the front of the skirt into their belts.

When visiting each other or going to a market, the Bedu men of Arabia also like to wear silver or gold belts fitted with highly decorated curved daggers called *khanjar*. These have much more than a

> ### BEHIND THE MASK
>
> Young Bedu in search of an eligible wife can be driven to distraction by skilful flirting.

decorative value, being a daily tool for cutting ropes and killing and skinning animals. Further north the Bedu use straight bladed knives.

Belts designed for carrying bullets are *de rigeur* for men, as are rifles and pistols. It is a common sight in any gathering of Bedu to see the men fully armed as if the desert was on the verge of a war. Firearms and knives are still very much a part of a man's costume and are integral to his sense of manhood and independence.

All Bedu girls cover their hair once they reach puberty. Head scarves are often lacy and semi-transparent showing off any earrings or necklaces the girl is wearing. Among virtually all tribes in the region it is the custom for a girl to veil her face covering it with a *burqa*, a striking mask, made of cotton and dyed with indigo, more like an ancient Greek's visor than a veil. Details of design vary a great deal. Within the general custom of her tribe, a woman has the freedom to make her own mask how she likes. If a girl wishes to be more revealing she can cut the shape slightly smaller, especially around her chin, and cut larger eye holes.

Some young Bedu girls use this freedom to create their own fashions. Al Wahibi girls sometimes wear gold-coloured *burqas* which they style by bending the bottom half outwards. The result is that their masks are not only very eye-catching, but also reveal tantalising glimpses of the line of the jaw and the girl's typically high cheekbones, especially when their head is held in certain positions. Young Bedu men, in search of an eligible wife, can be driven to distraction

WOMEN'S WORK – WEAVING

Weaving, almost entirely in the hands of women, is one of the oldest crafts of the Arabian Peninsula, and the earliest illustration of the ground loom used by the Bedu is in an Egyptian fresco dating back to over 2000 BC.

Women spin using a simple stick with a cross head whorl and hook before dyeing the wool and then respinning the material, producing a double strand of yarn. In the past, natural dyes derived from plants were used; the modern synthetic dyes give access to brighter and more varied colours.

Most decorative motifs are geometric but the repertoire also include stylised representations of familiar objects and animals, such as coffee pots, scissors and

camels. The patterns are repeated to the edge of the piece, reflecting the infinite horizon of the desert.

The tent curtain, the largest decorated piece of textile made by the Bedu, is a warp-faced textile usually in black and white. The white is commonly cotton yarn but can be white camel hair. A narrow pattern, it runs the length of the textile and uses symbols and designs including geometric representations of household objects. Designed to run from the back wall to the front, it is made extra long so that it can be extended into the open space at the entrance of the tent, creating a private space for the women. The curtain is hung with the good side facing into the men's half of the tent.

by this skilful flirting. Young girls think of the veil not as a form of repression, but as a sign of their coming to maturity. They look forward to covering their faces in the same way as Western girls long to wear make up.

Changing times

Today the Bedu are facing a challenge that is testing the strength of their culture. Throughout the Middle East the life of the desert is in a state of transition. Mass production of the motor vehicle and the birth of nation states with political identities have irrevocably changed the Bedu lifestyle. Modern employment, schools,

easy – and the house – cutting the Bedu off from his view across the desert – have alienated him from the environment and deprived him of the roots that give meaning to his sense of hospitality and honour.

The governments of the Emirates and Oman are not blind to the special needs of their nomadic peoples, but finding a meaningful alternative for them, without destroying their culture, is not easy. So much of the Bedu traditions is about surviving in a harsh world where starvation and thirst were constant threats. The oil companies and governments have dug new wells and helped the nomads make the transition to motor vehicles

hospitals and industry are not designed for a nomadic population. To find jobs and take advantage of schools, the Bedu have had to give up their migrations and adapt traditions never designed for a sedentary lifestyle.

One old Bedu sheikh explains this with the example of a man in his house who, on hearing a knock at his door, calls out, "Who is there?" In the old days, seeing a traveller from afar, the man would prepare fresh coffee and go out to meet his visitor with words of welcome. For him, the car – that makes travel too quick and

ABOVE LEFT: Harasis Bedu girl.
ABOVE: preparing a feast in the Wahiba Sands.

by providing grants and simple employment. Deep bore holes provide reliable water where previously there was none. Tanker trucks can now deliver water to the herds, cutting out days of travelling to water sources. Animal feed, bought in town and trucked out to the camps, reduces dependence on pastures. Modern communications and four-wheel drive vehicles make weather forecasting and the search for pasture quicker and more reliable. Once the Bedu were fighters protecting their herds from theft; peace has left them without a role. Lack of demand for their camels has reduced the size of their herds.

The Bedu, without a role that gives value to their traditions, are doomed to disappear.

مستشفى الصقور يرحب بكم
ساعات الدوام من الثامنة صباحاً
حتى الواحدة ظهراً

LCOME TO FALCON HOSPITAL
ECIEVING HOURS FROM
800 A.M TO 1300 P.M ONLY
UNLESS AN EMERGENCY

FALCONRY

Hawking is an old and much-loved pastime in the Gulf. Falconers pay huge sums of money for the very best birds and pamper them accordingly

Falconry is a passionate sport in the Gulf. It has its origins as the hunting technique par excellence of the Bedu, who admired the birds' courage, cunning and proud appearance and took pleasure in their skills at training them. During winter, on the edge of any major town, it is common to see members of the local falconry club exercising and training their birds in the cool of the afternoon.

The main source of falcons in the Emirates is the livestock market in Sharjah, where three or four dealers import birds from Iran and Pakistan. Aged between six months and three years, a bird can be worth anything between US$240 and US$32,000 depending on its species, age, general health and looks, and also the length of its tail feathers, an indication of a bird's flying abilities. Females are preferred over males as they are on average one-third larger.

Although it is illegal to trade in wild birds, they are favoured over more docile captive-bred falcons, which lack the natural instinct to hunt. Fledglings, taken from the nest in the wild, are also less sought after for similar reasons. By contrast, mature wild birds, used to their freedom, are hard to train. These attract more experienced falconers. Properly trained, mature falcons make exceptional hunters.

The best time to capture a bird is on its first autumn migration as it passes over the desert on its way south. These immature wild birds are relatively easy to train, but already have a developed hunting instinct.

The saker, from the Arabic *saqr*, is the most popular bird on account of its size, toughness and versatility. Known for its intelligent hunting tactics, it predicts the movements of its prey and uses the landscape to hide its attacks.

Smaller and more fragile than the saker is the peregrine falcon. Built for speed, it is designed to kill on the wing and is vulnerable on the ground. Difficult to keep in captivity, peregrines have become increasingly rare and valuable. The lanner, or *shahin wakri*, is a small falcon, like the peregrine, but with the qualities of the saker. The gyr has also appeared in Arabia in recent years, but they are exotics, not desert falcons, imported from the Arctic north of Europe and Canada, and desired for their size (twice

that of a peregrine) and good looks.

The season for hawking is very short, lasting from October to January and coinciding with the autumn migration of the game birds, mostly houbara. Falcons are also migratory and cannot stand the desert summer. It was once common for falconers to release their birds at the end of each hunting season. Now owners hang onto favourite or valuable birds throughout the year, caging them in air-conditioned environments.

Falconry has become a sophisticated pastime of the wealthy. All the Gulf sheikhs engage vets to staff private falcon hospitals in an effort to improve the captive conditions of these essentially wild creatures.

PRECEDING PAGES: falcon and owner, Abu Dhabi.
LEFT: a visit to Dubai 's falcon hospital.
ABOVE RIGHT: putting on the leather hood.

ALL THAT GLISTERS – JEWELLERY

Jewellery performs much more than a decorative purpose among the Bedu of the Middle East – it can be a talisman or even the family safe deposit

Oman is particularly rich in silver jewellery which the Bedu, notably the Al Wahiba, still wear in great quantities. The jewellery of the Bedu is not very different in style from that of the townspeople of the region. Never having their own silver or goldsmiths, the Bedu would buy or commission pieces from village jewellers during visits to markets. At other times, travelling traders of *Haj* pilgrims passing through tribal areas would sell their jewellery as well as wares, carpets and firearms to fund their journey.

Jewellery is worn almost exclusively by women and children (though men use silver accessories such as toothpicks, tweezers and ear spoons). Women make up their own pieces with beads and chains bought individually, adding coins, amulets and pendants either received as gifts, earned through the sale of produce, or found and kept for their magical powers. A woman's jewellery is technically her own, but she often also acts as the family bank, a custom dating from the days of raiding when women were immune from robbery. Even today, silver and gold provide a more trusted way of hoarding wealth than putting money into a bank.

PROTECTIVE PROPERTIES

A woman's wealth, worn as necklaces, bracelets, anklets and decorated veils, is much more than a financial reserve. Silver amulets, boxes and cylinders contain fragments of Qur'anic verse to protect the wearer against accidents, snake bites and scorpion stings. In Oman large round silver pendants called *sumt*, believed to contain an imprisoned *djinn* (demon), are popular.

△ **A FAMILY AFFAIR**
The combination of adornment and costume allows women to create tribal identities recognisable by their neighbours. Children, especially male babies, are protected from the evil eye by charms hung around their necks or anklets.

◁ **IN THE MAKING** Muttrah, Bahla, Rustaq, Nizwa and Sur are traditional centres of silver jewellery production in Oman. Each of these centres has its own distinctive style. Sur, for example, favours flower or geometric patterns, Nizwa produces etched lines and Nizwa appliqué.

△ **RINGS ON HER FINGERS**
Rings are commonly engraved with religious dedications, verse or even moons and stars representing the planets, symbols of pre-Islamic beliefs. First finger rings are normally pointed, second finger rings round or rhomboid, third finger ones square, and little finger rings the only ones with a stone.

THE RUSH FOR GOLD

Originally silver was the main metal used in jewellery, with heavy gold pieces such as the necklace above belonging to people of importance (the piece above, now in the TSR Museum in Kuwait, belonged to an Omani princess). But now gold jewellery, largely produced by Asian craftsmen, is replacing silver as a means of hoarding and displaying wealth.

This is as true amongst the Bedu as it is townsfolk. A Bedu woman may walk barefoot and live under a tree, but around her neck she wears several hundred dollars worth of gold and has earrings to match.

Urban centres like Abu Dhabi, Dubai, Sharjah, Muscat and Salalah are the best places to buy gold (which is usually 22-carat). Price tags are governed by current gold prices plus a little extra for the work.

Gold is an essential component of the bride's price. Most brides expect to receive a full complement of gold jewellery – headdress, rings, necklaces and bracelets. Often this will b e specially commissioned.

▽ THE ROLE OF COINS
Coins are often incorporated into jewellery. Among the old silver coins used are the Marie Theresa thaller (originally called riyals by the Bedu), which has an 80 percent silver content.

COMMON TALISMAN
selection on *hirz*, worn for protection against the evil
e. Sometimes a *hirz* will include a compartment
ntaining fragments of paper on which verses
m the Qur'an have been written.

THE EXPATRIATES

For years the Gulf was run by expats who came in search of tax-free salaries and first-class benefits. Times are now changing as nationals reclaim the plum jobs

Expatriate foreign workers are a long-established feature of the oil-rich Gulf countries. In most people's imagination the archetypal members of the species are oil industry workers brought to the country for their technical skill and valued for that but isolated from the mainstream of life. But in reality there is a huge range of expats in both the UAE and Oman and the result is a rich mix of different, interacting nationalities each making its own contribution to society.

Both the UAE and Oman have had non-nationals living in the countries for centuries, but after the oil boom of the early 1970s expatriate labour became essential if the Gulf countries were to become the effective economies they wanted to be. They needed the outside labour to make their national dreams happen.

This was particularly the case in the UAE, where populations were made up of small communities of Bedu or traders, plus some modest farmers in the northern emirates. In Oman there were sufficient numbers of people, but their education and training levels were woefully inadequate.

Situations vacant

The UAE, in particular, actively cultivated its open image and marketed its attractions to foreigners. Both the UAE and Oman, for example, allow relatively free access to alcohol. Though purchase for home consumption is limited to residents with licences and forbidden to Muslims, alcohol can be bought by anyone in larger hotel bars and restaurants. This is an important indication of the open style of thinking which distinguishes these countries from others in the region that do not tolerate alcohol at all or only permit it in expatriate compounds.

But this deluge of people with very different lifestyles and customs has not been without cost for the local populations. Many nationals have

felt their values and society to be under threat. This issue has been particularly crucial in the UAE, where over 75 percent of the population is now expatriate. Such a huge number of non-national residents tends to set the tone of the country, and the nationals are conscious that they are a minority in their own state. In Oman,

the situation is almost the reverse, where 72 percent of the population is Omani, but the very high level of economic and technical influence of the 28 percent of expatriates has triggered a drive in Omanis to take control of their own economy.

Who are the expats?

The most established expatriate communities in the UAE and Oman are the Indians, Pakistanis, and Iranians. A reciprocal pattern of settlement has gone on for generations, with people from both sides often taking nationality in the process. There are Omanis in Pakistan, Indians in the UAE and Oman, and Iranians in the UAE.

PRECEDING PAGES: golf on the "brown".
LEFT: Asian dockers pass time on Dubai Creek.
ABOVE RIGHT: wadi-bashing, a favourite with expats.

To the outsider many Indians, Pakistanis and Iranians are indistinguishable from true nationals: they wear the same clothes, talk in Arabic, have friends in the national community, and are part of the social and business scene.

Another wave of expatriates to come to the UAE during the 1960s and 1970s comprised other Arabs, who found that just as the oil boom was creating a need for skilled technicians, businessmen and managers in the Gulf, their home countries of Palestine, Jordan, and Lebanon were going through terrible political convulsions with war and civil strife. At the same time, Egypt's massive population was looking for profitable work as the grim impact of Arab Socialism under Gamel Abdel Nasser began to be felt by the Egyptian population.

Many families simply packed their bags and sought security and good salaries in the Gulf rather than try to live in the middle of a war zone or in Egypt. To this day, the Lebanese and Egyptian communities are large and important in the UAE.

Westerners make up the third major category of expatriate. In both countries, Britain played an important role as the imperial power until 1971 when it stopped many of its active political involvements east of Suez. The important legacy of British involvement in the machinery of state in Oman and the UAE gave the British community a standing way above that justified by their numbers. However, in recent years British sway has receded and the Americans have taken over as the dominant foreign influence in the region.

The right to nationality

However important the expatriates are to the economy, they remain expatriate. They are not, for example, entitled to the many state benefits enjoyed by nationals. UAE nationals can claim free education, free health care, and grants of free land available for commercial exploitation from which to derive an income, as well as free electricity and water. Oman has similar benefits, but since the population is larger and the government revenues smaller, the scale of the benefits is more modest.

Most importantly, however, expatriates do not have any automatic right to residency, nor are they allowed to claim nationality or own property. In theory it is legally possible in both Oman and the UAE for an expatriate to obtain nationality, but in practice this is rare. Any implication that there should be a right to nationality is a very sensitive issue, since any legally defined access to nationality would mean that many long-term expatriates would find grounds to claim it.

However, in the UAE many expatriates who came in the early oil boom days of the 1970s are still there and their children are growing up in

IN LIMBO LAND

In theory it is legally possible for an expatriate to obtain nationality, but in practice this is rare.

the Gulf. As a result, the UAE is developing twin societies of nationals and expatriates who grew up together at school and are used to interacting, yet remain separate.

However, some have married into other cultures. Young women from many different countries have come to the region for work, but ended up marrying into a large Arab or Indian family.

This social dynamic has yet to unfold to its full potential, as members of the second generation of expats have only recently finished their education and come onto the job market. But it does mark the start of a population which includes expatriates who were brought up in the UAE and know no other country.

The good life

Expatriates have a high standard of living. The cities are clean, with little crime, and the infrastructure is excellent. Company benefits often include accommodation, health care and plane tickets for annual leave home. Salaries are tax-free and opportunities for promotion more forthcoming than in countries with tighter management and union practices. Many individuals come to the Gulf to do one job, find an opportunity to move up the ladder quickly, or to move to a totally dif-

TRAPPED BY SUCCESS

Some become prisoners of their expatriate packages of salaries and benefits and cannot return home.

nomenon is common among Europeans, it is more intense among Asians, whose home economies cannot offer anything like the savings potential of the Gulf. The result is that many will do any job in order to remain.

This is the dangerous downside of a life which offers many positive aspects, including the excitement of absorbing the cultures of many different people in one place. The bond of expatriatism allows all sorts of people to mingle, people who might never get near one another in any other context.

ferent field, and prosper, all within a few years. Similar achievements elsewhere might have taken decades.

As a result, people want to stay in the Gulf even though the very high salaries of the 1970s have dropped away. They commit to large mortgages, heavy school fees, and a lifestyle they would not be able to afford at home. They can become a prisoner of their package of salaries and benefits, unable to return home without a drastic loss of income. While this phe-

ABOVE LEFT: working on the expat tan, Dubai.
ABOVE: Filipino chemist working in the Amouage perfume factory, Oman.

TIME OFF

The only gap in many Western expats' lives is the lack of a Western cultural life. This is compensated by excellent recreation facilities. Fabulous beaches and watersports are features of both the UAE and Oman, and the desert interiors of both countries offer opportunities for overnight expeditions, camping, or simply picnic lunches in the sand dunes or wadis. There are also some great holiday destinations in easy reach. Jordan, Israel and Egypt are only a short flight away, India only two hours, and even the Maldives and Seychelles are within range for a long weekend.

KINGS OF THE TURF

How the Maktoum family of Dubai transformed international flat racing and made Dubai the setting for the richest horse race of all time, the Dubai World Cup

In Britain it's long been customary to talk about horse racing as the Sport of Kings. The present Queen Elizabeth, like her mother before her, is both a knowledgeable and enthusiastic student of bloodstock and racing form. No Derby or Royal Ascot meeting would be complete without her avid attendance in the royal box. But considering her resources and the number of horses she has had in training, her big race successes have been surprisingly few. And you have to go back to her Silver Jubilee year in 1977 to find the last occasion on which she won a classic horse race in England.

Royalty's influence on the Turf may have waned but its continuing association with the sport has acted as a magnet for other wealthy and ambitious individuals from all corners of the world. American industrialists, Japanese tycoons and international aristocrats like the Aga Khan continue to duel regularly on the racetracks of Britain, Ireland and France.

Yet however important and influential these figures may be, their activities still pale into insignificance when compared with the phenomenal investment in bloodstock that has been undertaken by a small group of powerful men from the Middle East. Racing may no longer be the sport of European kings but it is emphatically the sport of Arab sheikhs and princes. And within those heady circles not even such stellar figures as Saudi Arabia's Prince Khaled Abdullah, owner of the great 1986 champion racehorse Dancing Brave, can match the scale of influence now exerted over the Turf worldwide by the Maktoum family from Dubai.

The Maktoums

There are four Maktoum brothers. The eldest, Sheikh Maktoum bin Rashid a-Maktoum, became ruler of Dubai and Vice President of the UAE on the death of his father Sheikh Rashid

in 1990. Sheikh Hamdan, the second eldest and known to British racing lovers as the owner of the 1989 and 1994 Derby winners Nashwan and Erhaab, is Dubai's Deputy Ruler and the UAE's Minister for Finance and Industry. The youngest brother, Sheikh Ahmed, is in charge of the Central Military Command and shares his brothers'

enthusiasm for horses. But it's the third brother, His Highness Sheikh Mohammed bin Rashid Al Maktoum, Crown Prince of Dubai and the UAE's Defence Minister, who is by far the most dominant figure in international racing.

Sheikh Mohammed is an imposing man in every way and he has brought his formidable reputation to bear in pursuit of a lifetime's dream: to focus the world's attention on the Middle East through the thoroughbred, the beautiful and capricious creature that owes its very origins to this region. Every thoroughbred racehorse competing in the world today can trace its lineage back to three Arab stallions – the Godolphin and Darley Arabian and the

PRECEDING PAGES: late-night line-up of competitors.
LEFT: Sheikh Hamdan Al Maktoum (left) at the races.
ABOVE RIGHT: Sheikh Mohammed bin Rashid Al Maktoum, the driving force behind Godolphin.

Byerley Turk – that were "imported" into Britain more than three centuries ago to improve the speed and stamina of the domestic breed. The Sheikh's ambition to see the thoroughbred return in glory to its desert roots enjoyed its defining moment at Dubai's Nad Al Sheba racetrack in March 1996. The occasion was the first-ever running of the US$4 million Dubai World Cup, now the undisputed richest horse race in the world. But the journey to that star-studded event began more modestly in England nearly 30 years ago.

A dream in the making

It was while he was studying at Cambridge University in England in the late 1960s that Sheikh Mohammed first became attracted to the flavour and atmosphere of nearby Newmarket racecourse. The history and traditions of British racing so appealed to him that within 10 years he and his brothers all had horses in training there. Their first big classic win came when a horse of Hamdan's called Touching Wood won the 1982 St Leger at Doncaster.

The Maktoums' investment in bloodstock was soon flowing on a massive scale, though some outside observers felt that the family were spending their money not wisely but too well. One or two English trainers and bloodstock agents were talking openly about Arab patronage being the racing equivalent of a "magic carpet ride" to the bank. The Sheikhs duly wised up to the people who were trying to take advantage of them and adjustments were made. But not to the spending spree. By the end of the 1980s the Maktoums' involvement in racing had spread to unprecedented levels. Today, the family has more than 1,500 racehorses in training, at home in Dubai, in Europe and North America; treble that number in broodmares, their foals, weanlings and yearlings; and vast property interests in thoroughbred stud farms in England, Ireland and the USA.

At the time of Sheikh Mohammed's entry onto the English racing stage, the top man on the owners' list was the Vernons Pools heir, Robert Sangster. In alliance with the distinguished Irish trainer Vincent O'Brien he had built up a smoothly professional syndicate based around his Swettenham Stud breeding operation in England and the Coolmore Stud

stallion station in Tipperary. But once Sheikh Mohammed developed a taste for buying the best-bred yearlings on the market, he left Sangster and his partners trailing in his wake.

The American trade magazine *The Blood-Horse* has documented the Maktoum influence at the Keeneland Select Sales in Kentucky, the world's premier showcase sale of thoroughbred yearlings. Between 1980 and 1995, it says, the brothers spent a staggering US$402.9 million on 593 yearlings, averaging US$679,500 a horse. Dur-

ing that period they also featured prominently at the Tattersalls sales in Newmarket, at Goffs in Ireland and at Deauville in France. Not all of their purchases were successful ones. In 1982 Sheikh Mohammed spent US$10.2 million on an American-bred yearling called Snaafi Dancer who turned out to be so useless that he never even set foot on a racecourse. But there were still enough good buys for the Sheikh to finish top of the owners' table regularly in England, Ireland and France.

Dubai becomes the hub

The Maktoums' love affair with the big US breeding farms is over. The brothers' own breeding operations, stocked with broodmares bought as yearling fillies at Keeneland, are now almost self-sufficient. As buying scaled-down so the family in general and Sheikh Mohammed in particular began to focus their operations on Dubai. Vital to restructuring the brothers' largely English-based racing concerns was the Emirates' success in securing in 1991 a disease-free status for livestock movement, allowing rapid transport of horses in and out of Dubai.

Plans to develop Dubai as the family's main racing base have now intensified to the point where a thoroughbred revolution is underway there, unmatched by anything else in the world.

complex complements the Zabeel stables and training centre, built more than 25 years ago by Sheikh Rashid on grounds neighbouring his Zabeel Palace and designed for the use of a small team of Arab-breds.

Al Quoz and Zabeel are the launching pad for Godolphin Racing Stables, the audacious – and audaciously entitled – operation to ship mainly Maktoum-owned horses to all points of the globe in search of big race victories. Godolphin has enjoyed quite stunning results in the few years since its inception, especially in 1995 when it carried off classic and grade one prizes in England, Ireland, France, Italy, Hong Kong,

Major developments include Nad al Sheba, built in 1986 as a modest training facility, which has had a complete facelift, with the sand track upgraded for racing. Floodlights were installed around its 2,200-metre (2,405-yd) circumference; the grandstand was refurbished on opulent Euro-Arabic lines, with four levels to seat 4,000 and provide 14 suites; work began on a grass track inside the main sand-track and a golf course was developed on the in-field.

In addition, the royal Al Quoz stables were built on bare desert next to Nad al Sheba. This

ABOVE LEFT: spectators at the Dubai World Cup.
ABOVE: on the way to the finish, Nad Al Sheba.

ALL MOD CONS

The Maktoums expenditure on racing is estimated at around US$2.4 billion. No expense was spared in setting up the Al Quoz stables in Dubai or on improving Nad al Sheba and Zabeel training facilities. Each horse has two men looking after it, and the range of facilities includes an equine veterinary clinic that apparently leaves visiting leaders of the profession in awe, and a feed mill that custom mixes more than 8,000 kg (17,600 lb) of food daily for the royal family's menagerie of falcons, racing and breeding camels, livestock and, of course, Arab and thoroughbred horses.

Japan and the USA. Supreme among those triumphs was the hat-trick recorded by the blue-blooded colt Lammtarra, a son of the 1970 Derby winner Nijinsky and foaled by an English Oaks winner, Snow Bride. As a two-year-old Lammtarra had been trained in Newmarket, where he ran and won once. But he was then shipped out to Dubai during the northern hemisphere winter. He showed the positive effects of the warm Gulf climate and the innovative Godolphin training regime, by

GAMBLERS ANONYMOUS

Dubaians have no need to bring money with them as Islamic law forbids gambling. You certainly won't see a Tote kiosk or a bookie's pitch at Nad al Sheba racecourse.

and the Jebel Ali sand-oil mix track built in 1990 and noted for its steep incline 200 metres/yds from the winning post). Nad Al Sheba is the busiest centre, staging 37 racing days in the November to April season. About 20 meetings are spread between the three other tracks. A typical meeting offers a programme of six races, four of them for thoroughbreds and two for Arab-breds. Prestige outweighs prize money, with purses scarcely relative to the cost of training and feeding a racehorse.

arriving back ready to race off the plane the following May. He only ran three times as a three-year-old but achieved the historic and prestigious treble of the Derby at Epsom in June, the King George VI and Queen Elizabeth Stakes at Ascot in July and then the Prix de l'Arc de Triomphe at Longchamps in Paris in October. It was a feat only managed once before by the immortal Mill Reef in 1971.

Race meetings

Racing in the UAE takes place in Abu Dhabi (one grass track, one sand), Sharjah (a 1,380-metre/1,500-yd sand track within the Sharjah Equestrian complex) and Dubai (Nad Al Sheba

The six races in the International Jockeys Challenge are valued at 8,000Dhs (dirhams) each, roughly US$2,220, provided through sponsorship or heavy subsidies from the ruling family.

Attendances vary, with an average of 3,000 at a normal meeting, 9–10,000 at a feature event such as the Jockeys Challenge series and up to 15,000 for one of the handful of meetings at which a prestige international race has been scheduled. Dubaians have free entry to the car park and the race track and have no need to bring money with them as Islamic law forbids gambling altogether. You certainly won't see a Tote kiosk or a bookie's pitch at Nad Al Sheba. However, to add to the spectators' entertainment, the race club officials provide in the complimentary racecard an entry form for a "Pick Six" competition; entry is free and a prize of about 20,000 dirhams (US$5,500) is awarded to the entry that names the six winners of the meeting.

The Dubai Gold Cup

This kind of diversion would normally be regarded as strictly small beer by hardened British and US racing types, as attracted to their daily doubles and trebles as to their frequent visits to the bar between races. Sheikh Mohammed knew that in the early stages of his Dubai experiment, some visiting racing figures were happy

enough to accept his hospitality while sniggering behind their hands about the whole thing being just another case of a rich man wanting to play with his toys in his own backyard. To legitimise the operation in the eyes of the international racing community, he knew that he had to think up a contest so big and so spectacular and challenging that his international rivals would find it impossible to stay away. So he came up with the Dubai World Cup.

The inaugural running of the cup on 27 March 1996 offered total prize money of US$4 million,

the winner alone taking home US$2.4 million which is more than the total winning prize for the Derby and the Prix de L'Arc de Triomphe combined. When entries for the race closed in mid-October 1995, 48 of the world's best performing racehorses were eligible via a US$5,000 nomination fee, while another 20-odd were added at the second entry stage in January 1996 at double the original fee. Later that month, an international panel of handicappers determined the composition of the 14-strong field, at the same time drawing up a lengthy list of reserves.

To ensure a truly World Cup flavour, they had to choose four starters from the UAE, three from the Americas, three from Europe and two each from Asia and Australasia. Britain was represented by Pentire, second only to Lammtarra in the previous year's King George V1 and Queen Elizabeth Stakes. Godolphin's principal representative was Halling. And from America came the mighty Cigar, the raw-powered six-year-old bay horse, owned by aerospace tycoon Allen Paulson and coming into the Cup on a roll of 13 consecutive victories spaced over 14 months. It was a brave decision by Paulson, who didn't need the money, to risk his champion in a distant arena and on an alien sand surface far away from home.

In the end almost everyone got the result they wanted. Halling may have flopped and Pentire could get no closer than fourth place. But Cigar maintained his proud record in heroic fashion, fighting back in the dying stages of the race to outpoint fellow American challenger Soul of the Matter (owned by songwriter Burt Bacharach), by half a length, with the other American runner in third. Intense American media interest in future runnings of the Cup was guaranteed.

There was fulsome praise afterwards for the courage and class of Cigar and for the skill of his trainer Billy Mott. And even the most cynical observer was forced to admit that Sheikh Mohammed's race across the sand, beneath floodlights and against the darkening desert sky, had raised the princely sport of horse racing to new and previously unimagined levels.

PRIZE GIVING

Sheikh Mohammed had to think up a contest so big and so challenging that his rivals would find it impossible to stay away. He came up with the Dubai Gold Cup.

ABOVE LEFT: in training for the big race.
ABOVE: the green and pleasant Zabeel Stables.

CAMEL RACING

This unusual sport provides great entertainment for participants and spectators alike. But it is also a serious business

If you are looking for an indication of how seriously Arabs take their camels then you need look no further than Oman where the government actually has a department for camel affairs. Back this up with the fact that top racing camels often change hands for over US$160,000 and you'll realise that training these strange looking creatures can be a worthwhile investment.

The sport is still strongly influenced by the Bedu, who train the majority of racing camels and prepare them for the racing season, which runs from August to April. Purpose-built racetracks are found in both Oman and the UAE but you may also come across an impromptu practice race on your travels: an excited, colourful gathering of owners, trainers and spectators urging on their favourites.

The camels, which can reach speeds of 60 kph (37 mph), sometimes race until they are about 15 years old but they are at their peak when they are three to four years. Trainers pay a lot of attention to their camels' diet – which will include honey, ghee (a clarified butter), barley, alfalfa, eggs and dates – but they also place great store by secret concoctions. Family pedigree is highly respected and a well-bred camel will be trained until the age of two when it will enter its first race.

Even if you don't like sport generally the opportunity to attend a camel race should be seized. The camels, which can look quite fearsome at close quarters, are held down while the jockeys, often as young as six, climb on top, gripping tightly to trappings until the camels are released for the start of the race. In a flurry of dust and a volley of shouts from the crowd, the camels take off – sometimes the wrong way – with their teeth bared. Encouraged by the jockey's stick, they bolt down the track, often veering across the width of the course while their bobbing jockeys struggle to bring them into line.

Once the camels have settled into a steady rhythm it is usually worth switching your attention to the side-show, the assortment of vehicles following the race, each one vying for the position close to the course rails. A cacophony of noise pours from car horns and desperate spectators cling to parts of vehicles you never knew

existed. They follow as close to the race as possible, often within a whisker of the next car. You will probably be invited to climb aboard.

The winner of a race will normally receive a cash prize but prestigious events may award cars. However, the real money is in the selling of a successful racer, which will often attract buyers from other Gulf countries.

Races are normally held on Fridays and on public holidays; local newspapers carry details of the time and place. The informal desert tracks generally provide better entertainment for the casual observer than the better-organised stadium events. Either way it is a great way to witness locals in pusuit of sporting glory.

LEFT: camel race at Barka.
ABOVE RIGHT: jockeys can be as young as six

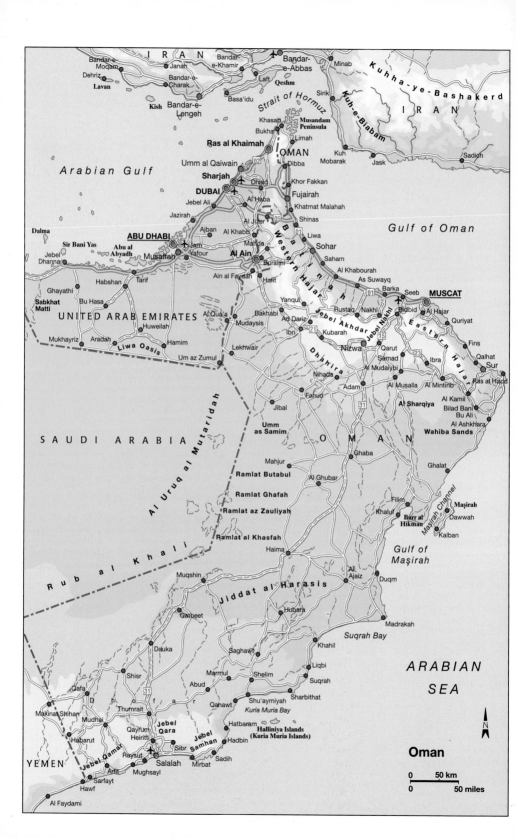

Oman

0	50 km	
0	50 miles	

PLACES: OMAN

*A detailed guide to the country, with the principal sites
cross-referenced by number to the maps*

Oman's potential as a tourist destination has yet to unfold, but all the right ingredients are here: unspoilt landscapes, wonderful beaches, a rich culture. Even Muscat, the capital, is beguiling. Though mainly modern, the low-level buildings are entwined in the folds of serrated hills. The city thus reveals itself gradually and never completely . It is still "the realisation of a pirate's lair as imagined by any schoolboy," as Cedric Belfrage, a visitor to Muscat, observed in 1936.

Oman's variety of landscapes isn't found anywhere else in the Gulf, likewise the range of climate. In summer, while temperatures in the north and interior soar to 50°C (122°F), the coastal area of Dhofar is wet and misty, the vegetation lush, with bananas and coconuts flourishing. And in spite of modernisation, you will still find perched mud villages in the mountainous interior, *barasti* (palm frond) houses on the Batinah coast, and round, thatched homes in the mountains of Dhofar, traditional modes of living not impetuously swept away as they so often were elsewhere in the region but preserved as a valuable part of the heritage.

Formidable natural barriers – the Rub al Khali (Empty Quarter), the Hajar Mountains, and the Jiddat al Harasis – mean that parts of the country are not easily accessible, at least not for humans. Remote regions of the Jebel Akhdar, southwest of Muscat, harbour the rare Arabian *tahr*, a goatlike creature unique to Oman, and an area of the Jiddat al Harasis is a sanctuary for the Arabian oryx, a creature once extinct in the wild. The Musandam Peninsula is one of the last refuges of the Arabian leopard *(see page 203)*, and over on the east coast, below Sur, are the world's largest breeding grounds for green turtles. Birdlife is also rich. The Daymaniyat Islands, north of Musct, are a designated bird sanctuary. More easily seen is the beautiful birdlife of Dhofar *(see pages 178–9)*.

It is possible to sample a little of each of Oman's regions in the space of about two weeks. Muscat makes a good base for the north, offering forays along the Batinah coast to Sohar; through the Sumail Gap to Nizwa, Jabrin and Bahla; and along the rugged east coast to Sur, a boatbuilding town with the dreamy air of a 19th-century watercolour of the orient. Salalah is the obvious base for Dhofar, a region well worth making a special effort to visit, preferably by air but also possible by road.

PRECEDING PAGES: sand dunes at sunset. Oman; Bahla's palmerie; Harasis Bedu.

MUSCAT

Map, page 134

Until 1970 Muscat locked its gates at night and its citizens weren't allowed out without a lantern. Today its long, slender tentacles reach from the airport at Seeb to the Al Bustan Hotel

The sleepy old town of Muscat, clinging to a small natural harbour, and its old port of Muttrah in the neighbouring bay are just fragments of modern Muscat. Since the 1970s, the city has blossomed with the help of oil money, and new business and office districts have sprouted in all directions. Modern highways and flyovers cut through a dramatic topography, leading from one tranquil district to the next up the coast towards Seeb International Airport and into the neighbouring valleys.

But one thing the rapidly developing city has tried to hold onto is its pride and traditions. Unlike Dubai, which has sold out to the Western way of things in many aspects of life, Oman holds on to its past with determination. Modern lifestyles are modified by the Omanis' love and respect for tradition, and past and present mingle. It is not unusual to see old women from the interior balancing bundles of alfalfa on their heads while a teenage Omani passes in the latest Mercedes sports car.

There are no skyscrapers and most of the large office blocks and ministries adhere to traditional Arabic designs, in keeping with the Muscat Municipality's book of acceptable architectural designs (pitched roofs are forbidden, satellite dishes and areas where clothes are dried must be screened from view). New buildings are either white or sand-coloured and surrounded by some of the cleanest streets you are likely to find anywhere. And presiding over it all is the image of Sultan Qaboos. Every shop and office has a picture of the Sultan hanging in its reception and many homes also get the royal touch.

Although not the wealthiest of Gulf states Oman does have its fair share of oil money and those families who latched onto the oil boom and its ensuing riches often boast the excesses for which the region is renowned. The city is also home to a huge expatriate Indian population which, together with strong trade links with India, has resulted in a big Indian influence. Some older buildings, especially in Muttrah, display Indian influences, perhaps in a window grille or the ornate trim on a minaret. Most restaurants can produce a fine curry, and Omani food, which is quite difficult to define, has absorbed numerous Indian ideas. Many offices and shops are staffed by Indians. Other nationalities prominent in the city are the British, Dutch and Americans, most of whom are linked to the oil industry.

City sights

Although Muscat's foundation dates from the 1st century, the town didn't gain recognition until the 14th and 15th centuries, when it attracted traders, and the 16th century when it attracted the Portuguese, who developed Muscat as their principal naval base and strength-

PRECEDING PAGES:
Old Muscat.
LEFT: into Fort Jalali.
BELOW: Muttrah's
fish market.

Entrance of Al Alam Palace. Though listed as one of the Sultan's homes, the palace is generally used only for formal affairs.

ened its defences – until 1650 when they were ousted by an Omani force. The great **forts** which stand high above the harbour in **Old Muscat** are Portuguese, both built by Philip of Spain. The western fort, **Mirani ⒶA**, was completed in 1587; the eastern fort, **Jalali ⒷB**, was finished in 1588. Following two sackings of the city by the Turks, the fortifications were extended in the early 17th century. Unfortunately, both forts are still in use today and so closed to the public.

The area of Old Muscat can be easily viewed on foot. One of the most striking buildings in the quarter, despite its modernity, is **Al Alam Palace ⒸC**, approached along Al Alam Street through **Kebir Gate (Bab Kebir) ⒹD**, the main gate in the old city walls. The palace, built in 1972 to replace the simple, two-storey old palace, has a story-book facade, with towering columns in blue and gold, made more eye-catching by the conformity of the buildings around it.

Old Muscat is home to some fabulous old mosques and houses. Several fine 18th-century buildings have served as embassies and consulates, including Bait Graiza. Among those still standing is the 18th-century Bait Fransa, the residence of French consuls until 1920, which now operates as the **Omani French Museum ⒺE** (Saturday to Wednesday, mornings only),commemorating Oman's historical links with France. Built by Ghaliah bint Salim, a niece of Sultan Said bin Sultan, it was presented to Paul Ottavi, the first French consul in Oman, to serve as the French Consulate by Sultan Feisal bin Turki Al Said in 1894. French ships carrying spices and sugar from the Indian Ocean had called at Muscat since the 17th century, and trade links intensified in the 19th century. The museum documents this fruitful exchange, with ship models, instruments of navigation, a reconstruction of the consul's office and a selection of old maps and lithographs.

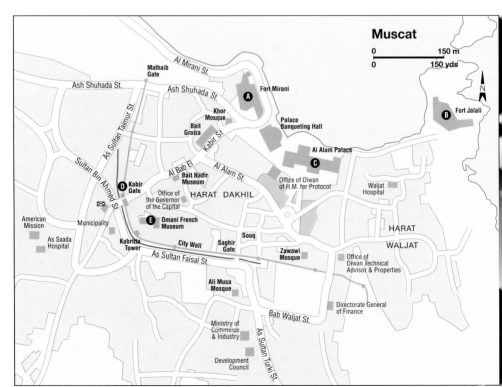

Muttrah

In the neighbouring bay to Old Muscat, less than 3 km (2 miles) along the dual carriageway winding along the waterfront, is **Muttrah**. Its majestic corniche makes it more memorable than its neighbour. But although opportunities for tourism abound, it caters primarily for trade and local fishermen and as yet not even a café to sit and enjoy the view exists. But the corniche has a few hidden gems leading from it.

The **Muttrah Souq F**, accessible from two points off the Corniche, is a must. Though modern – concrete booths replaced the original palm structures in the 1970s – the narrow lanes, heavy with the smell of frankincense and sandalwood, bustle with traders, money-changers and shoppers eager to do business. The *souq* , one of the most authentic in Arabia, is divided into various sectors, each dealing with a particular product – textiles, houseware, gold, silver, spices – punctuated by *halwa* (sweetmeat) sellers and coffee shops. The alleyways provide a glimpse of Oman's past (a palm frond roof has recently been added to recapture the mysterious fenestrated effect of a traditional souq) even though the products sold are rarely Omani. It is easy to get disorientated but one is never far away from the main thoroughfares. Two areas particularly worth exploring are the gold (22 carat) and silver souqs – the latter providing a good range of traditional items (*see pages 104–5*).

Standing close to the *souq* is the **Liwatiya quarter G**, housing a Shia religious sect of the same name who were traditionally merchants and originated from Hyderabad. Their residential area is walled and off-limits to outsiders – guards sit at the gates to make sure that only those who live there enter – but the houses back onto the Corniche, where the lattice grilles and balconies offer enticing glimpses of what lies behind.

Standing at one end of the Corniche is the **fish and vegetable souq**. Small fishing boats unload their catch directly at the side of the *souq* and the fish are spilled onto woven mats for likely purchasers to examine. There is an amazing array of different species, ranging from the popular hamour to sharks. Bartering, for those wishing to purchase, is a necessity.

South of Old Muscat and Muttrah

One of the highlights of the coast 6 km (4 miles) south of Old Muscat is **Al Bustan Palace Hotel H**, completed over two years between 1983 and 1985 for a Gulf Co-operation Council summit and one of the man-made splendours of the Middle East. Regularly voted the top hotel in the Middle East the hotel stands majestically in its own bay.

The site and design were chosen after long consideration of other possibilities. To make way for the hotel, a hill had to be blasted away and the old village of Al Bustan, which had once served as a leper colony, was moved to a new site just behind the small *jebel* (hill), on the beach. Based on an octagon, a recurring theme in Islamic architecture, the design of the hotel was intended to reflect the hierarchy of the delegates at the Gulf summit, with heads of state level at the top, then crown princes or ministers, and ordinary delegates in the bottom tiers.

Map, pages 136–7

The incense burner monument above Riyam Park, Muttrah, built to celebrate Oman's 20th National Day.

BELOW: shopping in the *souq.*

The *pièce de résistance* of the hotel is the atrium, which is high enough to house an up-ended Boeing 747. It is clad in Blue de France and White Dionysus marble, just some of the 800,000 tonnes of marble, from France, Greece, Italy and elsewhere, that was used in the hotel's interior alone.The building's plinth, pilasters and towers are faced in stone from Rajasthan, each piece of which was hand-chiselled on the ground in India before being shipped to Oman. Even the soil in which the luxurious gardens grow is special – it was brought here from Shinas near the border with Fujairah in the UAE.

Outside the entrance to the hotel, a roundabout commemorates the voyage of the *Sohar*, a 1980 replica of an ocean-going Omani sailing ship which sailed to Canton to mark the historic trading links between Oman and China.

In a bay between Old Muscat and the Al Bustan Palace Hotel is the new **Marina Bander Al Rowdha ❶**, visible from the coast road, which is attracting some stunning boats. It also caters for those who want to try their hand at game fishing. Standing above the marina is the **British Ambassador's residence** and in the next bay the **Capital Area Yacht Club ❶** accommodating more sea-going vessels.

North of Old Muscat and Muttrah

In recent years, as wealth has filtered through the city, Muscat has spread up the coast and inland. From Muttrah heading up to Seeb Airport is a succession of prosperous districts – Ruwi, Qurm, Medinat Sultan Qaboos and Al Khuwair – housing the main business and residential districts. Included in these are a number of museums, such as the **Sultan's Armed Forces Museum ❸** (Sunday, Monday and Wednesday, morning only), in the Bait al Falaj Fort in Ruwi, which

BELOW: Selecting a *khanjar* in Muttrah Souq.

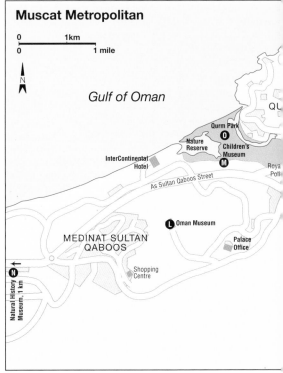

Muscat Metropolitan

0 — 1km
0 — 1 mile

N

Gulf of Oman

QL

Qurm Park ❶
Nature Reserve
Children's Museum ⓜ
InterContinental Hotel
Roya Poli
As Sultan Qaboos Street

❶ Oman Museum

MEDINAT SULTAN QABOOS
Palace Office

Natural History Museum, 1 km ⓝ

Shopping Centre

Map, pages 136–7

gives an interesting glimpse into Oman's crucial military history and reflects the determination of the current sultan, who gained his own army training at Sandhurst, England, to turn the limited defence forces of Oman in 1971 into the three highly trained and equipped forces it has today; the **Oman Museum** , (Saturday to Wednesday, mornings only), Muscat's first museum (opened in 1974) dedicated to different strands of the national heritage, from seafaring to fort-building, the **Children's Museum** Ⓜ (Sunday to Thursday), otherwise known as the Science Museum, off Sultan Qaboos Street in Qurm, with lots of hands-on, educational displays; and the **Natural History Museum** Ⓝ (Saturday to Thursday, morning only), in Al Khuwair, one of the most engaging museums of its size and kind anywhere but especially welcome in a country where background information is still relatively hard to come by. The "Oman Through Time" exhibition traces the fossil history of Oman from the Precambrian age 800 million years ago, while "Oman – Land of Contrasts" explains the different characteristics of the six distinct physical regions: Musandam, the Northern Mountains, the Batinah, the Interior, the Dhofar Mountains and the Islands.

Further out, in the suburb of Ghala, and visible on the way to and from the airport, is the new **Sultan Qaboos Mosque** commissioned by the Sultan in 1995. Designed by architects Quad Design, who won the contract through an international competition, the mosque, the largest in Oman, can accommodate over 15,000 worshippers. It is not open to non-Muslims.

Outside the entrance of the Natural History Museum are the fossilised remains of a 260-million-year old fir tree.

Shopping, nightlife, beaches and excursions

With soaring summer temperatures of over 50°C (122°F) in the hottest months it is not surprising that Muscat is more lively through the night than the day. The

TIP

A dhow cruise is a great way to spend the early evening. Boats leave from the Al Inshirah Restaurant on Muttrah's corniche.

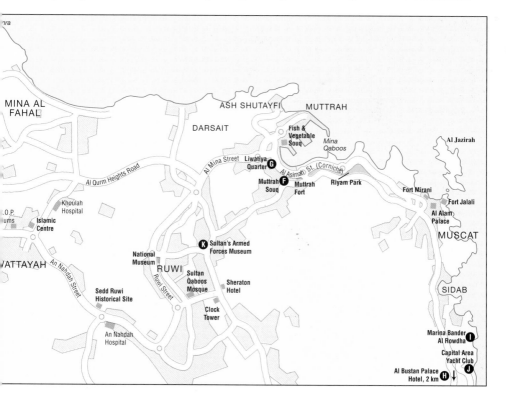

Café society in the InterContinental Hotel's coffee shop. Night-time entertainment generally centres on the hotels.

BELOW: bagpipe band in Qurm Park.

scorching sun forces people to keep within their air-conditioned vehicles and homes during the day from May to September.

The main **shopping** areas are in Qurm and Ruwi. Ruwi caters mainly for the Indian market (it's a good place to go for tailoring) whereas Qurm has several complexes which combine so-called "traditional souqs" and designer stores. The cooler night temperatures encourage people to descend on Qurm in their droves in the evenings. Apart from shopping, night-time entertainment, such as it is, generally centres on the big hotels. If you are looking for a wild time then look elsewhere because Muscat's night life is pretty sedate. Apart from a couple of hotel discos and a few bars, there is very little. However, a saving grace is the choice of quality restaurants (*see Travel Tips section*).

One of the nicest things about Muscat is that you never have far to go to find a quiet beach. Whether it is the long stretch of golden sand that leads from the base of the Gulf Hotel way past the InterContinental Hotel or one in the string of secluded bays south of Al Bustan Palace Hotel, there is always a place to relax, have a barbecue and try out a watersport or two. Emphasis has been placed on recreational facilities within the city and the parks are attractive. **Qurm Park** **ⓞ**, which has a boating lake, water fountains and a 4,000-seat amphitheatre, is especially pleasant.

Life never seems to be rushed in Muscat and the languid nature of the place makes it an ideal springboard for excursions to the wadis and forts of the interior or along the coast to Sohar or Sur and the Wahiba Sands. Unlike in the past, Muscat is the central focus for modern Oman and the power base for both government and business. Mobile phones are more in evidence than *khanjars* but the sights and sounds of old Oman are never far away.

Towering Strength

Whether you are wadi-bashing in a deserted region or sightseeing in Muscat, you can bet that a fortification stands not too far away. Wherever you go in Oman there is a constant reminder of the country's divisions and troubled past, from the massive structure of Bahla Fort in the Interior to the small watchtowers which cluster atop most jebels. Oman's topography has proved ideal for defence measures and in areas which have needed to be strong historically, forts and watchtowers, in varying states of repair, fill the skyline.

Sultan Qaboos has attempted to save as much of Oman's heritage as possible during his time in office, instigating a restoration programme that has brought many of the majestic fortifications back to life. Moroccan craftsmen were employed (the necessary skills having died out in Oman) and traditional materials, such as mud bricks, palm fronds and limestone, used.

If you are staying in Muscat you don't have to travel far to see impressive examples. Oman's forts were heavily influenced by the Portuguese and Persians but Arab designs are also evident. When the Portuguese occupied Muscat in 1507, they chose the most commanding places, high above the city, to build the forts of Mirani, Jalali and Muttrah. The two great forts which sit on either side of Muscat Harbour are Portuguese, both built by Philip of Spain. The western fort, Mirani, was completed in 1587. The eastern, Jalali, in 1588. They are simple in design but very strong. Both these and Muttrah Fort are still in use, either by the military or the police.

One of the most impressive forts in Oman is the one at Jabrin, which has been restored to its former glory. Its interior, unlike the compact, basic design of a military fort such as Al Hazm, is palatial, with carved doorways and painted ceilings. Unlike military forts which were built principally for defence, castle forts were built with a bit more comfort in mind. Some castle forts, such as Jabrin and Birkat al Mauz, housed the government. Others such as Bait Na'man and Al Hobe were used as retreats and rest-houses for travellers on their way by camel from Muscat to Nizwa or Sohar.

Generally, forts protected the towns and populated areas while watchtowers were used to guard inland trade routes and water supplies. At the sight of invaders, warning shots would be fired to alert people nearby. Other watchtowers were built close to forts for obvious reasons. The highest concentrations of watchtowers are along the main mountain passes – Wadi Sumail, Wadi Jizzi, and Wadi Hawasinah.

The forts at Rustaq, Bahla, Sohar and Nizwa are considerable in size. Sohar's once required more than 1,000 men for its defence, and the great fort at Nizwa, which was built in the 17th century, took 12 years to build.

Interesting features to note when visiting any fort are its dungeons, slits above doors for channelling boiling honey, oil or water, and the well – vital in case of seige.

Forts to visit include Nizwa, Nakhl, Jabrin, Bahla, Rustaq, Al Hazm and Sohar.

RIGHT: Fort Mirani.

SOHAR AND THE BATINAH COAST

Map, page 144

The flat and fertile Batinah Coast north of Muscat leads to Sur, once the most important trading centre on the Arabian Peninsula. Today the region is famous for its dates

he Batinah Coast north of Muscat is said to derive its name from an Arabic root meaning "to be hidden", and from out at sea the tawny-coloured Hajar Mountains glowering over the narrow coastal plain do indeed conceal it from sight. The Batinah, accessible by a dual carriageway extending 270 km (168 miles) from Muscat to the UAE border, is completely different from the rollercoaster terrain between Muscat and Sur. Here the landscape is flat – an unbroken line of grey-sand beach is lapped by a gentle sea, and the plain, never more than a kilometre wide, is extensively cultivated. Date plantations, some hundreds of years old, line large stretches of the highway.

Modern buildings are springing up along the Batinah, but old-style *barasti* houses made from date palms are still seen in quiet villages, and the biblical *shasha*, a canoe made from palm fronds, is still used for fishing. Such things have disappeared elsewhere in Oman. A drawback of the area for travellers is that the highway rarely runs alongside the sea, and without a detour or two the journey from Muscat to Sohar, the administrative capital of the Batinah, can be dull. By including the Rustaq loop (*see page 148*), you can make the journey more rewarding. Three splendid forts punctuate the circuit and a date-processing factory in Rustaq adds further interest.

The best way to sample the region is to drive to Sohar, stay the night, and then take the Rustaq sidetrip on your return. The southern Batinah, including the Rustaq circuit, can also be visited in a day trip from Muscat.

From Muscat to Sohar

Seeb ❶ is the first settlement north of Muscat. **Seeb International Airport ❷** (35 km/22 miles from Muscat) is the official gateway to Oman. The nearby **Sultan Qaboos University ❸**, which opened in 1986, has an enrolment of 3,600 students of whom 65 percent are women, a remarkable achievement considering that just 30 or so years ago schooling for girls was officially forbidden. A fairly unremarkable town, Seeb acts as a market depot for local fishermen and farmers with a busy *souq* catering to domestic needs. Camel races are staged on National Day (18 November) and on other festive occasions, with bullfights alternating between here and Barka on Fridays during winter (starting at around 4pm, free admission). Fight rules are simple – the referee pairs animals roughly based on equal height and weight and they are lead out and set against one another. When one bull takes a tumble in the dust the other is declared victor (*also see page 272*). Most contests last less than 5 minutes but should the fight turn vicious, a rope

PRECEDING PAGES: sunset at A'Sawadi, a typical Batinah fishing community. **LEFT:** traditional palm-frond *shasha*. **BELOW RIGHT:** harvesting dates.

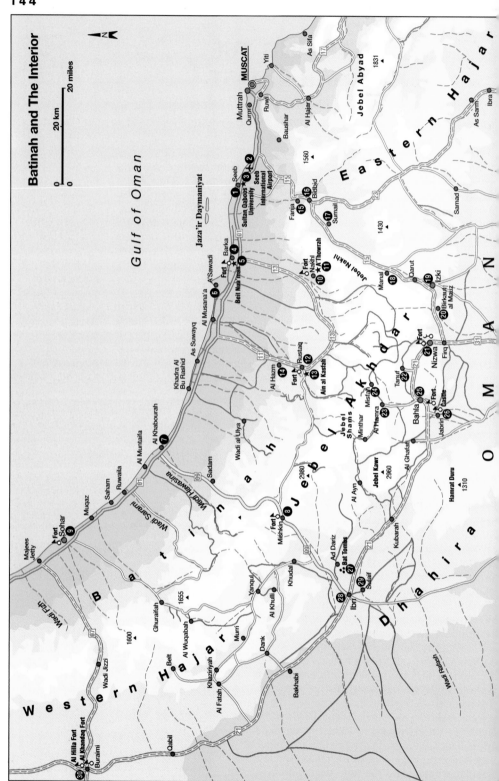

secured to the front leg of each animal allows their owners to keep control. As in camel and horse racing, there is no betting, and the crowd, exclusively men, is content simply to have a jolly day out.

Map, page 144

Barka ❹ (43 km/27 miles from Muscat) is the next town of significance on the coast and the springboard for the Rustaq Loop (*see page 149*). To get to it, ignore the first sign to Barka that you come to (10 km/6 miles) and continue along the highway to the Toyota showroom. Turn right here along a palm-lined avenue, right again at the roundabout and then left at the watchtower. This road, lined with tea-shops, ends at the beach where fishing boats are pulled up below a coastal *souq* selling, among other things, anchors, ropes, hooks, pegs, chains, salt and baskets of dried fish.

Barka Fort (7.30am–6pm; free admission), dating from the early Ya'ruba period (*see page 49*) and restored in 1985, is 400 metres (440 yards) west of the main crossroads in town. The former wali's quarters has a fine exhibition of imported china in the master bedroom, and a tower gives a panoramic view of the surroundings. **Bait Nua'man ❺** (flexible opening hours; free admission), the restored house of a wealthy merchant is a 4.8-km (3-mile) drive along the highway beyond the fort plus a further 1.9 km (1¼ mile) left on a graded road. The house is an interesting example of old Gulf Coast architecture.

A'Sawadi ❻ (63 km/39 miles from Muscat) is a large fishing community 9 km (5 miles) along a turn-off at a "prancing horses monument". The tarmac stops opposite a group of rocky islands at the end of a long beach from where A'Sawadi, a typical Batinah town with single-storey, flat-roofed houses and boats pulled up on the sand, is a 20-minute walk. As in Dhofar, a considerable portion of the sardine catch is dried for animal fodder – all along the Batinah, the smell of drying sardines leads to a small fishing hamlet. A modern hotel here has the last Western-style facilities (licensed to sell alcohol) before Sohar.

Mud-brick houses in **Al Khabourah ❼** (128 km/79 miles from Muscat) are dotted among the palm groves between the highway and the sea. The wives of local fishermen and date farmers make many of the hand-woven articles on sale in Muscat, in particular the distinctive black, brown, cream and red-patterned mats and wall hangings. Someone at the BP station may be able to direct you to a weaver's home. The adjoining Arab World Restaurant has a clean toilet and sells cheap *biryani* and kebab-type meals.

Al Khabourah is built on the junction of one of several major passes through the Hajar Mountains to the Interior. The major part of the road is a track passing few villages and winding in and out of dusty wadi beds. Blacktop (tarmac) runs from **Mishkin ❽** over the Western Hajar to Ibri (126 km/78 miles) (*see Nizwa and the Interior, page 155*).

The Batinah Coast is the food basket of Oman, and citrus fruit orchards, date plantations, fields of melons, aubergines, cabbages and other crops line the highway. One of the most famous products of the region is the small round loomi lime. The British writer Ian Skeet, who spent two years in Oman during the 1960s, wrote in his book *Muscat and Oman*: "the particular tang of the Muscati lime is the *sina qua non* of local rice spicing

My journey with Sultan was to take us through this populous province: now along the golden beaches, past little Arab ports ever associated with Sindbad the Sailor and little fishing villages whose men go forth to grope under the sea for precious pearls.
– BERTRAM THOMAS
Alarms and Excursions in Arabia

BELOW: Barka Fort.

and equally a compulsory addition to a cup of tea." Iraq was historically a major importer of Oman's limes and India and Pakistan remain important takers today – in fact in the 1970s the export of limes was second only to that of oil. The limes are dried before export, turning a black colour; this does not impair the flavour in any way.

Taking any right-hand turn north of Al Khabourah leads to small fishing villages. Today most fishermen own a modern boat obtained through the Fishermen's Incentive Fund, but the traditional *shasha*, a palm-frond boat, is not entirely obsolete, though these days it may have an outboard engine. Prone to capsize and becoming quickly water-logged, it has only ever been used for inshore fishing. Two people can construct a *shasha* in just two days.

Birds to look out for: an Indian Roller (top) and a European Bee-eater (bottom), both photographed near Sohar.

Sohar

The approach to **Sohar ❾**, the Batinah capital, is marked by a huge arch across the highway: a road to the right off the "date palm roundabout" cuts through a new, business district to the old centre on the sea. Sohar is a pleasant town whose clean streets lined with white houses and tropical gardens indicate civic pride but there is nothing left to suggest it was once one of the most important trading centres on the Arabian Peninsula: "Its traders and commerce cannot be enumerated. It is the most developed town in Oman," wrote Ibn Hawqal in *The Oriental Geography*, a 10th-century manual of the region.

Archaeological excavations date the city to the 3rd millennium BC when it was capital of the Magan Empire (*see page 22–4*) and a major exporter of copper mined in Wadi Jizzi. The fabulous Emporium Persicum near the Straits of Hormuz mentioned in a 5th-century Byzantine text is almost certainly Sohar,

BELOW: Sohar.

the home port of Sindbad the Sailor of the *Thousand and One Nights*. The city rose to prominence following the decline of the frankincense trade in Dhofar and the weakening power of the Caliphate in Baghdad, reaching its zenith in the 10th century, when it thrived on trade with Africa and Madagascar. The city was destroyed and most of its inhabitants slain by the Buyids of Baghdad in 971. Nonetheless, a description as late as the 12th century mentions 12,000 houses elaborately constructed of brick and teak and of traders from a dozen different countries rubbing shoulders in its sprawling *souqs*.

The seaport was absorbed into the Persian Kingdom of Hormuz in the 14th century but following capture by Portugal in 1507 its fortunes began to ebb. For the next hundred years, Portugal maintained a trade blockade which slowly choked the commercial life out of Sohar. Even after the Portuguese left Oman in the mid-16th century, the city's fate was sealed by internecine disputes. As a result, shipping from India and East Africa discharged in Sur and Aden and many local merchants and sea captains moved elsewhere. Sohar sank into a state of torpor from which it is only now recovering.

Agriculture, fishing and commerce remain the main occupations, but there is also a revival of the city's ancient copper-smelting industry, with reserves estimated at around 15.2 million tonnes. Two hotels cater mainly to domestic tourists and overland travellers between here and the UAE.

Sohar has a large seaside *souq* selling fresh fish and produce from the Batinah but a white-washed **fort** (Saturday to Wednesday 8am–2pm, Thursday and Friday 8am–noon and 4–6pm; free admission) at the eastern end of the corniche is its main attraction. The original building, believed to date from the early 14th century and crucial to the defence of the Straits of Hormuz, is said to have been

Map, page 144

BELOW: a camel gets a ride in Sohar.

so large that it took 1,000 men to defend it – though it surrendered to Albuquerque without a single cannon being fired. A Portuguese miniature shows the fort with six towers and surrounded by palm groves but today only a single tower rises from its courtyard. This has been converted into an interesting museum with exhibits on the geography and geology of the region including a section on the copper-mining industry in nearby Wadi Jizzi which dates back more than 1,000 years. Also on display are handsome, brass-studded chests and fading photographs of former rulers of Oman.

Ask a guardian to point out the **tomb of Sayyid Thuwaini bin Said bin Sultan Al bu Said**, one of two sons of the great Sultan Said bin Sultan under whom Oman regained prominence in the 19th century (*see page 50*). On the demise of Sultan Said, Thuwaini became ruler of Oman and a colony on the Makran Coast of what is now Pakistan, while his brother was awarded Zanzibar and Omani possessions in East Africa. Sultan Thuwaini ruled for only a decade. In 1866 he was shot by his son while asleep in the fort during preparations for a military expedition to recapture Buraimi Oasis.

Five km (3 miles) north of Sohar is a turn to **Majees Jetty** and an isolated strip of beach suitable for swimming. North of here, Route 07 cuts off for the Buraimi Oasis. The journey along a tarmac road takes around two hours (travellers to Abu Dhabi take this route). For Dubai, continue north through the town of Liwa and turn west through Wadi Hatta (*see page 236*).

Hajar Mountains and Wadis

The **Hajar Mountains**, rising behind the Batinah Coast, stretch from the border with the UAE for some 300 km (186 miles) to the Sumail Gap, where they become the Eastern Hajar extending into Sharqiya province. For the Western Hajar, including the 3,000-metre (9,842-ft) Jebel Akhdar (Green Mountain) massif, see *Nizwa and the Interior, page 155*).

New tarmac roads have been laid through several wadis leading from the coast to the interior. The main access is through the Sumail Gap to Nizwa, the historic stronghold of the Imamate (*see page 157*). The Rustaq Loop (*see below*) skirts the foothills of the Jebel Akhdar and rejoins the coastal highway. A third important pass cuts off at Al Khabourah and winds through **Wadi Hawasina** to Ibri, while Route 05 crosses the Northern Hajar to the UAE border.

These roads are motorable in ordinary cars, but secondary wadis cutting into the Batinah side of the Hajar are accessible only by four-wheel drive. Wadi-bashing (*see page 165*) is the term coined by expatriates for tackling these rough, winding tracks to remote hamlets built on the mountain terraces. Wadis **Abyadh**, **Bani Auf**, **Bani Kharus**, **Mistal** and the formidable sounding **Ghubrah Bowl**, a rocky amphitheatre beyond Wadi Mistal containing the perched village of **Wekan**, are minor expeditions falling into the category of adventure travel.

Excursion to Rustaq

The reward for making this detour off the road to Sohar is the chance to see two of Oman's finest forts, at Nakhl

TIP

For more information on off-road explorations of the remote secondary wadis of the Hajar Mountains consult *Off-road in Oman* by Heiner Klein and Rebecca Brickson (Motivate).

BELOW: exploring Wadi Bani Auf.

and Rustaq. A third smaller fort at Al Hazm can also be visited, but the massive Qalat al Kesra, dominating Rustaq, is alone worth the journey. To reach the turn-off, follow the coastal highway from Muscat to the Barka roundabout and turn left onto Route 13 signposted Nakhl 32 km and Rustaq 83 km. Heading towards the Jebel Akhdar, the blacktop road crosses a limestone plain studded with low-level *saumur*, a common tree of the acacia family with roots reaching deep into the water table. A Shell petrol station is located 10 km (6 miles) inside the wadi.

Crowning a spur at the wadi's head, **Nakhl Fort** (7am–5pm; free admission) is an awesome tribute to the skills of ancient Omani stone masons. Soaring to a height of 30 metres (98 ft) above ground level and covering an area of 3,400 square metres (36,597 sq. ft) it is built of limestone and wood covered with the terracotta-coloured mud and cement cladding common to more than 100 forts, palaces, watchtowers and other defences restored by Oman's Ministry of National Heritage and Culture. The fort's foundations are believed to pre-date Islam with maintenance work in the 9th, 16th and 19th centuries. To enter the fort, climb the stone stairs and bear left through the heavy teak door.

Nakhl was entirely self-contained with well-water and storage rooms for stockpiling in event of a siege. The wali lived on the mezzanine level in winter and on the breezy upper terrace during the hot summer months. His *majlis* is lined with handwoven carpets with muskets decorating the walls. The harem is spread with carpets and cushions while a master bedroom contains a large double bed. A sweeping panorama can be enjoyed from the top of the fort – early morning is the best time for photography.

Nakhl ❿ is a small, nondescript village in walking distance of the fort, with several grocery shops and a café catering to bus and taxi drivers. The main road

Map, page 144

These pots for sale near Sohar are used for storing dates

BELOW: beekeeper in the Ghubrah Bowl. In Northern Oman bees often nest in date palms.

through Nakhl continues 2 km (1 mile) to **A' Thowrah** , a shady oasis with a stream running under the date palms. The water here is warm enough to poach an egg. Locals picnic around the hot spring on Friday.

The fort at **Rustaq** ⓬ (51 km/32 miles from Nakhl) has stood on the site for more than 1,000 years. It looms over the date palms only to disappear from view as the road from Nakhl dips around the mosque before climbing an incline into the town. It seems curious to lose track of such a huge edifice so suddenly, but turn left at the second set of traffic lights to find it planted defiantly in front of you again. In fact, this is the rear of the fort. For the entrance, follow the dirt lane around the exterior walls, 10 metres (33 ft) in height and decorated with more than 2,000 triangular crenellations. Access is up a ramp and across the area between the outer and inner walls to a gate with the usual holes above for pouring boiling date oil or honey onto intruders.

The biggest fortification in Oman after Bahla, Rustaq is built over the site of a spring which gushes around its base – the stone structure to the left of the steps is an ablutions chamber. The ground-floor rooms were used to store dates and ammunition while the first floor appears to have been the harem with meeting rooms, a mosque, and a swimming pool supplied from the spring. The four huge towers – the Red Tower, Satan's Tower, Al Hadieth Tower and the Wind Tower – typify Omani defensive architecture.

Rustaq Fort is thought to have been founded by the Persians in the pre-Islamic period. It became the first capital of the Ya'ruba Dynasty under the Imam Nasir bin Murshid (died 1649) and was rebuilt under Imam Saif bin Sultan (died 1711), who was responsible for a massive building programme all over the interior. Saif bin Sultan also repaired the *falaj* and planted more than 30,000 date palms

Imam Nasir bin Murshid, who made Rustaq the capital of the Imamate, is reputed to have had mystical powers. As well as working miracles – such as feeding 100 men for several days on a basket of dates and rice – he is supposed to have had an aura that lit up a corner of Rustaq's mosque.

BELOW: Nakhl Fort.

around Rustaq. He is buried in the western corner of the Wind Tower.

The first Imam of the Al bu Said Dynasty, Ahmed bin Said (died 1783), also ruled from Rustaq, where he exercised control over both the interior and coast. This broke down under his sons Said and Sultan, who split the Imamate, with Said based in Rustaq, and Sultan, the more powerful of the two brothers, ruling from Muscat.

Rustaq is a rather soulless town built on the hillside leading up from the mosque. A **date processing factory** (closes midday) near the mosque is worth a visit although technically permission is required. It employs around 70 women responsible for washing, stoning, steaming, drying and other steps in machine-processing more than 800 tonnes of dates a year from all over Oman (except Dhofar where the date palm does not flourish), but especially Rustaq. The governorate counts more than 200 *falaj* watering its lush plantations, but bursting out of the limestone, 1.5 km (1 mile) from the town centre is **Ain al Kasfah** ⓭, a hot spring. *Biryani*-type cafés are found near the BP station from where it is a 20-km (12-mile) drive to Al Hazm.

Al Hazm ⓮ is basically a fort surrounded by a few houses to the left of Route 11 to the coastal highway. The three-storey limestone and wood structure, 17 metres (56 ft) high with two cylindrical towers, was built in 1708 by the Imam Sultan bin Saif II who moved here from Rustaq – an inscription on the right of two decorated wooden gates identifies him as the builder. The climb up to the bastions passes Portuguese cannons, bearing the crest of the Portuguese monarch, which were captured during sea battles in the 17th century and brought here by the Imam Azzan bin Qais. Sultan bin Saif II, who also built the fine *falaj* supplying Al Hazm, is buried in the western tower of the fort.

Map, page 144

BELOW LEFT: sorting dates at the factory in Rustaq.

STORY OF THE DATE

A staple food of the Bedu, a symbol of hospitality to strangers, the traditional break to the Ramadan fast, an essential ingredient at weddings, circumcisions and feasts – the date is revered throughout the Arab and Islamic world. Wilfred Thesiger, in *Arabian Sands*, recalls how when he once threw a date stone into a camp fire his Bedu companion leaned over and picked it out. In the 19th century dates were Oman's biggest export, with India and the USA its chief markets. Ships would leave Oman laden with dates and return with rice, coffee, sugar, spices, cloth, china, gunpowder and paper. Today, though date production is no longer essential to the economy, its potential is being reconsidered as part of ongoing efforts to wean the country away from oil. There are some 10 million date palms, occupying around 60 percent of cultivable land, and annual production is estimated at 150,000–175,000 tons.

NIZWA AND THE INTERIOR

Map, page 144

Historically the power base of the Imamate, the Interior is a rich and rewarding region to visit. Nizwa and Bahla are particularly interesting

The area of Oman historically known as the "Interior" refers to the region lying beyond the Hajar Mountains where, from fortified strongholds, the imams contested the authority of the sultan in Muscat. Hence the name 'Muscat and Oman" to describe the country prior to 1970 – Muscat being the capital enclave and Oman what an Australian might call the Outback.

Locals continue to speak of "going into the interior," more specifically meaning **Al Jauf**, a rugged central plateau extending from the western flank of **Jebel Akhdar** (Green Mountain) to the arid expanses of Al Wusta province abutting Saudi Arabia. Counting Nizwa, capital of the illustrious Imam Sultan bin Saif Malik Al Ya'ruba, and Bahla, whose giant fort is a UNESCO World Heritage Site, Al Jauf is the kernel of traditional Oman. The new towns growing up along Highway 21 may create an illusion of the present but only a few steps off the road lie ancient villages.

The lay of the land

North of Al Jauf is the sparsely populated **Dhahira** province whose main towns are Ibri and Buraimi (shared with Abu Dhabi). **Al Wusta**, covering a swathe of central Oman, is a waterless gravel desert rich in oil, gas and mineral deposits and little else. Apart from travellers using the Muscat–Salalah Highway, it is visited only by geologists and engineers working for the PDO (Petroleum Development Oman).

Immediately south of Al Wusta lies the isolated **Jiddat al Harasis**, the preserve of the Harasis, Arabia's last true nomads, who share the area with small herds of oryx re-introduced to the area in Operation Oryx launched in 1975 when oryx in the wild had been hunted to extinction. There are now around 300 oryx roaming the Jiddat al Harasis

This then is the Interior, a dusty cameo of the past and present with tourism knocking on its door in Nizwa. Still living within a tightly knit tribal society, its inhabitants wear their national costume with elan and live a symbiotic existence with their date palms.

A four-wheel-drive vehicle is not essential to visit Nizwa and the immediate villages, but is for venturing into some of the wadis of the Jebel Akhdar, such as Wadi Ghul (*see page 160*). From Muscat take the coastal highway to the Sahwa Tower Roundabout and turn onto Route 15 through the Sumail Gap.

Sumail Gap to Nizwa

Wadi Sumail, a natural break between the Western and Eastern Hajar Mountains, has been the artery between the coast and the Interior since time immemorial. The broad dry valley was the obvious course for the dual

PRECEDING PAGES: pisé village.
OPPOSITE: Nizwa fort.
BELOW: donkey days.

carriageway from Muscat to Nizwa, 166 km (103 miles) of relaxed driving.

The first of the many settlements along the Gap is **Fanja ⓯** (35 km/22 miles from Muscat). Typically, the new town lies along the road while the old town nestles against the hillside, accessible via a right-hand turn after the bridge. Fanja enjoys a reputation for pottery sold on the edge of its *souq* but most of this is imported from Iran. Further along the highway is a turn to **Bidbid ⓰** whose restored fort used to guard the junction of the old trade routes from Muscat, Nizwa and Sur. These now meet at a new fly over crossing the northern Sharqiya to Sur.

The town of **Sumail ⓱** lends its name to the pass. The old village boasts an unusual upright rose-pink fort. It stands back from the fast-flowing **A'Samdi Falaj**, the second-biggest *falaj* in Oman after the Daris Falaj in Nizwa. Ask directions to an ancient *falaj* sundial which measured the use of water by so many minutes, hours or days per week. Each plot of land would have a prescribed allocation of time, and this could be measured by the sundial. Generally access to the *falaj* for irrigation purposes had to be paid for and access rights were sold with the land, but drinking water (generally drawn from higher up a *falaj* system), and water for ritual ablutions and domestic purposes was available to everyone. Maintenance of a *falaj* was usually the responsibility of the landlord or main shareholders.

On either side of A'Samdi Falaj are palm groves and market gardens growing, among other produce, bananas, marrows and limes. Sumail dates, renowned for their quality, were exported to California in the late 19th century where they now flourish around Palm Springs. Muezzin Ya'ruba, the first Omani to make the pilgrimage to Mecca, came from Sumail.

BELOW: view of Birkaut Al Mauz.

Manal ⓲, guarded by seven watchtowers perched on spurs in the foothills of the **Jebel Mahil**, is one of the most picturesque villages on the Sumail Gap. Between here and the poetically named **Umtydumty** are two petrol stations. The new town of **Izki ⓳** lies on the highway 103 km (64 km) from Muscat; in the old village against the protective flank of the *jebel* are a tower, a mosque and one of the oldest *falaj* in Oman.

Many inhabitants of **Birkaut Al Mauz ⓴** combine date farming with careers as civil servants commuting daily to Muscat (117 km/73 miles). Their Gulf-style houses festooned with television aerials reflect their high standard of living. A right turn off the highway passes a *falaj* splashing down the hillside.

The old town of Birkaut Al Mauz, a maze of crumbling pisé buildings, is stacked into the side of the Saiq plateau around 2,000 metres (6,562 ft) above Wadi Muaydin beneath the Jebel Akhdar. It was bombed by the British Royal Air Force in the 1950s during the Green Mountain War, a rebellion by the Beni Riyam tribe that controlled the Jebel Akhdar and approaches to it from the south.

The tiny pink roses used in the making of attar of roses – once an important export from Oman – are cultivated up here in the brisk mountain air. A hike up to the plateau, requiring a local guide, is attempted by an occasional expatriate but technically much of the Jebel Akhdar is a military zone.

Nizwa

Curling around a final bend, Route 15 deposits you gently in the historic town of **Nizwa ㉑** at the head of Wadi Sumail. Upon visiting Nizwa in 1350, the North African geographer Ibn Battuta remarked on its massive fort, the magnificent *souq* redolent with smouldering incense and crowded with turbaned tribesmen, and of the number of mosques and *madrassas* (religious schools). Protected by the *jebel* and deeply conservative, it was an obvious choice as capital of the Imamate more than 300 years later.

The town of Nizwa, surrounded by square mud walls and houses entered by wooden doors and stairways, is essentially unchanged. The **Daris Falaj** irrigates its vast date plantations, each palm individually owned and providing fuel and building material as well as sustenance – a bridal dowry for poorer farmers. Around 60,000 people living in Nizwa and environs are farmers and traders with a few producing crafts and goods related to tourism. The town centre has been restored by the Ministry of National Heritage and Culture, but the result is bland, with everything – shops, banks, *souq* and fort – painted a uniform Revlon bronze. Nonetheless, after Muscat Nizwa is the most popular visitor attraction in Oman. Most tourists stay only for a day, but to see Nizwa properly and to visit other interesting places in the Interior requires two or three days. Local accommodation is limited but comfortable.

Nizwa's **fort** (daily 7.30am–4.30pm, until 5pm in summer; free admission) was raised over a period of 12 years by Imam Sultan bin Saif in the late 17th century. According to one source it was financed by spoils from Ras al Khaimah while a second theory claims it was financed by an Omani attack on the tiny Portuguese colony of Diu on the Malabar Coast of India. Whichever is correct,

Map, page 144

TIP

Wednesday and Thursday are the best days to stay overnight in Nizwa. That way you can rise early to see the livestock market in full swing near the fort (*see page 159*).

BELOW LEFT AND RIGHT: life around the local *falaj*.

Nizwa's importance in the long struggle between Muscat and the Interior is reflected in its fort, built here to guard the Sumail Gap while also acting as a residence and administrative centre for the Imams .

Big rather than aesthetically pleasing, it consists of a massive circular tower with foundations sunk 30 metres (98 ft) deep to withstand vibrations from mortar fire. Several of more than 400 gun emplacements still have mortars in situ, one of them inscribed with the name of the Imam Sultan bin Saif and another a gift from the city of Boston to the first Omani ambassador to the USA. A narrow staircase leading up to the tower is kinked at each level, leading to a false door with gun emplacements and apertures in the ceiling to pour boiling oil onto any invader who managed to penetrate this deep inside the fort.

The easy climb opens into the drum of the tower with 120 positions for askars to stand guard duty on the parapets. The top – 40 metres (131 ft) above the *souq* – commands a panoramic view of the landmark blue-domed **mosque** next to the fort, the maze of flat-topped houses and the belt of palms surrounding Nizwa like a *cordon sanitaire*. To the northeast, the Jebel Akhdar is angled menacingly against the sky with its highest peak Jebel Shams (3,009 metres/9,872 ft), the highest point in eastern Arabia, usually swathed in cloud.

Less than two decades ago Nizwa had one of the largest *souqs* in Arabia, a warren of interconnecting lanes lined with hundreds of tiny shops, some no bigger than cardboard boxes where each trader sat like a spider in a web of paraphernalia. There was no space to squeeze inside, so customers would stand outside pointing out what they wanted and bargaining a price. Shafts of sunlight filtered through palm matting roofs hoary with centuries of cooking smoke. Queen Elizabeth II, who visited Nizwa with Sultan Qaboos on her state visit to

High up in the Jebel Akhdar lives the Arabian tahr, a shy goat-like creature unique to Oman. The Wadi Sarin Nature Reserve was set up to protect and increase their numbers.

BELOW: on the ramparts of Nizwa Fort.

Oman in 1979, was said to have been fascinated by the *souq*, remarking that she could never have found her way around alone. In fact, the *souq* was organised as well as any supermarket, with crafts and trades grouped together for comparison and convenience. It had a street of butchers, another for incense blenders, a street for spice sellers, several streets of tailors, a corner for dates, another for gunsmiths, silversmiths and so on.

Map, page 144

Alas, this traditional *souq* has now moved into a modern arcade, though the shops remain small with their owner usually found squatting behind a glass showcase containing anything from sticky sweetmeats – *halwa* is a Nizwa speciality – to silver jewellery and accoutrements for which the old Ya'ruba capital is equally well known. Luxury goods – rich fabrics, perfumes, embroidered hats – are found in the *kissaria* opposite the mosque.

Most silverware – the *khanjar* dagger worn by men, and the bangles, rings, anklets, necklaces and *kohl* cases beloved of women in the Interior – is still handcrafted locally. In the old days jewellery was made from silver obtained by melting down Maria Theresa dollars, which along with the Indian rupee was used as currency. These days it is fashioned from imported ingots.

Al Akur, an authentic Omani restaurant above an interesting crafts/antiquities shop on the square off the *souq*, is an excellent place for lunch. Such things as fried locusts, spicy fish and goat's tripe stew are served in clean surroundings.

On Thursday and Friday, between 7am and noon, an area next to the car park becomes a livestock **market**, where traditionally attired men, many with a *khanjar* in their belts, a cane to hand or perhaps a rifle slung over their back, bid for goats, sheep and cattle. The market is especially busy before *Eid al Adha*, the Muslim feast of sacrifice, when every family buys an animal to slaughter.

Nizwa's kissaria is the place to buy luxury goods such as a richly embroidered hat.

BELOW: view from the top, Nizwa Fort.

On the edge of the market veiled women sell onions, cheese, honey, dates and woven date-palm mats. Potential customers will slide their bare feet up and down the mats to test for knots which will make sitting uncomfortable. Pottery items come from Bahla, a 40-km (25-mile) drive north on the tarmac highway through the Dhahira (*see page 161*).

Around Nizwa

Coming out of Nizwa, the road passes the first of two detours to the ruined town of **Tanuf** ㉒, the former capital of the *jebali* (mountain) warlord Suleiman bin Himyar. As well as being bombed, the town had its *falaj* cut as a reprisal for supporting the Imamate revolution of 1954–9 (*see page 19*). A second sign leads to the new town (4 km/2½ miles) where a factory bottles the popular Tanuf mineral water.

Al Hamra ㉓ (17 km/10 miles from Nizwa) is considered one of the most elegant and unusual towns in the interior. It has no defences and, curiously for this rugged part of Oman, it has an almost Italianate feel, with terraced gardens and a piazza, from which a flight of steps leads to a street of grand three- and four-storey houses with green wooden window shutters. The lower terrace by a gushing *falaj* is a pleasant picnic spot.

A turn- off the Al Hamra road to **Wadi Ghul** is motorable a little way by car. At the end of the valley a track in poor condition ascends **Jebel Shams**. With ample notice Muscat travel agents can organise an enjoyable expedition up Jebel Shams, taking in spectacular scenery, including Oman's "Grand Canyon", ancient rock carvings and remote villages, camping out overnight and well rugged up against the cold.

BELOW: the ruined town of Tanuf, a casualty of the 1954–59 rebellion.

Misfah ❷, accessible up a steep road from Al Hamra, is a pretty village where houses cling to the cliffside. A tank filled by a *falaj* running off the *jebel* is a favourite spot for village boys, who delight in diving in and splashing any visitor. Steps beside the tank lead down to a tiny mosque.

Bahla to Ibri

Bahla ❷, 40 km (25 miles) west of Nizwa, is another town whose massive fortress fills the horizon. The Nabahina rulers of Oman from the 12th–17th century raised the **fort** on pre-Islamic foundations and also built the 12 km (7½ miles) of mud-brick surrounding walls. Covering a hilltop west of Bahla, the fort, pierced by seven gates, has been listed as a UNESCO World Heritage Site following painstaking restoration.

Bahla's once-flourishing pottery industry is reduced to only two potters working in a dusty village beyond the *souq*, where a sign "Pottery Made and Sold" is tacked on a date palm. One of them still throws pots on a traditional kick-wheel operated by a Bangladeshi. Its Omani owner welcomes visitors who are shown the clay pits and ovens and invited to have a glass of tea. The unglazed objects – incense burners and water jars – are mainly for local use.

Another 10 km (6 miles) west, and 4 km (2½ miles) off the highway, is **Jabrin Castle** ❷ (daily 8am–5pm; free admission), the finest example of residential architecture in Oman. Despite the imposing battlements, Jabrin was not a fort but a retreat for the Imams as well as a seat of learning for students of Islamic jurisprudence, medicine and astrology. Certainly its location, set back from the mountains on an open gravel plain, does not suggest that its builder, Imam Bil'arub bin Sultan Al Ya'ruba, felt under threat of attack.

Map, page 144

On the battlements

BELOW: a potter in Bahla.

Built in 1671, the three-storey rectangular building has 4-metre (13-ft) thick stone walls with north-south towers. In the high-ceilinged rooms with Moghul-style arches are traces of what must have been a sumptuously decorated palace, tastefully restored by the Ministry of National Heritage and Culture in 1983. Swirling Islamic inscriptions in the plaster walls are cut as delicately as hand-embroidered lace, rosettes cover the pine-carved ceilings while astrological designs in what is called the Sun and Moon Room have no parallel in Oman. In contrast to the splendour are small plain cells used by students off the third-storey courtyard. Go up a final flight of steps to the top of the castle for a view of the *jebel* quivering in the heat haze.

A guide is essential to see everything, including Imam Bil'arub's tomb (he died in 1692) and the curious upstairs room for the Imam's horse. An interesting exhibition records the castle's impressive restoration.

To Ibri

West of Jabrin, the Route 21 continues to Ibri. The **Bat tombs** ❷ off the highway between Ibri and Kubarah are best approached from Kubarah (20 km/12 miles from Bat), with a left turn before the village of Al Ain. Linked to the Umm an-Nar civilisation (2500–2000 BC) of Abu Dhabi (*see page 216*), the curious beehive tombs outlined against the misty blue of Jebel Misht make an impressive sight perched on the stone rubble of an ancient village or necropolis (the ridge is climbed in 10 minutes from the river bed). Also here are round towers of the period, one of which is 20 metres (65 ft) high.

Ibri ❷, 36 km (22 miles) from Kubarah , is the heart of the Dhahira, the north-west shoulder of Oman wedged between the Western Hajar and the Empty Quar-

BELOW: Jabrin Castle.

ter. Historically it was a buffer against Wahhabi nationalism although many disputes were started by Imams pitching in with the Saudis, a root cause of the Imamate revolt in the 1950s.

A 19th-century visitor to Ibri wrote: "The neighbouring Arabs observe that to enter Ibri a man must either go armed to the teeth, or as a beggar with a cloth." Tribalism remains strong but it does not affect travellers who tend to pass through quickly en route to somewhere else – on their way from Nizwa to Buraimi or crossing the Hajar Mountains via Wadi Hawasina to the Batinah Coast. Petrol stations, mechanics, foodstores – all with plastic brick shopfronts – line Route 21 beside a huge new mosque. Set back off the highway is the old village with a traditional *souq* and a small restored fort .

Sulaif ㉙, a crumbling village a few kilometres east of Ibri was deserted by its inhabitants some 40 years ago when the *falaj* dried up. The old fortified town built on a rock is entered through a small black door in the city wall – note the inscription over it – which would have been shut at nightfall. Sulaif's houses are in a ruinous state and the wooden *souq* is being eaten by termites, but it is worth a quick visit before rejoining Route 21 for Buraimi, 126 km (78 miles) further west.

The drive up from Ibri skirts the edge of the Empty Quarter, and sand spits across the highway. The **Dhahira** is barren except for scattered "bag trees", so called because their thorny branches trap wind-blown plastic bags. At 46 km (28 miles) is a Shell petrol station and foodstore, but beyond only signposts on the highway indicate the presence of villages hidden in the *jebel*. Nearing Buraimi the road swings close to the rocky outcrop of Jebel Hafit in Abu Dhabi where archaeologists have discovered ancient tombs. A winding road up offers

Map, page 144

BELOW: the Bat tombs outlined on the hillside.

Map, page 144

a spectacular view of the huge oasis watered by some of the longest *falaj* in Arabia. One of two main feeder canals supplying the date plantations, **Falaj Sa'ara**, is 16 km (10 miles) long.

Buraimi

The truth about Buraimi ㉚, one of several villages in the Buraimi Oasis, is that visitors to Al Ain – on the Abu Dhabi side – are excited to dip a toe into Oman while Omanis cannot wait to cross to Al Ain which is livelier with cheaper shopping. There are no checks at the border cutting through the centre of the oasis, but coming from the Ibri road travellers must negotiate 30 km (19 miles) of the UAE before entering Oman again. A road pass – issued in Muscat – is essential and Oman Customs make a thorough check for any opened bottles of alcohol.

New and sprawling, Buraimi lacks character, but its modern hotel with a pool and a licence to sell alcohol is appreciated by travellers from the dry Dhahira. The main buildings – the hotel, a mosque and Al Khandaq Fort – are linked by roundabouts where lifesize fibreglass oryx graze on real grass. A small *souq* supplies limes, dried fish, tobacco, canes, ropes, camel halters, paraffin and other Bedu needs. The occasional old coffee pot or silver necklace is priced for the day visitor from Al Ain whose shops are stocked with electronic goods.

Al-Hilla Fort, behind the *souq* on the edge of the oasis, is gradually being restored. The larger **Al Khandaq Fort** (Saturday to Wednesday 8am–6pm; Thursday and Friday 8am–1pm and 4–6pm; free admission), surrounded by a deep if dry moat and with crenellated battlements flying the flag of the Sultanate, makes a suitable end to a circuit of Oman's forts. There are no displays, but the dramatic architecture and a little imagination make a visit enjoyable.

A coffee pot – a symbol of hospitality all over the Middle East.

BELOW: weaving palm fronds in Buraimi.

Wadi-Bashing

The major cities and towns of Oman and the UAE are linked by asphalt highways but to fully explore what the region's landscape has to offer, weekenders and naturalists should find themselves a seat in a 4X4 and hit the dirt and the dunes.

Wadi-bashing, as off-road driving is popularly known, is both a means to an end and an end in itself: not only will it get you from inhabited point A to isolated point B, but you'll have a lot of fun on the way.

Bouncing along a boulder-strewn wadi is like flying through bad turbulence with the "fasten seatbelt" sign on. Those who are not strapped in can become unwilling headbangers. But those who are usually emerge from the experience unscathed with the exuberance of children after their first spin on funfair dodgem cars.

Off-road driving should not be attempted in ordinary saloon cars. The all-terrain traction provided by four-wheel-drive vehicles is essential. It's also safer if more than one vehicle takes to the wilds at a time: that way, one can tow the other out of trouble if the need arises.

The person behind the wheel needs the handling skills of a rally driver, which is why if you're a first-time wadi-basher it's a good idea to have someone else do the work. While 4X4s can be rented, less worrisome off-road tours with experienced drivers are provided by hotels and specialist tour companies.

But even those who are most adept at judging the conditions can get stuck in a sand dune. A little forethought can prevent major problems, and the experienced wadi-basher hopes for the best but prepares for the worst. A long rope, shovel, tyre jack and base (to stop the jack from sinking in the sand) are musts. A small ladder or large sheet of tarpaulin can be placed under the wheels for traction. Extra fuel, water (in the desert, one person needs 4.5 litres/1 gallon a day), a spare wheel and tyre pressure gauge are also important features of a successful trip.

Wadi-bashing depends on tyre pressure as much as skill – lower pressure for driving through sand and desert, and higher for mountain driving. When stuck in soft sand reducing the tyre pressure and reversing over your own tracks may allow your vehicle to be driven, instead of towed, out of trouble.

To avoid getting stuck, don't change gear in soft sand, as the vehicle will lose the momentum needed to pull it through. And avoid stopping where you can't start again. If engines are over-revved at the first sign of trouble, the wheels dig further into the sand.

When ascending and descending sandy slopes, the wheels should be kept straight and the most vertical route taken. Attempting to cross a slope diagonally is an invitation for disaster. When going down a slope, the vehicle should be in low gear with the engine instead of the brakes used to slow it down. That way, it's less likely that the front wheels will become stuck and that the rear end will swing around, precipitating a roll.

Wadi-bashing is a great means by which to appreciate the raw beauty of the desert and mountains. It can be done year round, as long as the bashers are mindful of wadis where winter flash floods have occurred in the past.

RIGHT: wadi-bashing is fun and exhilarating

SUR, THE EAST AND THE WAHIBA SANDS

Map, page 171

This region offers a beautiful coastline, the characterful old ship-building city of Sur and the dunescapes of the Wahiba Sands. It makes an ideal three- or four-day excursion from Muscat

This part of Oman combines rugged coastline, sandy plains and the spectacular Wahiba sand sea. It lies within Al Sharqiya province southeast from Muscat and easily accessible from the capital. Sparsely populated, its main coastal towns are Quriyat, an important fishing community, and Sur, an historic boatbuilding and trading centre. Sanaw, Ibra and Al Mudaiybi are among half a dozen Bedu market depots on the edge of the sands.

Unlike the road to Sohar, Route 17 east travels largely along the coast passing picturesque fishing villages and coral-ringed bays. The round-trip via Route 23, a tarmac inland road, can be accomplished in two days and nights, with stops in Sur and Al Qabil on the edge of the Wahiba Sands. The journey can also include a visit to the turtle-breeding headland of Ras al Hadd, the most easterly point in Arabia.

It is essential to have a four-wheel-drive vehicle for sightseeing off the main road, and experience of desert driving and a local Bedu guide are imperative for the Wahiba Sands. Petrol stations and foodstores are found at regular intervals along the inland road and in the larger coastal villages, but follow the golden rule when travelling anywhere in Oman and take extra water and petrol in case of an emergency.

Quriyat ❶ (87 km/54 miles) from Muscat is a quiet coastal town of no special interest. Turn right at the old fort on the roundabout and drive across the wadi to the bay, an animated spot when the fishing boats return and lay their catch out on the beach. The current sweeping around the headland off Quriyat offers one of the richest fishing grounds in Oman, and sharks, including hammerheads, are seen with other species of pelagic (open water) fish. In earlier times horse-breeding on the plains between here and the Eastern Hajar was also important. Affonso D'Albuquerque, who sacked Quriyat in the early 16th century, mentioned the export of horses.

At the eastern end of the beach is a rocky outcrop crowned by a watchtower which you can wade out to at low tide. A creek, today silted up, before the turn-off to Sur was in all probability Quriyat's old port. A small hotel is popular with Omani families.

Around 10 km (6 miles) beyond Quriyat a rough track cuts off the broad valley known as Wadi Suwayh into the Eastern Hajar. Winding through **Wadi Daiqa**, it eventually rejoins the tarmac near Hail al Ghaf. The **Daiqa Gorge ❷**, with clear pools for swimming, is a favourite wadi-bashing circuit, but the road ahead has more interest for visitors. Stock up at the BP service sta-

PRECEDING PAGES: Wadi Tiwi. **LEFT:** Dhow painting at Ras al Hadd. **BELOW:** fishing for fun.

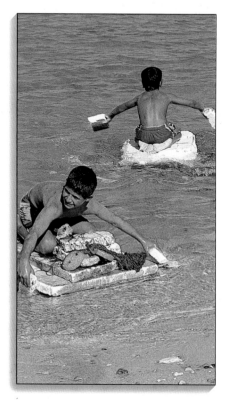

tion at the turn-off to Hail al Ghaf (82 km/51 miles from Muscat) before leaving for Sur, a four- to five-hour drive on a graded surface. The road crosses the dusty floor of **Wadi Suwayh** winding 36km/22 miles inland before reaching the sea again at Dibab.

A small cairn of stones on the right of the approach to Dibab indicates the turn to **Dibab sinkhole**, a large blue sinkhole in the limestone ridge. Around 100 metres (330-ft) in circumference, the sinkhole is one of several in Oman, the biggest being found in Dhofar. Marine species including sponges indicate a connection with the sea. At the time of writing the hole was unfenced and easily accessible for a refreshing swim.

When the donkey work is over in the fishing village of Bimmah.

Dibab ❸, **Bimmah** and **Fins** are small fishing villages on the rugged coastline. Houses in **Ash Shab ❹** (76 km/47 miles from Quriyat) cling to the side of a steep cliff. A wadi with shallow lagoons and shady trees is a delightful spot. **Tiwi ❺** has a superb white sand beach strung like a hammock between the cliffs. Like Shab, it has a lush wadi with cultivated terraces and is a perfect spot for swimming and a picnic.

Qalhat

A little further down the coast is the ancient city of **Qalhat ❻** (*see page 32*). "This city has a very good port, much frequented by merchant ships from India... since it is a centre from which spices and other goods are carried to various inland cities and towns," wrote Marco Polo, who visited **Qalhat** in the late 13th century. "Many fine war horses are exported... to the great gain of the merchants." The Moroccan explorer Ibn Battuta, who visited Qalhat some 50 years later, remarked on its splendid Persian mosque.

BELOW: in ancient Qalhat.

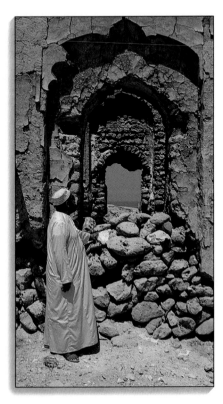

The city is believed to have been founded by the Persians around the 2nd century, reaching the height of prosperity under rule from Hormuz in the 13th to the 14th century. Damaged by an earthquake and sacked by Albuquerque in 1508 (who found "a great entrepot of shipping, which comes thither to take horses and dates to India"), Qalhat's remains are scanty. Drystone walls which once surrounded the city run down the hillside, and there are remains of ancient water cisterns and the scattered headstones of a cemetery.

The most notable feature is a shrine in poor repair named after a saintly woman known as Bibi Miriam. Ibn Battuta described it as "one of the most beautiful mosques. Its walls are tiled with qashani, which is like *zalij*, and it occupies a lofty situation from which it commands a view of the sea and the anchorage."

Qalhat's location on a narrow ridge between the mountains and the sea seems a strange choice when compared to Sur, 26 km (16 miles) further along the coast in a sheltered bay with a deepwater creek. But Qalhat probably had access to water via a *falaj* system (*see page 156*) from the mountain catchment area while Sur to this day remains short of drinking water.

Sur

From Qalhat the road descends to **Sur ❼** (126 km/78 miles from Quriyat), a major trading port with East Africa until early in the 20th century and still the biggest wholly traditional port in Oman. Sur finally gave in to the better shipping facilities of Muscat-Muttrah, but new housing developments on the western approach to the town indicate its fortunes are again improving. Untouched by the current construction boom based on commerce, old Sur and the small suburb of Aija, on the east bank of the creek, continue to provide visitors with a pastel cameo of the past.

A couple of silverware shops apart, the business district of Sur surrounding the bus station holds few attractions except for a restaurant under the Sur Hotel which serves reasonable chicken and seafood grills. Sur is renowned for fresh fish with much of the catch sold in Dubai coming from here by road.

The **dhow yards** are 6 km (4 miles) out of town on the banks of a blue tidal creek. Access to the yards is free and the workers, mainly Indian, do not mind being photographed. The shipyards were famous throughout the ancient world, and were especially associated with the magnificent *baghala* and the smaller *ghanja*. Both these vessels featured small windows set in a high stern designed like a Portuguese galleon. Describing the 200-tonne baghala *Hope of Compassion*, Alan Villiers who sailed on a number of Arab craft in the 1930s wrote: "Her windowed stern was especially lovely. Its elliptical area of ancient teak was covered with intricate patterns of excellent carving and her curved bow swept upwards from the sea as gracefully as the breast of a swan." The Sur craftsmen who used no drawings were renowned for carving beautifully decorated poops and sterns with only simple tools – a chisel, adze, hammer and a bow drill. Electrically powered tools have replaced traditional ones but the hulls are still sealed with shark fat and gypsum .

From the eight dhows built and launched in Sur in 1874 demand is down to

Map,
page 171

TIP

The route into Sur from Qalhat passes the Sur Resort Beach Hotel, offering comfortable Western-style facilities on Sur's main beach. It is the only place in town licensed to sell alcohol.

BELOW: new architecture in Sur.

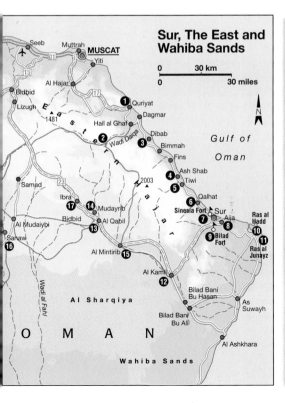

Sur, The East and Wahiba Sands

0   30 km
0   30 miles

N

Seeb
Muttrah
MUSCAT
Yiti
Al Hajar
Bidbid
Lizugh
1481
Hail al Ghaf
Quriyat
Dagmar
Dibab
Bimmah
Fins
Gulf of Oman
Ash Shab
2003
Tiwi
Samad
Ibra
Qalhat
Mudayrib
Sinesia Fort Sur
Bidbid
Al Qabil
Aija
Ras al Hadd
Al Mudaiybi
Bilad Fort
Sanaw
Al Mintirib
Ras al Junayz
Al Kamil
Al Sharqiya
Bilad Bani Bu Hasan
As Suwayh
Bilad Bani Bu Ali
O M A N
Al Ashkhara
Wadi al Fahl
W a h i b a   S a n d s

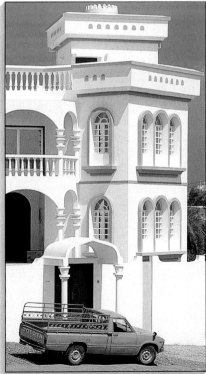

The old part of Sur is known locally as "Makkah", doubtless because the wealthy owners that originally lived here were able to perform the haj (pilgrimage).

one, or two a year. Half a dozen builders working full time take about five to six months to complete a vessel costing between OR 10,000–50,000 depending on her fittings. Around seven *sambuqs* are built each year. One or two of these and a traditional *jalibut* are usually moored in the harbour, but most craft are bum boats identified by a beaked prow and angled stern. Around 2,000 boats use the creek as an anchorage.

Local craftsmen have also left their mark on many fine merchant houses in the old part of Sur. Diverse patterns on green and blue wooden doors and windows reflect Indian, Persian and Zanzibari influences indicative of Sur's widespread trade contacts.

Old merchant-style houses are an equal attraction in **Aija ❽**, reached in a three-minute ferry crossing from the dhow yards. The little whitewashed community was founded in 1928 by rebellious sheikhs from Beni bu Ali who established an independent customs post and ran up their own flag which took the sultan, aided by the British Resident in the Gulf, two years to remove. At low tide the view of Aija from Sur crosses extensive mud flats and beached bum boats, which in the evening are bathed in rose-coloured sunlight; at high tide this is one of the most charming corners of Oman.

Two forts guard Sur. The main one, **Sinesia Fort** (7.30am–6pm; free admission), with its four distinctive towers, is built on a hill overlooking the sea approaches to Sur. Inside the courtyard are a mosque and a small prison, while to the far left a wooden door gives access to the water cistern. A second defensive structure, **Bilad Fort ❾** (7.30am–6pm; free admission) is 6 km (4 miles) from the town centre off the inland road to Al Kamil. It has a large courtyard, also with a small mosque, and a *mihrab* prayer niche in the western wall indi-

BELOW: fishermen haul in their boat.

cating the direction of Mecca for the overflow of worshippers. Close to Bilad Fort, next to the Arobah Sports Club, is a small, private **museum** (8am–noon and 4–7pm; free admission) with early photographs of Sur, costumes, traditional fishing and navigation equipment, and model boats.

Map, page 171

Ras Al Hadd

The jutting headland known as **Ras al Hadd ⑩** is the first point in Arabia touched by the rising sun. One of the world's largest concentrations of green turtles nests on this 40-km (25-mile) section of coastline. To visit Ras al Hadd, follow a section of new tarmac around to Aija. Winding inland for some 30 km (18 miles), a graded road then drops down to Khor Garama, a shallow inlet providing a safe mooring for fishing boats. A score of houses around a restored fort, Ras al Hadd spreads across an exposed headland. An airport here, its runway cracked and overgrown, was used as a staging post by Britain's Royal Airforce during World War II.

Around 20,000 green turtles lay their eggs on Oman's beaches during the summer breeding season. A female always returns to the beach where she herself hatched out.

Ras al Junayz ⑪, the main turtle-nesting beach, is 23 km (14 miles) along the coast (it is a protected site and you will need a permit from the Ministry of Regional Municipalities and Environment to visit it). The turtles come ashore at night, dig a hole in the sand and lay their eggs, covering them carefully before returning exhausted to the sea. The eggs, which may number up to 100 per turtle, take about 60 days to hatch, after which the tiny turtles must burrow their way to the surface and head as quickly as they can for the safety of the sea.

From Ras al Junayz there are two choices – either go back to Sur and return to Muscat on Route 23 via the Wahiba Sands, or continue on to **Al Ashkhara**, which is as far as the graded road currently goes.

BELOW: tuna on the beach.

The Beni bu Ali who installed themselves in Aija were the only tribe in Oman to subscribe to the conservative Wahhabism sect of Islam followed in Saudi Arabia. Their ancestors living in the **Bilad Beni bu Ali** ("territory of the Beni bu Ali") and Al Ashkhara remain extremely conservative. Women visitors are advised to dress with decorum if visiting either place; and swimming should be done well out of sight of any locals.

Al Ashkhara has historically survived on fishing, but its future will change radically if a planned holiday complex goes ahead. At present it is a quiet, down-at-heel old town with a couple of foodstores, a ship's chandlers and a tackle shop. This is the end of the road for most tourists, but equipped for four to five days camping, adventurous expatriates continue down this savagely beautiful coastline to Salalah. Flamingos are among thousands of migratory birds seen on the mud flats and lagoons sheltered by Ras an-Nuqdah.

The island of **Masirah**, though linked by ferry from An-Nuqdah and having an air link with Muscat, is not promoted as a tourist destination as there is no accommodation for visitors. Sharing Masirah with seabirds and turtles, Masirans are exclusively fishermen, living in a time warp.

Al Kamil ⓬, 75 km (46 miles) north of Al Ashkhara via Route 35 is a roadside town of traditional mud-brick buildings. On the junction of Route 23 from Sur (63 km/29 miles), it has a petrol station, mechanic, *biryani* cafés and several foodstores. Al Kamil is a 50-minute drive from **Al Qabil ⓭**, where a small but comfortable rest house (171 km/106 miles from Muscat) makes a good base from which to visit the Wahiba Sands. Close by (a 10-minute drive towards Sur) is **Mudayrib ⓮**, a busy community with a lively Friday *souq* and a restored fort but no hotel.

Masirah is a breeding ground for loggerhead turtles, which are even more numerous than the green turtles on the beaches south of Ras al Hadd

BELOW: in the Wahiba Sands.

Wahiba Sands

Map, page 171

Sunset and sunrise provide spectacular photo opportunities of this unique desert covering 10,000 square km (3,860 sq. miles) of the eastern Sharqiyah. Nigel de Winser the project director of a British Royal Geographic Society expedition to the Wahiba in 1985, described it as "a perfect specimen of sand sea".

The 35 scientists in the expedition spent four months studying the ecosystem of the Wahiba Sands and discovered 150 species of plants including extensive woodlands of native ghaf inland from Al Ashkhara. Among the desert's most valuable trees is the *Proposis cinera,* which helps stabilise the shifting sands as well as provide fuel, shade and food for livestock. A hardy tree, it sends down an immensely long tap root to the water table, but most desert plants are sustained on dew.

A rare dew-drinking beetle was among 16,000 invertebrates collected by the R.G.S. team. Two hundred species of mammals, birds, amphibians and reptiles were also logged. Early-risers here will probably see patterns made by nocturnal creatures in the sand – the swishing trail of a side-winding viper, the hip-hop footprints of a hare and the pad marks of a Rüpell's sand fox to name a few. During the day the desert is devoid of life as the creatures burrow away from the intense heat.

The Al Wahiba Bedu are famous weavers, producing fine camel saddle bags and superbly detailed girdles. This black and red design is characteristic of the region.

The dune systems of the Wahiba Sands are believed to have existed before the last pluvial period in Arabia around 4,000–6,000 years ago. Aligned mainly east-west and soaring upwards of 60–80 metres (200–260 ft), the dunes commence less than 1 km (½ mile) off the road between Al Qabil and Al Minitrib. With four-wheel drive, you can venture a little way into the desert. If you want more than a taste, Gulf Explorers, in Muscat, using Bedu guides and camping

BELOW: Wahiba Bedu.

out, cross the sands in three to four days. The entire sand sea can be circum-navigated in three days.

An easy point to access the dunes is to turn off the tarmac road at the Bank of Muscat outside the village of **Al Minitrib** . Drive past the fort and a concrete-faced *falaj* onto the sandy plain and bear east of the date plantation. Stop here and reduce your tyre pressure. Ranged ahead are soaring mountains of sand. Do not proceed from here without a Bedu guide.

Around 3,000 Bedu live on the fringes of the Wahiba Sands, mostly herders keeping sheep, goats and a few camels. Coastal families living south of Al Ashkhara double as fishermen while men around Al Qabil and Al Minitrib act as drivers and guides for local tour operators. They will usually take small parties of visitors to a Bedu encampment, where they will be invited to drink coffee and nibble dates and probably purchase simple crafts – *burqa* (the characteristic Bedu mask), brightly tasselled key fobs, masks and maybe larger woven items. Sanaw and Ibra are two of the most important Bedu market towns. **Bilad Bani bu Hassan**, near Al Kamil, is a centre for pottery.

Sanaw (171 km/106 miles from Muscat) is reached in about 40 minutes from the turn at the Shell petrol station. Its *souq* is a melting pot as Bedu come from miles around to sell their animals and exchange news (traditionally a very important aspect of Bedu life). Women sell handmade mats and masks to tourists. Lining the walls around the market are small shops filled with bric-a-brac essential to desert life. Silver jewellery and rustic pottery are found in several dusty outlets. Before 11am on a Thursday or Friday morning are the best times to visit the *souq*, which is inside distinctive green gates in the centre.

Ibra (150 km/93 miles from Muscat) has a general *souq*, but more interesting is the vibrant women's *souq* held here on a Wednesday morning from 7am until noon. To find the *souq*, turn left at the Oman National Bank: it is ahead on the left with dozens of pick-up trucks parked outside. While a husband, or a son, may drive the women into Ibra, men are barred from trading on Wednesday. Run exclusively by women, the Wednesday *souq* caters to women's and household needs.

As many as 60–70 Bedu women, young as well as old, unveiled and caparisoned in multi-patterned cotton robes, squat on the ground selling bolts of silk and satin brocades, jewellery, *kohl* eye make-up, sandalwood (*dahl oudh*) and other exotic perfumes, incense and kitchen goods, utensils, spices, goat's milk cheese, vegetables, eggs, and date-palm honey. Mothers, aunts,sisters and female cousins are seen shopping with prospective brides.

Times and distances

Ibra to the Nizwa-Muscat Highway is about a 70-minute drive on a low-altitude but winding road. Both Ibra and the Wahiba Sands (around 360-km/224-mile return trip) can be seen in a day's drive from Muscat. Sur is an 8–9 hour return journey via the same good tarmac road. Coming from Muscat on the Nizwa highway (Route 15), the turn off is left onto the new fly-over at the Sur/Muscat sign beyond Fanja. At the road branch take the direction to Sur.

TIP

Most women at Ibra's women's *souq* do not object to having their picture taken, but always ask first. "*Mumkin asawarak*" is a phonetic translation of "May I take your picture?"

BELOW AND OPPOSITE: trading at Ibra's women's *souq*.

THE BIRDLIFE ALONG DHOFAR'S COAST

The special climate of coastal Dhofar in southern Oman has made its wadis, hills and creeks particularly rich in birdlife

Clouds in mid-summer; verdant mountain-tops; deep wooded valleys bathed in mist; freshwater creeks sheltered from the ocean swell; and all inhabited by a very special birdlife near Salalah, the capital of Oman's southwestern province of Dhofar.

From June until mid-September moisture in the southwest monsoon condenses into fog and cloud as it crosses the wind-whipped cold sea and strikes the low Dhofar Mountains, enlivening the parched vegetation and scenery to the joy of the many visitors. But this part of Dhofar has another surpise: it has a superlative variety of birds, many of them African in character, within easy reach of Salalah, and not to be seen in the north. As a bonus, if you visit in spring or autumn you can expect to find many Eurasian migrants dropping in to rest and feed on their way between winter quarters in Africa and their breeding grounds far to the northeast.

GARDENS AND FARMS

In Salalah's gardens and farms there will be resident Rüppell's Weaver (but no House Sparrow), Abyssinian Sunbird, African Silverbill, as well as the more mundane Graceful Warbler and Yellow-vented Bulbul. Here even the widespread Palm or Laughing Dove is of a southern race, darker than the birds in the north. You may also see Black Kite and Fan-tailed Raven, the former perhaps nesting here in winter, the raven foraging from its cliff roosts and nests.

▷ **TRISTAM'S GRACKLE**
Listen for the loud fluting calls of Tristam's Grackle, a red-winged starling found only in Arabia, above Raysut's cliffs where red-billed Tropicbirds scream.

▷ **WADING OUT**
Egrets of many kinds visit Dhofar.

△ **A WALK IN THE HILLS**
A walk in the hills or up a valley is rewarding. From April the Didric Cuckoo (above) and the Grey-headed Kingfisher (*above left*) will be calling and nesting, while Singing Bushlark stand and buzz from any prominence and Cinnamon-breasted Rock Bunting sing in the trees. Further up you may see Arabian Red-legged Partridge.

ALONG DHOFAR'S CREEKS

Good views of waterbirds are to be had at most of the fabulous creeks called *khor*. Khor Salalah is a fenced bird sancturary and usually thronged with resting or feeding birds, but open creeks eastward to Khor Rawri (near Taqah) have their individual interest.

Visiting Greater Flamingo, egrets and herons of several kinds, Glossy Ibis (above) feeding on the grassy banks with resident moorhens and coots, gulls and terns gathering on the shore nearby – these creeks are always busy with birdlife. The many ducks in autumn will include Cotton Teal (Indian Pygmy Goose), and there may be Pheasant-tailed Jacana, occasional lapwing species, three or four species of snipe, roosting Yellow Wagtails, and a variety of waterbirds from the large visiting Eurasian Curlew and Black-tailed Godwit to the diminutive spring-nesting Kentish Plover. More birds can be 'scoped from a headland just east of Mirbat.

Don't neglect the surrounds of the creeks, where Little Pratincole may roost unseen, and a flock of Alpine Swift may mill over your head, or (early on a May morning) you may find the bushes bursting with fat Marsh Warblers, dawn arrivals from wintering in Africa and now on their way to nest in Europe.

◁ **SPOONBILL**
Spoonbill, identified by the spoon-shaped tip of their black bills, resting at Khor Taqah. Spoonbil may be seen in creeks all year round.

BIRDING ADVICE
Visitors wanting more information on Oman's birdlife can contact the Oman Bird Group, C/O the Natural History Museum, PO Box 668, Muscat 113, Tel: 605400.

◁ **PINK VISITORS**
The Greater Flamingo comes to Salalah's creeks from its breeding grounds in Asia. It wanders in parties in search of invertebrate food (molluscs, crustaceans, diatoms and plants) which it filters from the water and mud through its bill.

◁ **BIRDS OF PREY**
The fish-eating osprey (left) can often be seen perched above the creeks near Salalah. Other birds of prey include eagles and harrier (autumn), Lesser Kestrel and Amur Falcon (spring and summer). A good place to see these are the fodder farms near Salalah.

شواطئنا جميلة فلنحافظ
على نظافتها وسلامتها
الرجاء

DHOFAR

The only part of the Gulf that is visited by the southwest monsoon, Dhofar is a lush summer retreat for northern Omanis. Its rich history is rooted in the ancient frankincense trade

Maps pages 184, 186

he southern province of Dhofar, a ruggedly beautiful region, is quite different from the rest of Oman. Its mountains attract the *khareef* (southwest monsoon) blowing off the Indian Ocean, resulting in a cool wet summer (June–September) when the rest of the country is paralysingly hot. Waterfalls pour off the *jebels* into coastal wadis and low-hanging mists occasionally disrupt air services to the capital Salalah. Lush woodland is sustained by rainfall of 27–150 mm (1–6 inches) a year, but beyond its limits you can die of thirst. "To the south, grassy downs, green jungles and shadowy gorges fell away to the...Indian Ocean...whereas immediately to the north a landscape of black rocks and yellow sand sloped down to the Empty Quarter. I looked out over the desert. It stretched away unbroken for 1,500 miles to the orchards around Damascus," wrote Wilfred Thesiger in *Arabian Sands*.

Occupying about one-third of the total area of Oman, Dhofar adjoins the Rub al Khali (Empty Quarter), first crossed by Bertram Thomas in 1930 and then by Thesiger in the 1940s (*see pages 66–7*). The province shares a border with Yemen to the south (Yemen and Oman completed their demarcation of the border in 1995), and in the north melts into the gravel plains of the Jiddat al Harasis. Thirty kilometres (18 miles) offshore are the five rocky Hallaniya Islands – formerly known as the Kuria Muria Islands – once part of British-administered Aden but presented to the sultan of Oman in 1967. A few fishermen inhabit Helaneea, the largest of these, but none is accessible to tourists.

Dhofar has six *wilayat* (governorate), but the majority of its estimated population of 400,000 lives in Salalah. This figure includes many workers from the Indian subcontinent who manage shops and other small enterprises on behalf of locals. As on the Batinah Coast in northern Oman, the inhabitants of the coastal villages are fishermen and farmers.

Southern tribes

About nine mountain tribes known collectively as *jebali* live in the coastal ranges – Jebel Qamar, Jebel Samhan and Jebel Qara – rising behind Salalah. Brown skinned and with rounded heads, in appearance they resemble Ethiopians more than either Omanis or the long-skulled Bedu of the Jiddat al Harasis and Wahiba Sands. *Jibali* dialects are related to pre-Semitic languages spoken by the ancient Minaeans and Sabaeans. Short like the Yemenis, men are often bare-chested, or wear a long shirt over a sarong and carry a rifle (which may be used should you photograph them without permission). Most are herdsmen running stocky mountain cattle and keeping camels for prestige. During the monsoon, as the weather in the mountains cools down, they move their tents to the coastal plain around Salalah.

PRECEDING PAGES: Darbat Lake during the monsoon. **LEFT:** blowholes at Mughsayl. **BELOW:** Dhofari woman in typically vibrant attire.

TIP

Although a daily bus service crosses central Oman to Salalah, the 12-hour journey is monotonous, relieved only by one or two stops at petrol stations en route. Air travel is preferable.

BELOW: mixing business with pleasure on the beach at Salalah.

Salalah

Most people travel to Dhofar by air, a spectacular 90-minute flight across the Wahiba Sands from Muscat. On the approach to **Salalah** ❶ the brown terrain is flecked with green and the drop down onto the coastal plain is sudden and exciting. Likewise 1,000 km (620 miles) after leaving Muscat, the highway sweeps into Salalah, flanked by lines of flame trees and coconut palms, which here replace the date palm of the north.

Local development has been rapid following the end of the Dhofari War in 1975 (*see page 19*), and Salalah is too new to have character. The General Post Office and Salalah Museum are on A' Nadhah Street which cuts across A'Robat Road to the seafront. The *souqs* surrounding the bus terminal can be explored on foot, but walking from one end of A'Nadhah Street to the other takes at least an hour and more often than not it is too hot.

The city's markets are filled with locally grown tropical fruits such as coconuts, pawpaws, melons and bananas. Other local buys include seafood, spices and gold jewellery (**Gold Souq Ⓐ**), but it is the **Incense Souq Ⓑ** with its exotic aromas that deserves most attention: outside each small shop a woman of African slave descent sits tossing a pinch of this and a pinch of that onto a smouldering incense burner. Buyers squat down to sniff and select what they like. The operculum of the tulip shell *Fascilaria trapezium* ground with aloe and mixed with frankincense is a popular fragrance for the home.

Salalah Museum Ⓒ (Saturday to Wednesday 8am–2pm; free admission) in the Cultural Centre on A'Nadhah Street, is worth a visit, not least for the exhibition in the ante-room of photographs by Wilfred Thesiger, who set off on his first crossing of the Empty Quarter from Salalah in 1946. Extracts from *Ara-*

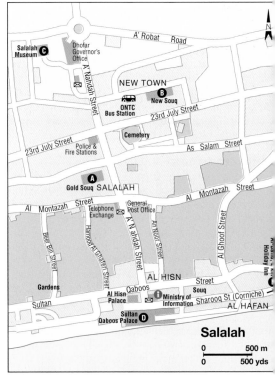

Salalah

0 ────── 500 m

0 ────── 500 yds

bian Sands, Thesiger's record of his journeys caption the pictures, some of which are portraits of his Bedu travelling companions, including Bin Kabina, a young member of the Rashid tribe who faithfully followed "Umbarak" during his five years travelling in southern Arabia.

Map page 184

The other rooms in the museum contain a variety of interesting displays, including tablets bearing Himarytic script from the ancient frankincense port of Sumhuram, model dhows, traditional fishing tackle, regional costumes and domestic items and jewellery.

At the end of A'Nadhah Street is a 10-km (6-mile) long golden sand **beach** flanked by **Sultan Qaboos's palace ❶** and, to the east, the Holiday Inn, currently the best hotel in Salalah, with pool, tennis courts and licensed restaurants. Tall, slender coconut palms create a tropical impression which is all the more curious with the desert starting just 50 km (30 miles) inland. Behind the palm groves lies **Old Salalah**, whose once-elegant coral-stone houses are in disrepair, their carved wooden doors removed. Strewn with masonry and garbage, the old town is a sad but interesting spot to stroll through and like everywhere in Oman perfectly safe, including for a woman on her own

The ruins of **Al Balid ❷**, the ancient city of Dhofar (*see box below*), are a short walk west of the Holiday Inn. During the Middle Ages, the town prospered from the frankincense trade and the export of Arab horses. It was visited by both the North African explorer Ibn Battuta and Marco Polo on their journeys along the Arabian Sea littoral. Describing the City of Dhofar in the 14th century, Ibn Battuta observed that it had numerous mosques with the main mosque not far from the palace in the northwest part of the city and the main gateway in the west wall of the city.

[Salalah] was the Sultan's Balmoral.
— JAMES MORRIS
Sultan in Oman 1957

ABOVE: desert rose.
BELOW: tropical fruits, including bananas, flourish.

ARCHAEOLOGICAL EVIDENCE

In 1952 the archaeologists working at Khor Rawri (*see page 187*) also started work at Al Balid where they located the west gate described by Ibn Battuta and the large mound which probably represents the palace. More recent excavations uncovered the Great Mosque in the northwest of the site. Today Al Balid is partially surrounded by two inlets which once formed a "moat" surrounding the entire landward sides. At the west end of the site the foundations of a bridge over the moat have been excavated. Further gates to the city have also been located, and it appears that the site was divided in half with the main buildings in the west. In the course of excavations, smaller mosques were located, many with finely detailed architectural elements. Pottery found on the site indicates that it was well established by the 13th century and in receipt of imports from as far as China.

Excursions from Salalah

Salalah is a comfortable springboard for a variety of mountain, desert and coastal trips. Allow one week to explore the area properly with time off for swimming and snorkelling in tranquil coastal inlets. There are food stores in larger towns such as Taqah and Thumrait, but it is prudent to pack a picnic and drinks on any trip you take. Always carry more water and petrol than you are likely to need especially on an excursion to the Empty Quarter. Most towns are linked to Salalah by tarmac roads, but four-wheel drive is essential beyond Sadih to the east and Raysut to the west. Cars can be rented locally, but most of the following excursions can also be made by taking an organised tour (*see the Travel Tips section, at the end of the book, for details*).

East to Mirbat

The day-trip to the old fishing community of Mirbat (74 km/46 miles from Salalah) is a pleasant drive, offering interesting diversions inland to Jebel Samhan and the Tawi Atayr sinkhole (*see page 188*) and, close to Salalah (25 km/15 miles), **Ain Razat ❷**, a lush picnic spot around a spring. A graded road runs to Sadih, a tiny hamlet known for abalone diving, but four-wheel drive is essential to continue on to Hadbin and beyond.

Taqah ❸ (36 km/22 miles from Salalah) is the second largest town in Dhofar. The majority of its 12,000 population are fishermen netting huge catches of sardines during the winter migration season beginning in December. When the vegetation dies off, dried sardines become an important food supplement for *jebali* (mountain) cattle. Where there are no roads the stinking sacks of fish are still carried into the mountains by camels. Plank sewn fishing boats were used in

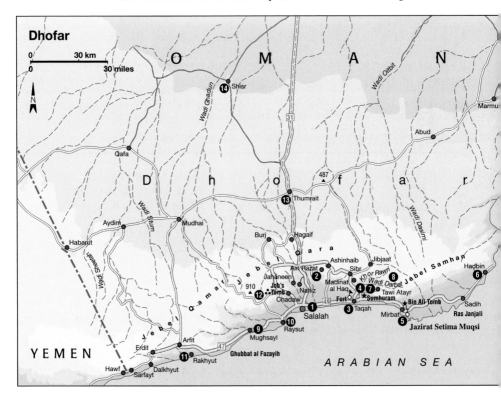

Taqah until as late as the mid-1970s, but today most fishermen share a fibreglass vessel powered by a Japanese outboard. A **fort** of no special interest (Saturday to Wednesday 7.30am–2.30pm, free admission) is open to visitors.

Khor Rawri ❹, 2 km (1 mile) long, is the largest of a dozen creeks between Salalah and Sadih. With a particularly low salt content, it supports freshwater fish from small guppies to ponderous milk fish of 80 cm (31 inches) in length. Pelican, stork, spoonbill and flamingo are among 186 species of birds recorded in the vicinity. Higher up in the head of the wadi is a breeding ground for Arabian Red-legged Partridge. Ruined **Sumhuram**, a beautiful site on the banks of Khor Rawri, was an important port for the export of frankincense during antiquity. A right turn off the tarmac road before Mirbat leads to an unusual white double-domed mosque enshrining **Bin Ali Al Alawi**, a 14th-century Muslim divine from Yemen. Access to the tomb is forbidden, but you may walk around the cemetery to see early Islamic headstones.

Mirbat ❺ is the most picturesque town on the coast of Dhofar. Its tiny whitewashed fort with a row of cannon pointing seawards offers good views (including to Jebel Samhan behind the Mirbat plain, *see page 188*). Beyond the headland the old town has similar fine old houses to Aija, near Sur. Set further down the hill, the new town has a score of shops plus a fish and tobacco market held in the early morning.

It is a one-hour drive from the petrol station outside Mirbat to **Sadih**, at present the end of the line. Crossing the rocky coastal shelf, the road affords wonderful views of Jebel Samhan. Sheltered from the force of the monsoon wind, a few straggly frankincense trees grow in the wadis and stops in the shape of incense burners indicate a local bus service. On reaching Sadih, turn left at the

Map, page 186

This inscription at Sumhuram records the foundation of the city by colonists from Shabwah.

BELOW LEFT:
Khor Rawri.

SUMHURAM

In 1952 archaeologists excavating Khor Rawri confirmed that the site dated from the pre-Islamic period. This was indicated by a bronze plaque bearing an inscription in the south Arabian script typical of the civilisation in the Yemen at this time. The inscription showed the name of the site to be "Smhrm", and further inscriptions revealed that it had been founded by a king of Shabwah specifically for the shipping of frankincense. The excavations also revealed a temple dedicated to the moon god Sin, the main deity of the Hadhramaut region. Other buildings have the appearance of store rooms, possibly to hold incense. Objects found in the excavations help date the site to the same period as the *Periplus of the Erythraean Sea* (around AD 50–200). These include sherds of Roman pottery from the eastern Mediterranean, a statue of a dancing girl imported from India and a statue of a bronze bull of south Arabian type.

Abalone Roundabout and drive down to a tiny harbour where a few boats are usually moored. Local women as well as men work as abalone divers wearing only goggles and diving to depths of 10 metres (30 ft) to prise the shells off the rocks. They bring up an average of 10–20 kg (22–44 lb) of abalone a day during the season (November to December). A café in Sadih sells soft drinks and plates of *biryani*.

Historically, **Hadbin** ❻ (170 km/105 miles from Salalah) was linked to the export of frankincense, but today, like Sadih, it relies on fishing and occasional abalone diving. It has several small foodstores, but no other facilities. Travel beyond here is strictly by four-wheel drive with a back-up vehicle.

Jebel Samhan and Tawi Atayr

Jebel Samhan, the green coastal range behind Mirbat, can be seen in a half-day trip from Salalah. On the main road turn left at the signpost marked Tawi Atayr, 6 km (4 miles) from Taqah, and climb. During the summer rainy season, the run-off from Jebel Samhan forms an impressive cascade down the valley into Khor Rawri which is itself occasionally broached by high seas whipped up by the strong monsoon winds.

The mountain top is lush and green with brilliantly coloured birds flitting about the woodland. Pigeons feast on wild figs and eagles soar at eye level 1,000 metres (3,280 ft) above the coastal plain. Among the botanical wilderness look out for the curious *Adeium obesum* whose pink blossoms grow straight out of the trunk.

The plateau town of **Tawi Atayr** ❼ has a few foodstores. The sign to the sinkhole is posted "Kisais Adheen", a right turn off the main road then a further

BELOW LEFT: spring cleaning.
BELOW RIGHT: waterfall off the *jebel* in September.

1.5 km (1 mile) to an ablutions site where you can park and ask one of the young boys to act as your guide. The enormous limestone cavity plunges 100 metres (328 ft) below. Taking care, you can scramble down a rugged path to the bottom in around 30 minutes. A subterranean stream leads out of the sinkhole, but no one has yet managed to follow it to the end. A lagoon surrounded by shady forest trees in **Wadi Darbat ❽**, a 30-minute drive from Tawi Atayr, is a popular picnic site.

West of Salalah

Leaving Salalah, the road west to Rakhyut winds through dusty wadis behind soaring cliff-tops with spectacular ocean views. Travellers currently require a pass from the military authorities to travel beyond Rakhyut, and the Yemen border is closed, but the situation may change so it is worth checking. A four-wheel drive vehicle is essential for the trip and because of the switchback nature of the road it is sensible to return before dark.

For **Mughsayl ❾** (45 km/28 miles from Salalah) follow the road to the modern port of **Raysut ❿** (10 km/6 miles from Salalah) and bear inland at the roundabout. A rocky track on the left leads to cut-off cliffs with a view back to Raysut.

Mughsayl is known for giant blowholes which spurt water up to 30 metres (100 ft) high on an in-coming tide. Walking along the rock shelf you can hear the eerie sound of the sea rushing beneath your feet. Mughsayl has a good swimming beach and the creek at the southern end is popular for birdwatching. Between December and February and April and June, herons, grebes, egrets, ducks, flocks of fairy terns and even flamingos are among the visitors.

Map, page 186

TIP

On a clear day look out for dolphins, packs of sharks or even a whale or two off the coast at Mughsayl.

BELOW: summer dampness caught in a spider's web.

Map,
page 186

Before 1988 the only way to visit Rakhyut was to make a 400-km (148-mile) detour inland via Thumrait and over Jebel Qamar from Salalah. Today access is by the "Furious Road", literally carved out of the cliff-face by engineers. In 5 km (3 miles), the road rises some 400 metres (1,312 ft) in height and includes eight hairpin bends at frightening gradients of between 10 and 12 percent. Some 6.4 million tonnes/tons of rock and 160,000 tonnes/tons of asphalt went into building the road which cost around £75 million (US$120 million).

Rakhyut ⓫ (148 km/92 miles from Salalah) is a small village built under the lee of the cliffs with a couple of basic foodstores and nothing else. There is a camping area behind the beach, but you should ask the wali's permission to use it; this is always granted.

The road to Dalkhyut and Sarfay, near the border with Yemen, remains closed following the 1994 civil war in Yemen when the South Yemen cabinet decamped by air to Salalah.

Job's Tomb

Job's Tomb ⓬ (open 24 hours) lies to the north of Salalah. Famed in the Old Testament for maintaining his faith in God in spite of the great sufferings sent to test him, Job (Ayoub in Arabic) is revered by Muslims as well as Jews and Christians.

To reach the site held by Muslims to be the patriarch's tomb, take the road into the *jebel* behind the Hamdan Plaza Hotel in Salalah. After about 30 km/18 miles turn left at a sign to Al Nabi Ayoub, then drive 1.4 km (1 mile) to a road fork and bear left. Enter the gate beside the mosque and walk down the path to a white shrine with a gold dome. A single long grave, the tomb is covered with

ABOVE: Job's tomb
BELOW: the "Furious Road".

shrouds, garlands and pages from the Qur'an left by faithful pilgrims. Non-Muslims are allowed to enter the shrine, but must cover their heads and remove their shoes first.

Map, page 186

The Empty Quarter

Frankincense trees are guaranteed on the 200-km (124-mile) round trip from Salalah to Thumrait (from which you will need a four-wheel drive to dip a toe in the Empty Quarter). The tarmac road to Thumrait, part of the Desert Highway to Muscat, starts climbing into the Jebel Qara 5 km (3 miles) outside Salalah, a gradual rise into an increasingly inhospitable landscape. The inland side of the mountains forms a plateau which dips gradually to the north, eventually giving way to gravel hills dissected by numerous wadis and the desert. The best-quality frankincense comes from this baking plateau. You may see some of the Bait Kathir Bedu, a famous tribe who own hereditary rights to the trees, either cutting or collecting the resin. Keep money handy if you wish to take their picture.

Road to somewhere, on the edge of the Empty Quarter

About midway between Salalah and Thumrait is **Hanun**, site of a permanent pool of water and an ancient storehouse for frankincense. The site, first excavated in 1962, is small and simple and consists of a building divided into a number of long narrow units which give the appearance of being store rooms, not unlike those excavated at Sumhuram at Khor Rawri (*see page 187*). In addition there are the remnants of one larger room and a small detached building. The latter appears to have been a small shrine or temple dedicated to the moon god Sin, the main deity of the Hadhramaut region. An inscription discovered at the site gives the local name of the site as Sa'nan and states that it was located in

BELOW: come fully prepared.

Map, page 186

Sa'kalhan – confirmation that Dhofar was the country of the Sachalites. It is probable that frankincense stored here was subsequently transported to Khor Rawri. It is likely that the frankincense was then shipped to Cana and then overland to Shabwah, from whence the builders of Sumhuram had come.

Thumrait ⓭ is a survival post on the edge of the Empty Quarter, with foodstores and cafés, a public telephone and a petrol station. From here, a graded road cuts off to the west through a featureless landscape relieved only by shimmering mirages. Follow the scores of tyre tracks until a black petrol drum looms up on the right of your vehicle and then, keeping a solitary rock outcrop to your right, head towards a second drum on which is written "By-By". Stop here and reduce tyre pressure. Unless you have previous experience of desert driving, or a local Bedu guide, get out and walk about on foot.

The high dunes have a strong mystical appeal, especially when there is a full moon. But the "Mother of Deserts" is a threatening place if you do not play by the rules. Should it be windy, keep close to your vehicle as sand soon covers any tracks and you may not find the way back easily. If driving back to Salalah after sunset, watch out for loose camels on the Jebel Qara road.

The Lost City of Ubar

In 1992, while excavating at **Shisr** ⓮, 140 km (87 miles) northwest of Salalah and noted for its freshwater wells, archaeologists found what is believed by some to be the ancient lost city of Ubar, known as Irem in the Qu'ran, whose riches, founded on the frankincense trade, were legendary. They had been alerted to its whereabouts by infrared satellite photographs taken of the Empty Quarter in 1984. The radar recorded miles of ancient camel tracks which abruptly disappeared under a vast sand dune only to reappear on the other side.

BELOW: girl in green. **OPPOSITE:** in the Rub al Khali (the Empty Quarter).

Like the Bible's account of Sodom and Gomorrah, the Qur'an relates how the citizens of Irem were punished for their excessive lifestyles and how the city which was built over the top of a huge limestone cavern at some point collapsed and was buried under drifting desert dunes. The historian Al Hamdani, writing in AD 6 hailed Ubar as one of Arabia's most priceless treasures – " a city lying astride the fabled incense routes with imposing architecture, vast orchards and fabulous wealth". More recently, in 1995, Ubar was commemorated by a new Omani perfume created to celebrate the sultan's silver jubilee. It was intended that the name Ubar should conjure up the exotic essence of ancient Arabia and the frankincense trade.

Archaeologists and explorers – including the British explorer Sir Ranulph Fiennes (who wrote about his search in his book *Atlantis of the Sands*, published in 1992) – have spent years trying to locate Ubar in the parched desert of the Empty Quarter. Excavations at Shisr have so far uncovered the rubble of eight towers and the walls of what are believed to be the city precincts. Greek, Roman and Syrian pottery has also been found, some of it dating back 4,000 years. While there are known to have been many *caravanserais*, placed at strategic distances along the frankincense route to the Gulf, it seems likely that this is Ubar.

FRANKINCENSE – THE PERFUME OF THE GODS

The fashion for frankincense is not what it was, but a new initiative has resulted in Amouage, a costly frankincense-based perfume produced in Oman

Frankincense made a considerable contribution to the wealth of southern Arabia in ancient times. Greece and Rome bought massive quantities for their religious rites, with Emperor Nero burning more than the annual harvest of Arabia at the funeral of Poppaea alone. But gradually demand dwindled and prices fell accordingly, though it remained popular in the Arab world, where it was used to create a convivial and festive atmosphere on social occasions.

A RENAISSANCE

Then in 1983 His Royal Highness Sayyid Hamad bin Hamood Al bu Said of Oman attempted to revive the tradition of perfume-making in Oman and commissioned the Parisian perfumier Guy Robert to create a new perfume that would incorporate frankincense, rosewater and myrrh. Robert, the nose behind perfumes for Chanel, Dior, Hermès and Gucci, came up with Amouage. Noted for its beautiful packaging – Aspreys of London designed and produced silver bottles plated with 24-carat gold – it is the most costly perfume in the world, more expensive than Joy by Jean Patou. Top-of- the- range products such as a silver gilt and black onyx bridal set retail for a cool US$7,360 in London. But in 1988, with an eye on the many more modest-sized pockets of ordinary mortals, the company launched its Cristal range – the Amouage fragrance in replicas of the original bottles – and in 1995 it created Ubar, named after the "lost city of Ubar", which is sold in duty-free shops worldwide for about the same price as other big name scents.

△ **A RARE TREE**
The best quality frankincense is found in the area of the Nejd in Dhofar, inland of the mountains affected by the monsoon. Some trees grow near the foothills on the seaward side of the mountains but it is probable that these were purposely planted. The tree (*Boswellia sacra*) grows in small gullies or on wadi beds to a height of up to 5 metres (16 ft), with a cluster of main branches extending from the base. Incense is first harvested when the trees are about three years old, in March, April and May before the monsoon.

△ AROMATHERAPY

Frankincense is used for many purposes apart from on religious and ceremonial occasions. On a day-to-day basis incense burners are passed around after meals and the aromatic smoke allowed to perfume the recipients' clothes, hair or beard. On other occasions clothes are arranged over burning incense to fumigate them. Frankincense is also used in culinary and medicinal recipes.

AN ANCIENT TRADE

A ruined settlement on the banks of Khor Rawri in Dhofar (see page 187) is believed to have been one of the main ports for exporting frankincense in ancient times. Inscriptions show that its name was Sumhuram, which archaeologists think was synonymous with Moscha mentioned in *The Periplus of the Erythraean Sea* written in the 1st century. *The Periplus* contains a description of trade between the Roman world of the east Mediterranean and the Red Sea, East Africa, the southern coast of Arabia and India.

Mentioned in this are the Sachalites and their frankincense country. It records how ships arrived at a port called Moscha that had been established for the receipt of Sachalitic frankincense and beyond which lay mountains, high, rocky and steep, inhabited by cave dwellers. The ships exchanged their cargoes of cloth, wheat and sesame oil for frankincense which was then shipped to the port of Cana and from there overland to Shabwah, the capital of the Hadhramaut.

The description of the country behind Moscha, inhabited by cave dwellers, is an apt description of the Dhofar Mountains. Indeed, excavations between 1952 and 1962 confirmed Dhofar as being the country of the Sachalites.

◁ PERFUMED PRESENTS

Frankincense can be bought all over Oman, but the best choice is in the incense *souq* in Salalah where women sort, weigh and package the crystals according to quality.

△ PRECIOUS DROPS

The gum resin is obtained by making an incision in the bark. The white latex-like substance that exudes is later collected and, when dried, becomes crystalline.

THE MUSANDAM PENINSULA

Map, page 199

Separated from the rest of the Oman by part of the UAE, this rugged peninsula, with its soaring cliffs and desolate interior, has only recently opened up to the outside world

The Musandam Peninsula, the mountainous northern tip of southeast Arabia, is separated from the rest of Oman by part of the UAE. Pointing towards Iran, with which it has traded for centuries, it creates the constriction at the southern end of the Gulf that forms the Strait of Hormuz, one of the busiest sea lanes in the world.

Until recently, Musandam was a strictly military zone. However, as Oman has gradually opened up to tourism, so has Musandam, reckoned by many to be the most beautiful region in the country.

Approaches

Travelling along the Gulf coast towards Ras al-Khaimah from Dubai via Sharjah, Ajman and Umm al-Qaiwain, the coast road passes through a landscape of *sabkha* (sand and mud flats), lapped on the west side by the waters of the Gulf and by encroaching sand dunes on the landward side. Further north the mountains that form the spine of the UAE and Oman home into view and at Ras al-Khaimah the road offers a first glimpse of the Musandam Peninsula with its steep limestone cliffs, some with distinct bands in contrasting colours. At Ash Sham, a little further north, these mountains drop precipitously to the sea.

Until recently these mountains presented an impenetrable barrier; it was impossible to travel further around the coast by land and the only option was to proceed by boat. The same was true if you approached from Dibba on the east coast.

However, this situation changed with the construction of a coastal road from Ash Sham, north of Ras al-Khaimah, north to Bukha and then to Khasab, and a second, inland road linking Dibba and Khasab.

Geography

The mountains of Musandam are quite different from those elsewhere in the UAE and Oman, a distinction seen clearly along a line drawn roughly from Ras al-Khaimah to Dibba. South of this the mountains are of mainly igneous rocks with irregular peaks, fringed by lower foothills and dissected by numerous wadis. North of the line the Ruus al-Jibal ("heads of the mountains") is characterised by a limestone massif, the rock faces of which are more vertical and form a plateau averaging about 800 metres (2,600 ft) above sea level.

The limestone massif of Musandam has also been subject to faulting, and in the past 10,000 years has been forced downwards, resulting in a submerged coastline with many drowned valleys. This is what gives it its fjord-like appearance and accounts for the peninsula's incredible 600-km (370-mile) long coastline.

Such a landscape has had a profound effect on the dis-

PRECEDING PAGES: decoration on an old mosque in Bukha .
LEFT: dhow trip to Khor Shim.

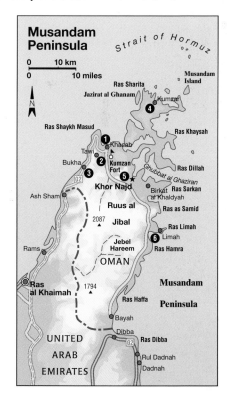

Musandam Peninsula

tribution of settlements and the way their inhabitants live. The main villages are along the coast, usually located at the mouth of a wadi, allowing a limited amount of agriculture. But there is strong reliance upon the sea for both food and communications since the main coastal towns and villages such as Bukha, Khasab, Kumzar and Limah were extremely isolated until the roads were built. Even today the peninsula's isolation mean that foodstuffs and other commodities are expensive

Places of interest

Khasab ❶ is the main coastal town of Musandam and the usual base for visitors (it has the peninsula's only hotel). At the mouth of a wadi, it has a relatively large area of cultivation, primarily based on dates and dependant on the building of terraced fields and well irrigation. As in other places on the Gulf coast, the town's traditional architecture employs a combination of traditional materials – coral, brick and palm wood – and reflects the influence of maritime contacts (wind towers are an indication of contact with Iran).

Khasab is developing fast, and it now contains roughly half of the peninsula's 10,000 population. But it is still a picturesque spot, particularly around the **port**, the liveliest place in town. The **fort** is thought to be built on the foundations of a fortified compound established in the 16th century by the Portuguese, an indication of the strategic importance of Musandam at that time. Another fortification, **Kumzan Fort**, is now a ruin.

Sights close to Khasab include **Tawi ❷**, inland from Quida 10 km (6 miles) north, which is visited for its prehistoric rock carvings, pictured on page 18 (in Tawi, ask someone to direct you, as they are easily missed). Further west around

BELOW: Musandam mountains.

the coast, a scenic 27 km (17 miles) from Khasab, is the peninsula's other main town, **Bukha ❸**, again with two forts, one of which is a ruin.

Accessible only by boat from Khasab (water-taxis available) and a popular excursion run by Khasab Travel & Tours is **Kumzar ❹**, a picturesque village on the northern tip. Remote even today, it has its own dialect made up of a mixture of languages attesting to an assortment of maritime contacts in the past. Accessible by car from Khasab is **Khor Najd ❺**, 25 km (15 miles) away. This attractive creek is a popular picnic destination.

Boatbuilding has always been important to the coastal towns and villages and was once exemplified by the *battil*, a slender fast boat which was used for trading and fighting. Other items typical of the area are ceramic incense burners, mainly made in the area around **Limah ❻** on the east coast, and the most distinctive and idiosyncratic item associated with Musandam, the *jerz*, a small axe traditionally carried by local men.

The interior of the peninsula

The tribe most commonly associated with Musandam is the once fearsome Shihu, which inhabits many of the coastal areas but also the even more isolated limestone plateau, accessible only by four-wheel drive. Most of the limestone uplands are completely bare with only sparse vegetation. Nevertheless, by utilising seasonal rainfall the Shihu have developed a means of adaptation to this landscape, enabling them to grow limited amounts of barley, wheat and even date palms, as well as herd goats.

Constraints on life in the mountain area are such that occupation is practical only in the winter months, when rainfall is more plentiful. From June to Sep-

**Map,
page 199**

Just off the Musandam Peninsula, in Khor al-Sha'm, is Elphinstone Island (Telegraph Island) where the British established the first telegraph station in the Gulf.

BELOW: irrigation.

Map,
page 199

tember the majority of inhabitants move to the coastal areas, some to help in the date harvests at Khasab or Dibba. Despite this, the mountain settlements of the Shihu can be quite substantial and exhibit many ingenious features. Settlements are often spectacularly sited, surrounded by deep ravines or on isolated mountain peaks.

Fields are usually formed by the construction of terraces and may be irrigated via small but long canals that meander along the mountainside. If necessary, a small aqueduct will be built to lead the water over an otherwise unpassable gully. Cisterns and large pottery vessels are used to conserve water supplies.

The architecture of the mountains is very different from that of the coast, as the only readily available building material is stone. The typical house, known as *bayt al qufl* (literally "cave house"*)*, is partly subterranean. A rectangular pit is dug 1 metre (3 ft) deep and lined with regular stone blocks. The superstructure rises only a small way above these subterranean foundations and is then roofed with a combination of timber and stone or in some cases by the judicious use of just large stone slabs. Either way, the roof is then sealed by a covering of earth. Entrance to the building is provided by a narrow, window-like opening less than a metre (3 ft) square and blocked on the inside by a wooden door. Since these houses are occupied primarily on a seasonal basis and used for storing personal items, a special form of lock has been developed for additional security. Often the size of individual stone blocks used in construction is staggering and can be described as Cyclopean.

The landscape and culture of Musandam are in marked contrast with the rest of Oman and the UAE, and remarkable ingenuity has been applied in overcoming severe physical obstacles.

BELOW: cormorants come to roost..

Arabian Leopards

L eopards in Arabia? Indeed it's true – but for how long? Persecuted by man as a threat to his domestic animals and perhaps himself, few survive in the recesses of mountain ranges in Oman, Yemen and Saudi Arabia. In the Musandam region, for instance, we know of their presence by the reports of fresh spoor and of yet another animal shot.

More leopards (known to some as "panthers") survive in the wild and rocky gorges of Jebel Samhan in Dhofar, far from human habitation, where they live by seizing the occasional ibex, and seeking any smaller wild animals that can be overpowered, including porcupines, birds and even insects. Secretive and usually hunting at night with a combination of cunning, stealth and luck, they will hunt by day when undisturbed. Solitary animals, the females occupy smaller territories than the wide-ranging males and raise small litters of two to three cubs, the young dispersing after 18 months.

Reports of spoor and of their rasping cough indicate that leopards wander (or live) further westward along the Dhofar Mountains and foothills, and old men recall that leopards once lived in parts of the Hajar Mountains.

The leopard is now mainly distributed from Africa south of the Sahara, eastward across Arabia to southern Asia, in several geographic races, but in many areas it is threatened or already exterminated. The Arabian race is called *Panthera pardus nimr* after its Arabic name of *nimr*. Although smaller and paler than some races, the *nimr* is a large powerful cat, some males reaching 2 metres (6 ft) in total length and 60 kg (132 lbs) in weight, but its short fur is always marked with the distinctive hollow rosettes on the back and flanks. It is more sturdily built than the cheetah, which has solid black spots and a black tear-stripe from each eye, and which is thought not to occur in the Gulf.

In the UAE, where Leopards reach its mountain borders with Oman, the private Arabian Leopard Trust (ALT) actively and successfully draws attention to the plight of this handsome beast. It has saved a caged male and arranged mating with a female from the Mammal Breeding Centre of Oman: it has raised funds, obtained sponsorship, and published booklets for children as well as making proposals for nature reserves.

In Oman, the public's interest in these persecuted carnivores has been kept alive since 1985 by displays in the Oman Natural History Museum, where two stuffed leopards (one from Musandam and one from Dhofar, saved after their unfortunate deaths) are shown in a realistic diorama of their rocky habitat. The Ministerial Decision in July 1993 which forbids the "hunting, trapping and shooting of animals and birds" in the Sultanate, gave added impetus to the setting-up of nature protectorates. The rangers who patrol them will also help to increase public awareness by visiting schools. In this way it is hoped to save the leopards and their habitat in Dhofar, and later in Musandam. But it may require all the ingenuity of the conservationists to persuade the people who live and tend goats in leopard country to live and let live.

RIGHT: Arabian leopard exhibited at the Natural History Museum in Muscat

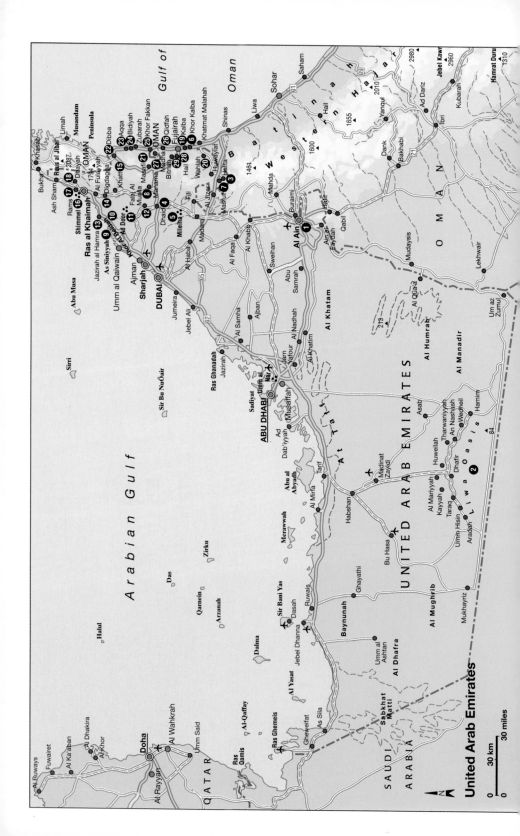

United Arab Emirates

0   30 km

0   30 miles

PLACES: THE UAE

Abu Dhabi and Dubai are well-known destinations. But each of the five other emirates also has something to offer visitors

The seven cities of the emirates are all on the coast – Abu Dhabi, the capital of the UAE, centres on an island; Dubai, Sharjah and Ras al Khaimah on creeks; Ajman, Umm al Qaiwain and Ras al Khaimah on sand spits curling around a lagoon. Abu Dhabi's territory is the largest (around 85 percent of the total area) and driest, a vast stretch of desert relieved only by the oases of Liwa and Al Ain. Ajman, by contrast, is so small that it is not much more than the city itself. The Places chapters of this guide begin with Abu Dhabi and work their way east to Fujairah.

Complicated tribal allegiances at the time the federation was formed mean that several states have enclaves away from their main territory. Fujairah, for example, is split by enclaves belonging to Sharjah and Oman, and on the border between Ras al Khaimah and Oman are tiny but lush parcels of Ajman and Dubai (Hatta). This pattern reflects the traditional tendency for the tribes to divide their time between two economic activities, one in the desert or the mountains and one on the coast. Herdsmen, for example, might have spent the winters in the mountains or the desert and the fiercely hot summer working the pearl banks or fishing. This economic split has a modern manifestation – it is quite common for a city civil servant also to have a country farm.

Abu Dhabi and Dubai are the richest emirates. Sharjah, at one time the federation's capital, is third in terms of wealth, while the other states are essentially subsidised by the richer members. Ras al Khaimah, however, is rich in agriculture, and Fujairah is considered the most beautiful of the emirates, cut of from the rest of the UAE by the dramatic Hajar Mountains that run up from Oman.

Modern infrastructure has transformed the cities, but the stark geography of the region – sandy desert merging gradually into limpid seas scattered with islets and sandbars – is unchanging. The ring of forts and watchtowers – some ruined, some restored – are evocative reminders of a different but not that distant era of tribal rivalries, piracy and pearls.

PRECEDING PAGES: sailing off Abu Dhabi; Abu Dhabi waterfront.

ABU DHABI

*Though short on "sights", the Capital of the Emirates has plenty to
offer visitors, from inspiring architecture to fabulous beaches.
Two hours away by car is the oasis town of Al Ain*

Maps,
pages
214, 216

Abu Dhabi

I n March 1948 Wilfred Thesiger emerged with four Bedu companions from
the great golden dunes of Rub al Khali (the Empty Quarter) at Liwa – a fertile crescent consisting of about 45–60 oases – and travelled another 240 km
(150 miles) across "interminable blinding salt flats" to reach the coastal village
of Abu Dhabi. Wading across the creek that separated Abu Dhabi from the mainland (now the site of the Maqta Bridge) they walked a further 16 km (10 miles)
across empty desert before arriving "at a large castle that dominated a small
dilapidated town along the seashore". The few palm trees offering shade near
Al Hosn (the fort) have now multiplied beyond recognition, and since the discovery of enormous oil reserves during the late 1960s the town has emerged as
a thriving international city.

Abu Dhabi ("father of the gazelle") takes its name from legend. In the early
1770s, the story goes, a party of hunters from Liwa followed the tracks of a
gazelle to one of the numerous coastal islands they knew in the Arabian Gulf. To
their good fortune they found a freshwater spring where the animal had stopped
to drink and began a settlement there in the 1790s.

Today Abu Dhabi is the capital and largest emirate of the UAE. At more than
225,330 square km (87,000 sq. miles) it occupies 86 percent of the country's
total area. The city is the headquarters of the UAE's
President and Ruler of Abu Dhabi, H.H. Sheikh Zayed
bin Sultan Al Nahyan (*see page 65*).

Al Nahyan, of the Al bu Falah tribe, have ruled Abu
Dhabi and the Dhafrah (Liwa) since about 1690. They
are a *fakhd* (sub-section) of the reputedly bellicose Bani
Yas. Like most tribes of the Arabian Gulf, the Bani Yas
trace their origins back to Yemen, yet unlike their coast-
hugging, seafaring cousins their ancestral home is at the
desert oases of the Liwa. They owned camels, some
donkeys and goats and lived in rectangular palm-frond
houses built into the sand dunes above carefully tended
date palm groves. During the summer many of the men
would go to Abu Dhabi to join the pearling fleet as
divers. In 1800, under Shakbut bin Dhiyab, the Al bu
Falah collectively left the Liwa to settle on Abu Dhabi
island.

Sheikh Zayed was born in 1918 in eastern Al Ain – a
territory fought over for centuries but finally ruled by
the Al Nahyan from about 1890. Sheikh Zayed was
named after his grandfather Sheikh Zayed bin Khalifa
Al Nahyan (Ruler of Abu Dhabi 1855–1909) known as
Zayed the Great. It is these two Zayeds that give their
names to Zayed the First Street and Zayed the Second
Street (otherwise referred to as "Electra Street") which
runs from east to west and changes name at the intersection of Sheikh Rashid bin Saeed Al Maktoum Street
("Airport Road').

PRECEDING PAGES:
view, Jebel Hafit
LEFT: high-rise
Silver Towers.
BELOW: silver sands.

In 1966 Sheikh Zayed succeeded his brother Sheikh Shakhbut bin Sultan Al Nahyan as Ruler. The extreme wealth generated by the discovery of oil has enabled Sheikh Zayed to build first-rate public facilities for his people, but his benevolence reaches beyond the UAE and is appreciated by many international charity programmes and Islamic communities.

City sights

Sheikh Zayed's enormous, gold-domed residence is located on the western edge of the island city. To catch a glimpse of the **Presidential Palace** follow the Corniche road past the Hilton Hotel, go straight on at two large roundabouts and turn right through an open boom-gate. Photography is strictly forbidden, but the surrounding Ras Al Akhdar ("Green Headland") is worth exploring. for its many beautiful public beaches, including the very private **Ladies' Beach Ⓐ** (Saturday to Wednesday 1–6pm; Thursday 12 noon–6pm; Friday 10am–6pm; admission charge) for women and children only.

Unlike the other historic cities of the UAE Abu Dhabi has few heritage sites. **Al Hosn Ⓑ**, the large white fort on the corner of Khalid bin Al Waleed and Al Nasr Streets was built in about 1763, and at one time was the only noteworthy building along the coast from Dubai to Doha, Qatar. Until 1972, when Sheikh Zayed moved to a new palace, it was the ruler's residence. The outer wall and towers were added at a later date, but the original fort was constructed to protect the town's well. Today it is used as a Centre for Documentation and Research and is open to visitors (Saturday to Wednesday 7.30am–1.30pm; Thursday 7.30am–12 noon).

The **Abu Dhabi Cultural Foundation Ⓒ**, opposite Al Hosn, on the corner of

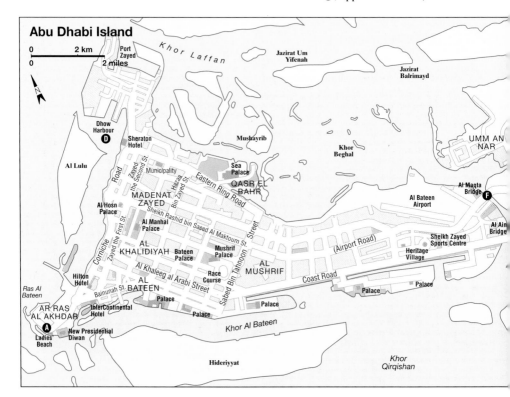

Abu Dhabi Island

Sheikh Zayed the First and Al Maktoum (Airport Road) streets, was developed under the patronage of Sheikh Zayed. International and local exhibitions, concerts, plays and film screenings are regularly held to continue the development of cultural growth throughout the region.

The Corniche is a long paved walkway that comes to life every evening with joggers and families enjoying the cool sea breeze. The **Abu Dhabi Fountain**, a large volcano-like construction set amongst the lush gardens that border the Corniche walkway, constantly erupts with water and coloured lights.

The view of the city's multi-storey and multi-coloured skyline is best seen from the water. **Al Dhafra Restaurant**, at the **Dhow Harbour D** on the city's far east side, offers evening cruises on traditional wooden dhows that slowly travel the length of the Corniche during the course of a fine Arabic dinner. Alternatively **Al Safina Restaurant**, a converted wooden boat donated by Sheikh Zayed, remains stationary on a built-up sandbar (to reach Al Safina turn right at the roundabout directly after the Hilton Hotel Beach Club – a road runs along a breakwater joining the sandbar to Abu Dhabi island). Once on the sandbar the restaurant is clearly marked on the right-hand side of the road.

Abu Dhabi is known for its striking modern architecture. In a competition to build the tallest building in the Middle East, the elegant blue-glass **Baynunah Tower E**, containing Abu Dhabi's second Hilton Hotel, was built in 1995. Some of the equally interesting architectural monuments of the city include the falcon-shaped club house of the Abu Dhabi 18-hole championship grass golf course, Forte Grand Hotel and the Etisalat Building (local telecommunications).

The **Maqta Bridge watchtower F** (built *circa* 1780s) and the **Central Souq G** give some sense of Abu Dhabi before its transformation. The *souq* is a small

Maps, pages 214, 216

A dhow cruise is a pleasant way to spend an evening.

BELOW: working-out in the Baynunah Tower Hilton

maze of relatively new shops that sell everything from gold and fabrics to electrical goods. To find this hidden treasure trove locate the Clocktower Roundabout on the Corniche, walk to the corner of Sheikh Hamdan bin Mohammed Street and turn left: the *souq* is on the left.

Until 1953, when a causeway was built across the Maqta, anyone wanting to cross to the other side had to wait for low tide and then wade through the shallow water.

The Maqta is the stretch of tidal water separating Abu Dhabi from the mainland. Coming into Abu Dhabi across the **Maqta Bridge** (built in 1968) the Eastern Ring Road offers the most scenic route, running parallel to the coastline and mangroves that grow on the eastern edge of the island. A watchtower stands opposite the bridge, surrounded by translucent, turquoise-coloured water.

On the way into the city, on Khaleej Al Arabi Road, near the Sheikh Zayed Sports Centre, is the **Sheikh Zayed Heritage Village**, celebrating traditional life in Abu Dhabi, from *barasti* (palm-frond) houses to handicrafts. On Friday it hosts a real *souq* and, on special occasions, festivals of dance and poetry.

Around Abu Dhabi city

Close to Abu Dhabi city is the island of **Umm an- Nar** (now the site of an oil refinery). Here settlement dates to around 3000 BC. Archaeological excavations were established on the island in 1958, but it was not until 1975 that a large circular collective tomb was uncovered. The Al Ain Museum exhibits the results of this excavation. Inhabitants of Umm Al Nar traded with the civilisations of Mesopotamia (Iraq) and the Indian Subcontinent (*see page 22–4*).

The Eastern Region of Abu Dhabi, around the oasis of Al Ain, is only two hours away from the capital by car (160 km/100 miles: watch out for unexpected, unusually wide, speed bumps), but in 1958 it was still a five-day journey by camel. Dubai to Al Ain is a mere 120 km (75 miles) on a fast bump-free high-

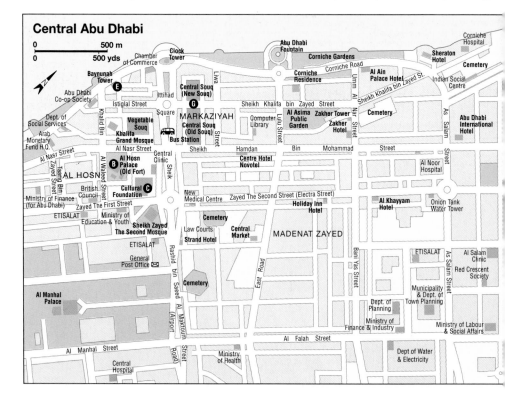

Central Abu Dhabi

way. To detract from the desert and halt the ever-shifting sands, thousands of trees have been planted on either side of Abu Dhabi's major roads. About 20 million trees have been cultivated in the emirate's Western Region, covering about 100,000 hectares (247,000 acres).

Al Ain ❶ ("the spring", previously known as Muwaiqih) is a popular destination during the hot summer months as it offers an escape from the humidity experienced on the coast. This lush oasis has been settled since about 3000 BC. A round tomb in the **Hili Archaeological Park** Ⓐ (daily 4–11pm; holidays 10am–11pm) was reconstructed by an Iraqi archaeology team in 1975 to show an important excavation of tombs from the Jamdat Nasr Period (3200–3000 BC) at Jebel Hafit, the 1,240-metre (4,000-ft) high limestone mountain south of Al Ain. A tomb discovered in the area of Qattarah between 1973 and 1976 was re-excavated in 1988 and exposed a burial layer below the foundations. Considered to be the richest 2000 BC burial site in the UAE, its contents indicate a thriving culture that had contact with the outside world.

Driving in Al Ain can be confusing. All the streets are lined with trees and have heavily planted central reservations, and maps don't give a true scale of distances. Hili Oasis, the Hili Fun City (amusement park) and Hili Archaeological Park (Hili Gardens) are indicated by purple tourist signs, but are most easily found from the Dubai road (Rashid bin Saeed Al Maktoum Road).

Al Ain Museum is reached by driving under the flyover in the heart of the town centre, turning left at the roundabout and taking the first right towards the Coffee Pot Roundabout. The renovated mud-brick **fort** left of the roundabout is the old prison. The large walled **Livestock Market** is straight ahead, off Zayed bin Sultan Road, and the museum is on the right, across a wide gravel area. Al

Map, pages 208, 218

150 m

Beware natural hazards of the open road.

BELOW: Hili tomb.

Ain Museum 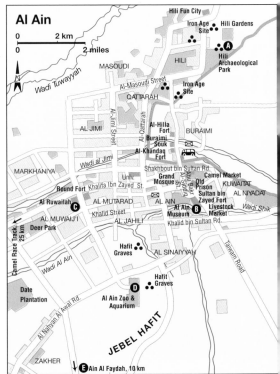 (Sunday to Wednesday 8am–1pm and 3.30–5.30pm; Thursday 8am–12 noon and 4.30–6.30pm (November to April 3.30–5.30pm); Friday 9–11.30am and 4.30-6.30pm (November to April 3.30–5.30pm); closed Saturday but open on official holidays) was built during the 1970s and consists of a low flat single-storey building and the Sultan bin Zayed Fort. The exhibits offer a good introduction into the emirate's archaeological heritage, local culture and natural history. The fort has two large black cannons at its entrance, a magnificent wooden gate and photographic displays in the *majlis*.

Scattered throughout Al Ain are a number of other forts and watchtowers. The most interesting are the Hili District defences. The two-storey **Al Ruwailah** fortified house (off Mohammed bin Khalifa Road at the end of a small street) has an intriguing octagonal defensive wall. On the other side of Mohammed bin Khalifa Road, opposite the Al Ruwailah building, is a tower-like fort. Raised on a large mound, this circular fort provided an advanced warning post should intruders approach the palm groves from the desert. The site appears deserted, but a watchman will open a small rear door to enable exploration of the 1-metre (3-ft) thick walls and rooftop stairway. Built from *sarooj* (mud brick and straw) the foundations of the fort may be more than 500–600 years old.

In the **Qattarah** district are four large fortresses set amongst palm groves. One is undergoing considerable rebuilding and offers good views from its high defensive walls (to find it from Mohammed bin Khalifa Road, pass the football stadium on the right, cross the Dolphin Roundabout and turn right into 3rd Street: the rear wall faces the road, but the entrance is on the right-hand side).

Al Ain Zoo and Aquarium (April to October 7am–6pm; November to March 7am–5.30pm) and **Ain Al Faydah** (mineral springs, family swim-

BELOW: mosque among the palm trees, Al Ain.

ming centre and accommodation) are in the southern part of the city. The zoo is clearly marked on Al Nahyan Al Awal Road. To reach Ain Al Faydah, turn right into Haza bin Sultan Road from Nahyan Al Awal Road and head towards Jebel Hafit. The mountain looms high on the left side of the road and is well worth a diversion, the view from the top is magnificent. The high dunes of the Empty Quarter look like a red carpet drifting off into the horizon beyond the village of **Wegan**, and the spectacular ridges of the lower rock formations below look like a dragon's tail disappearing under the lush Al Ain oasis. Ain Al Faydah is about 10 km (6 miles) from Jebel Hafit Road on the left-hand side.

Map, page 218

A dip into Oman

From Al Ain you can travel into the Omani oasis of Buraimi without a visa. For centuries Buraimi has been an important gateway into the desert regions of Abu Dhabi (linked to Britain by treaty from 1850–1971), Oman and Saudi Arabia. In 1952 the Saudis, supported by the American ARAMCO oil company, claimed the oasis for themselves. By 1955 all talks to expel the Saudis had foundered and a small ground-war broke out. The Saudis withdrew, but it was not until 1975 that negotiated borderlines were accepted.

To reach Buraimi, locate the large oval roundabout (it has five sets of traffic lights) on Shakhbut bin Sultan Road in Al Ain and follow the signs. At the first set of lights after the large blue and white "Peace Be With You" sign make a left-hand U-turn and head back towards Al Ain. The large renovated Al Hilla Fort and covered Buraimi *souq* are on the right. From the fort, walk down a small side road to the elegant, restored **Al Khandaq Fort** (Saturday to Wednesday 8am–6pm; Thursday to Friday 8am–1pm and 4–6pm; admission: free). Built

BELOW: keeping old skills alive.

by the Al bu Shamis, a division of the local Na'im tribe, in about 1780, it was strengthened between 1808 and 1813 by Mutlaq Al Mutairi, the leader of the occupying Wahhabis (puritanical Islamists). The fort has a wonderful 7.3-metre (24-ft) moat and four decorative crenellated towers. The pristine inner courtyard is complemented by well-proportioned rooms and towers.

The walled open compound beside the fort is a public prayer ground (note the *mihrab (*prayer niche) facing Mecca). The palm groves west of the *souq* and forts are also full of interesting old village dwellings, but respect should be shown at the public wash houses built over the area's extensive *falaj* system.

The Empty Quarter

The Western Region of Abu Dhabi encompasses the great red sand massif of the **Rub al Khali** (the Empty Quarter), the oil fields of Bu Hasa, Shah and Marzuq, and the fertile Liwa oasis. In 1948 Wilfred Thesiger was the first European to explore the Liwa's 80-km (50-mile) palm grove and scattered settlements in 60–90-metre (200–300-ft) dunes. Thesiger described what he saw in *Arabian Sands*: "The sands were like a garden. There were matted clumps of tribulus, three feet high, their dark green fronds covered with bright yellow flowers, bunches of karia, a species of heilotrope that was rated high as camel-food by the Bedu, and *qasis*, as well as numerous other plants which the camels scorned in the plenty that surrounded them."

Thesiger rode into the Liwa on a camel. Today the journey from Abu Dhabi is made easy with a tarmac road cutting through the desolate limestone ridges, drifts of white sand and stretches of gravel dotted with woody grass.

It is a three-hour trip by road from Abu Dhabi to **Liwa ❷**, and much longer if the dirt track through the dunes at the Rumaitha oil field is taken. This scenic dirt track route requires a party of at least two 4WDs and experienced desert drivers. It passes the "caravan field" of Abu Dhabi's Rainbow Sheikh (a well-known motor enthusiast whose logo is a rainbow), marked by an oversized red Dodge pick-up truck. The **Dodge Caravan** was built as a symbol of the exploration vehicles used during the 1950s and is at least six times bigger than the real thing. A two-storey **Globe Caravan** is located in the same field. Whether whims of fancy or feats of engineering and design, the Sheikh's caravans have become desert icons.

The Liwa crescent is well served by an amazing four-lane highway. Passing the villages of (from west to east) **Aradah, Taraq, Al Hilah, Qatuf, Kayyah, Al Mariyyah, Dhafir, Huweilah, Qumidah, Shah, Tharwaniyyah, Al Nashash, Jarrah, Wedheil, Al Kris** and **Hamim** it is difficult to imagine how the sparsely populated village of *barasti* (palm frond) dwellings and carefully tended date palm groves, subsisted here for hundreds of years. The concrete houses, guest house and irrigated farms were developed during the 1980s.

Any visit to the Liwa is a special experience. The effect of the remoteness and beauty of the sands is profound. Every day the dunes change and encroach on the farms nestling below. The scale of the big red dunes is best appreciated in winter, when it is possible to climb to the top of a dune without the heat burning through

Reduce your tyre pressure before venturing into the desert.

BELOW: a rough ride.

the soles of your shoes. Surprisingly, the Liwa has an extensive range of fauna. Hares, foxes, monitor lizards and other animals and reptiles flourish in the harsh, seemingly inhospitable desert environment.

Map, page 208

Industrial outposts

West of Liwa are **Ruwais** and **Jebel Dhanna**, but without a government pass it is impossible to visit either of them. Ruwais is the site of the country's largest oil refinery, started in 1978 and still expanding, and Jebel Dhanna an inhospitable coastal area where the export terminal for Abu Dhabi's onshore oil is sited. The oil, held in special storage tanks, is piped to tanker-mooring terminals 5km (3 miles) offshore.

Further west, heading towards the Saudi and Qatari borders, **Al Silas** and **Al Odaid** are rewarding sites for ornithologists and naturalists. There are no petrol stations this far west so adventurers should be prepared for harsh conditions and take sufficient water and petrol for the 18-hour return journey.

The islands

The many islands off the coast of Abu Dhabi are all privately owned. **Sir Bani Yas Island**, for example, is a private nature reserve owned by Sheikh Zayed (visits for ornithologists and naturalists can be arranged through the right authorities). In 1993 one of the oldest human settlements yet discovered in the UAE was excavated on **Dalma Island**, northwest of Sir Bani Yas Island and 50 km (30 miles) offshore. The settlement dates from the Ubaid period (4300–3500 BC) and excavated artefacts indicate that the inhabitants traded by sea throughout the southern Arabian Gulf region.

BELOW: ostrich at the nature reserve on Bani Yas.

DUBAI

*Dubai is the commercial centre of the Middle East,
but there is much more to the city than its famous duty-free
shopping, including a characterful creek and old quarters*

Maps
pages
226, 233

Abu Dhabi

UNITED ARAB
EMIRATES

Modern Dubai is characterised by the towering glass buildings that rose out of the desert sands in the 1980s and '90s, but for centuries it was known to traders of spices, gold, slaves, sandalwood and other precious cargoes as a safe haven. Dhows have moored on the shores of the Creek that runs through the city since it was first settled in the early 1800s. Archaeological sites in the areas of Jumeira, Al Qusaid (15 km/9 miles from Deira) and Mina Siyahi indicate that Dubai was an important station for caravans travelling between Mesopotamia and Oman as early as 3000 BC (*see pages 22–4*). Today, these ancient areas are joined by four-lane super highways and residential suburbs, and the city of Dubai is defined as the international commercial centre of the Middle East. But regardless of the city's obvious wealth and capacity for development, it has retained some of the atmosphere of the old trading port that existed before the 1960s.

Khor Dubai Ⓐ, or the creek, is a 300-metre (1,000-ft) wide, 10-km (6-mile) long saltwater inlet that divides the areas of Bur Dubai to the west and Deira to the east. It concludes near the Dubai Country Club with a bird sanctuary and flamingo breeding ground. Until 1963, when it was desilted and a breakwater was built at its mouth, the creek lapped the edges of the city and at high-tide often created a wading pool between the areas of Shindagha and Bur Dubai. Now the creek is a scenic thoroughfare for trading dhows, *abras* (ferries), luxury yachts and the occasional ship.

There are three ways of crossing the creek by car from Bur Dubai to Deira – the **Maktoum Bridge** (built in 1962), **Shindagha Tunnel** (built 1975) and **Garhoud Bridge** (built 1976). Both bridges provide breathtaking views of the cityscape, and like the 39-storey **Dubai World Trade Centre Ⓑ** – the third tallest building in Middle East (with daily tours and a magnificent view from the top) – offer good orientation points for exploring the city.

City sights

In spite of the overwhelming impression of high-rise office towers, five-star beach hotels, world-renowned horse-racing facilities, enormous shopping centres and PGA-standard golf courses, it is still possible to experience the atmosphere and character of old Dubai. A good place to begin is the **Dubai Museum Ⓒ** (open Saturday to Thursday 7.30am–2pm and 3–9pm; Fridays and holidays 3–9pm; Ramadan 9am–4.30pm and closed Friday), housed in **Al Fahidi Fort** (built *circa* 1787), located in the heart of Bur Dubai, on Al Fahidi Road. The museum not only displays archaeological finds dating back to the emirate's ancient past (approximately 5,000 years) but has exhibition halls that bring to life

LEFT: life on the creek.
BELOW easy rider.

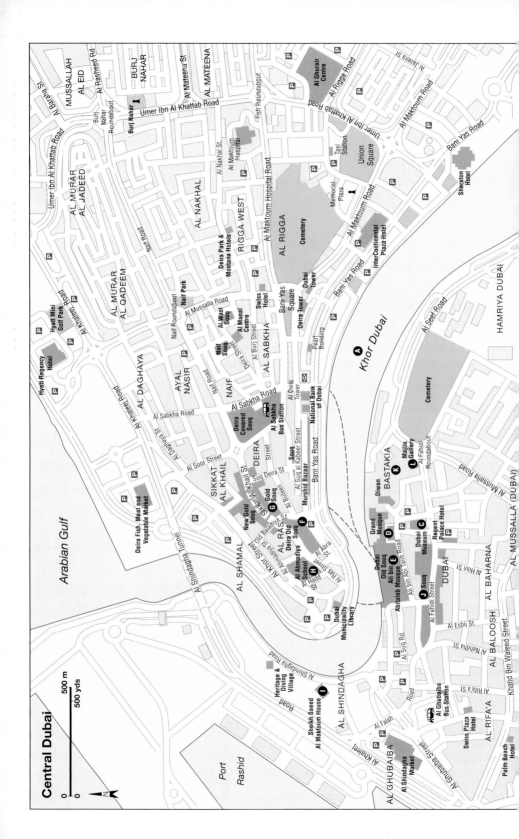

the atmosphere of the *souq*, traditional architecture, and the local community as it was prior to expansion in the 1960s.

Map, page 226

The fort was originally built to defend the city against foreign invasions, and was once home to approximately 100 men. Built with local materials – rectangular sea rocks, palm tree trunks, palm fronds, mud bricks and *sarooj* (mortar made from imported red clay, manure and water) – it has large towers at three corners and three vast halls facing the courtyard, which were added in about 1900. Initially built as barracks, the halls served as Dubai's jail as late as 1971. A round tower in the southwest corner is an example of the classic artillery defence style – in which the solid sand-filled base provides a strong platform for a cannon.

The museum has been incorporated into the fort without altering its original structure. The courtyard displays the old well, a 1785 bronze cannon, a traditional *majlis* (meeting room) and a collection of boats formerly used for fishing and pearl diving. An underground extension, completed in 1995, houses the new exhibition halls.

Al Fahidi Fort is the perfect place to begin a **Dubai Heritage Walk**. From the museum's entrance, walk towards the Diwan (Ruler's Office, not open to the public), the large white building on the opposite side of the street, facing the creek. Built in 1990, the arched windows and decorative iron screens present a sympathetic architectural addition to this historic area.

Taking an abra across the creek.

Wandering left, down Ali bin Abi Talib Road – a small but busy street lined with fabric shops – brings the Grand and Ali bin Abitaleb mosques into view. The **Grand Mosque ⓓ** is one of the oldest in Dubai, and although photographs dating from the 1950s suggest that it has had a recent refurbishment it adds great atmosphere to the narrow street. The **Ali bin Abitaleb Mosque ⓔ** features a towering minaret, splendid domes, gold and green mosaics and wooden screens. (Non-Muslims are requested not to enter the mosques.)

BELOW: visiting Dubai Museum.

At the T-junction turn right and wander towards the creek. A large wooden gateway now marks the entrance to the renovated "old *souq*". Prior to a recent renovation project the small, colourful fabric and clothing shops opened out onto uncovered lanes. Now a wooden roof covers the narrow streets of the meandering *souq*, almost as far as historical Bastakia, beyond the Diwan.

The Bur Dubai *abra* (ferry) terminal is found in the old *souq*, and provides one of the most authentic and inexpensive experiences available in the Emirates. Prior to 1962 *abras* provided the only means of crossing the creek. These little, open-sided, motor-powered wooden boats cross from here to three **Deira** terminals. The first terminal on Deira-side sits between the large trading dhows moored at Al Ras, on Bani Yas Road – which is the best place to continue on a journey into the spice and gold *souqs*. The second is a larger terminal further down Bani Yas Road near the intersection leading to Al Nasr Square, the main electronics *souq* in Dubai. A third terminal is in front of the triangular, blue-glass Dubai Chamber of Commerce building.

Ferry views of the buildings lining the creek expose the great contrast between old and new. The curved glass facade of the **National Bank of Dubai**, and the

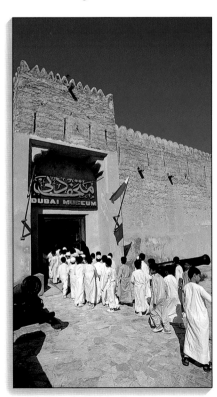

distant sail-like structure of the **Creek Golf Club clubhouse** are beautifully juxtaposed against the traditional windtower houses of Bastakia and two-storey mud-brick buildings on the opposite side of the water.

Abra captains will negotiate a charter fee (approximately Dhs 40–50 per hour) for journeys up and down the entire course of the Creek. Local families often hire a private *abra* to avoid the public ride. An alternative to hiring an *abra* is to take a guided dhow tour (Coastline Leisure operate daily from the quay in front of the National Bank of Dubai, Deira; Al Boom are located near the Garhoud Bridge).

Into the souqs

Large spice-filled sacks spill out into the tiny, shop-lined, covered walkways that form **Al Ras Spice Souq** (open Saturday to Thursday 9am–1pm and 4–8.30pm; Friday 4.30–8.30pm). Established as early as 1850, this *souq* has always been close to the dhow moorings for easy trading and unloading. Cardamom, paprika, nutmeg, cinnamon, dried limes, saffron, henna and frankincense are displayed amongst enormous cooking pots, weighing scales and tobacco. The area is always full of UAE nationals, and women should dress conservatively (permission should always be obtained before taking photographs of people).

The Al Ras area also incorporates the glittering **Gold Souq** . Here the narrow, wooden-roofed streets are lined with shops dealing solely in gold, their windows hung with 24- and 22-carat bracelets, chains, tiaras, diamond rings and solid gold wrist-watches. Designs can be intricate, with filigree work very popular locally.

TIP

Dubai is considered the cheapest place to purchase gold in the world. Unless complex jewellery-making is involved, items can be bought at the daily gold price, displayed at the entrance to the New Gold Souq on Al Khor Street

BELOW: in Al Ras Spice Souq.

At one time Dubai pearls were also bought and sold in this area. Pearling was of crucial importance to Dubai from the 1840s (*see page 35*), but the industry declined rapidly in the 1930s and 1940s with the advent of Japanese cultured pearls. The Old Souq in Sharjah (*see page 242*) is one of the last places in the Emirates where elderly merchants can be seen selling the highly-prized and valuable local pearls.

Leaving the Gold Souq via Al Khor Street, turn left down Old Baladiya Street and then right into Al Ahmadiya Street to discover the Al Ahmadiya heritage building project. The **Al Ahmadiya School** was established around 1903 by a wealthy pearl merchant called Ahmed bin Delmuk. The school taught Arabic language and grammar, Islamic studies and basic mathematics to about 200 'boys. Unlike pupils of the Qur'an schools, who sat on the floor, these boys sat at proper desks. It was a disciplined environment, and many of Dubai's older generation clearly remember their school days at Al Ahmadiya.

By the 1920s four main schools had been established by pearl traders, but following the 1930s depression in pearling they all closed. Al Ahmadiya was reopened in 1938, and by the 1950s approximately 500 students were enrolled. In 1965 the school was relocated elsewhere in Dubai, and the buildings were used as a religious institution until it was abandoned in the 1970s.

Great care has been taken to restore Al Ahmadiya School, Ahmed bin Delmuk's house (situated directly in front of the school), surrounding houses and the mosque. A merchant's house further along Al Ahmadiya Street shows how decorative the houses used to be in this area. Stucco panels, detailed window screens and finely carved wooden doors were largely the result of stylistic influences from India.

Map, page 226

Al Ahmadiya School's most distinguished alumni was Sheikh Rashid ben Saeed Al Maktoum, Ruler of Dubai 1958–1990 and regent for his ailing father, Sheikh Saeed, from 1939.

BELOW: shopping in the Gold Souq.

Al Ahmadiya Street joins Bani Yas Road, which runs parallel to the creek, at the **Dubai Municipality Library**. This modern institution conveniently divides the books into Arabic and English language sections. Although it is not possible to remove books, it offers an alternative to the British Council Library near Rashid Hospital and the Maktoum Bridge.

Return to Bur Dubai by *abra* and walk to **Sheikh Saeed Al Maktoum House, Museum of Historical Photographs and Documents of Dubai Emirate ❶** (open Saturday to Thursday 8.30am–1.30pm and 3.30-8.30pm; Fridays and holidays 3.30–8.30pm; Ramadan: 9am–1pm and closed Friday) on the sandy promontory of **Shindagha**. To get there, pass the Bank of Baroda, the green and white British Bank building and the old coral block Shindagha watchtower.

Born in 1878, Sheikh Saeed bin Maktoum ruled Dubai from 1912 until his death in 1958. The Shindagha house was originally built by Sheikh Maktoum bin Hasher Al Maktoum, Sheikh Saeed's father, in 1896, and served as home to his extended family. The house was abandoned in 1958, and became so derelict by the 1980s that it has been rebuilt next to the original site.

Photographs in the museum vividly illustrate many aspects of the social, cultural, educational and religious life of old Dubai. The nomadic lifestyle of the Bedu, well digging, date harvesting, falcony and camel racing illustrate the richness of the desert and its oases. Letters, treaties, maps, coins and stamp collections focus on the development of the emirate through official documentation dating back to 1822. The square-shaped building itself, with four fine examples of the traditional *barajeel* (windtower) and square shaped, is a vanishing symbol of Arab architecture.

BELOW: Dubai Municipality.

The return walk from Shindagha to the Al Fahidi Fort includes the core of the

Bur Dubai Souq ❹ on Al Suq Road, bustling Cosmos Lane and Al Fahidi Street. Electronic goods, fabulous fabrics and vibrant Indian saris are all good buys here.

Continue along Al Fahidi Road to the historical area of **Bastakia ❻**. Once the homes of wealthy merchant families, the houses that line the small paved streets are now mostly occupied by expatriate taxi drivers and their families. A heritage building project established by the Dubai Municipality is cleaning and restoring the area for tourist development. Most of the buildings, referred to as the "windtower houses", will form an open-air museum.

The **Majlis Gallery ❶** (open Saturday to Thursday 9.30am–1.30pm and 4–7.30pm; closed Fridays), located near the Al Fahidi Roundabout, is a commercial art gallery based in a converted windtower house in the heart of Bastakia. Enter through a low, decorative doorway into a cool, airy courtyard. All the rooms open onto the courtyard, although in the larger houses of Bastakia the courtyard is given more shade by a loggia running around three sides. The rear room, entered from a small verandah, houses the windtower. Windtowers became popular throughout the Arabian Gulf during the 1890s. They rise 15 metres (49 ft) above ground level and open into the main sitting room, or *majlis*. Built with X-shaped cross walls, providing an opening on all four sides, the tower catches the wind and channels it down an opening into the *majlis* below. The tower stops about 2 metres (6 ft) above floor level, creating a cool place underneath for sitting or sleeping.

The Majlis Gallery sells traditional artefacts such as the *khanjar* (curved dagger traditionally worn by UAE nationals until the 1970s and still common in Oman). The silver Bedu jewellery, studded chests, goatskin water bags, Ara-

Map, page 226

Windtower in restoration. The ingenious cooling device was introduced to the region from Persia.

BELOW: a cool and comfortable place to read.

bian coffee pots, incense burners, rosewater sprinklers and camel bags can also be bought in the *souq*. Many of the gift shops scattered throughout the city's hotels sell replicas of these items too, but treasure troves such as **Hassan Exhibition** on Khalid bin Waleed Street in Bur Dubai sell antique items.

To complete the Heritage Walk leave the Majlis Gallery, turn left at the roundabout, and continue straight towards the creek. **Al Seef Road** runs along the side of the creek, past the British Embassy, and ends at the Umm Hureir Roundabout not far from the Maktoum Bridge. It offers a scenic stroll, and uninterrupted views of Deira's interesting modern buildings across the creek.

Dubai's outskirts

Although mostly residential, the areas beyond the creek contain intriguing archaeological evidence that dates settlement in Jumeira to the first Islamic era (AD 600–700), and the Umm Suqeim Mound near Mina Siyahi to the Bronze Age (3000 BC). The Mound of Serpents at Al Qusaid, 15 km (9 miles) east of Deira, is thought to have been the largest settlement on the Arabian Gulf from 2000–1000 BC, with more than 120 graves uncovered by archaeologists. Traces of a city occupied in the Umayyad period (AD 660–730) prove that Dubai traded with the world for centuries prior to the discovery of oil in the 1960s.

It is possible to view the low walls of three buildings now uncovered at the **Jumeira** site **Ⓜ**. Approach from the Sheikh Zayed Road, exit at **Safa Park Ⓝ** (a public oasis on the right) and turn right at the roundabout on Al Wasl Road. Continue straight until the Eppco service station on the left. Take the first U-turn and turn right directly after Eppco. At the T-junction turn left and the archaeological site is straight ahead.

BELOW: desert kitsch in Wafi Shopping Centre.

An interesting open-air museum, **Al Ghorfa Umm Al Sheef**  (Al Ghureifa Majlis; (open Saturday to Thursday 9am–1pm) has been created at the summer house of Sheikh Rashid bin Saeed Al Maktoum, several streets away from the Jumeira dig. To get there, follow the winding roads to reach the Jumeira Beach Road, and turn left at the first U-turn after the **Jumeira Beach Park** 🅿. It is well sign-posted, in a small street near the No.1 Supermarket. The two-storey *sarooj* structure was built in 1955 to serve as a *majlis* and residence. The sea breezes at Jumeira offered relief from the heat of Dubai.

By sailing along the coast from the creek, Jumeira can still be reached in about two hours. Al Ghorfa Umm Al-Sheef was also a date palm farm that supplied its residents with a healthy food supply. The *falaj* system and *barasti* coffee shop are recent additions, and were incorporated to educate visitors on the broader aspects of the local culture.

Shopping in Dubai

Iranian silk carpets, Bedu kilims and Kashmiri rugs are available throughout Dubai and, due to the wide range and competitive prices, are affordable even on the smallest budget. Rug shops are scattered throughout the city. The ground floor of Deira Tower on Deira's **Al Nasr Square**, the **Bur Jurman Shopping Centre** (corner of Khalid bin Waleed Street and Trade Centre Road in Bur Dubai), **Markaz Al Jumeira** shopping complex on the Jumeira (Beach) Road, Mehreen Carpets on **Al Diyafah Street** in Satwa, and the neighbouring emirate's Sharjah Souq, are all reputable carpet-trading establishments. The most enjoyable way to experience the rug shops is simply to visit as many as possible. An hour or more can easily be spent in one establishment.

For many people shopping is a reason in itself for visiting Dubai. There is a huge range of goods on offer from electronic ware to locally made pottery.

BELOW: roll out the magic carpets.

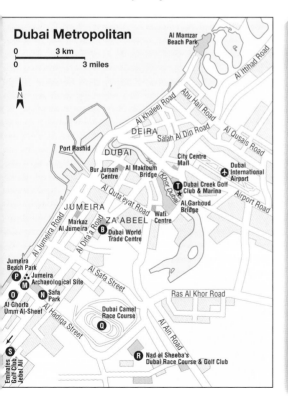

Dubai Metropolitan

Like most modern cities, Dubai has several large, air-conditioned shopping malls. Among the more interesting are the **Wafi Centre**, **Bur Juman** and **Deira City Centre**.

Sporting Dubai

Enormous resources have gone into creating superb sports and leisure facilities, including several world-class complexes. Camel racing is one of the most interesting local sports, and from October to May races are held on Thursday and Friday afternoons from 2pm (admission free). The **Camel Race Course Q** is located on the southern section of Al Hadiqa Street (Safa Park exit from Sheikh Zayed Road – the tent-like roof of the grandstand is immediately visible). Also worth visiting is the camel auction yard adjacent to the track, where Bedu camel trainers and herdsmen wander around looking at the camels and goods on sale. If you are here around sunset, jockeys can be seen meandering across the tarmac on their camels under a large, fiery sun to the pens and farms in the distant desert.

Fittingly, **Nad Al Sheba's Dubai Race Course and Golf Club R** is located on the same road as the Camel Race Course. Every Thursday evening in the cool winter months Dubai hosts a six-race meeting at the home of the prestigious US$4 million World Cup (*see* Kings of the Turf, *page 115*). The atmosphere is electric and the crowd a colourful, multi-cultural mixture.

Dubai Race Course and Golf Club, **Emirates Golf Club S**, the **Creek Golf Club and Marina T** are all international, 18-hole, grass golf courses created by American golf-course designer Karl Litten. They all boast distinguished architectural features, including Emirates' clubhouse shaped like a Bedu tent. The

TIP

Betting on the horses at Nad Al Sheba is illegal but punters can enter the free "Pick Six" competition to win a new Mercedes, Rolls Royce or Range Rover.

BELOW: on Dubai's public beach.

annual Desert Classic, the first Middle East tournament on the PGA European circuit, is held at the Emirates Golf Club.

But golf courses are not the only grass-covered oases in Dubai's sandy surrounds. Creekside Park, Al Mamzar Beach Park (on the north side of Al Hamriya Port), Jumeira Beach Park, Safa Park, Mushrif Park (turn right off Al Khawaneej Road, about 10 km/6 miles past Dubai International Airport) and Umm Suqeim Park have playground facilities, amenities, picnic areas and lush garden settings. As with many of the emirate's public works, little expense has been spared. The beautifully landscaped Creekside Park, for example, was completed at a cost of Dhs100 million.

A trip to Hatta

An hour away by road to the east, but within Dubai emirate, is Hatta, a recommended excursion from Dubai city. The journey there cuts through wide gravel plains, high red sand dunes, date palm oases and the rugged Hajar Mountains. From Dubai, set out from the roundabout near the bird sanctuary at the end of the creek and take the road signposted to Al Awir. At Hebeb the mountains come into view and the colour of the sand begins to change. After a few kilometres, Margum oil field will appear on the right, and shortly after that a large dune, knows as Big Red, looms on the left.

From the village of **Madam** the landscape flattens out into a gravel plain, and a wide wadi runs parallel to the road. Watch for camels during the next 30 km (18 miles) as there is no fence to keep them off the tarmac. A sign welcoming visitors to the *Wilayat* (Governorate) of Mahdah indicates that the road from Madam to Hatta passes through Omani territory – in fact, Hatta is surrounded by territory

Map, page 208

BELOW: aerial view showing Creek Golf Club.

Map,
page 208

belonging to Oman, Ras al-Khaimah or Ajman. No visas are required, for this is simply an anomaly that occurred when the borders were drawn: the borderpost for Oman is about 5 km (3 miles) east of Hatta.

The approach to Hatta highlights the enormous contrasts in habitat that exist in Dubai. Beautiful beaches and open desert country give way to rocky mountain ranges. At Hatta the air is cooler and the lifestyle less arduous than in the hot desert or along the humid coast. A large dam ensures a constant water supply, and the altitude enables farm crops to flourish.

The Hajar Mountains were formed over 90 million years ago beneath the Tethys Sea. Their rugged shapes are seen to best advantage on the road to the village of **Huwaylat**. Go straight on from the Fort Roundabout in front of the entrance to the Hatta Fort Hotel, and turn left at the signpost. The winding road is 10 km (6 miles) long and shows how undeveloped much of the mountain region has remained.

Return to the Fort Roundabout and turn left to the old village of **Hatta ❸**. A municipality sign marks the left turn to the **Hatta Heritage Village**. The square fort, several houses, a farm fed by a *falaj* , and hilltop watchtowers give visitors a closer look at life in the UAE before modernisation. Burial tombs found close to the village revealed that settlement in Hatta dates back to 3000 BC.

Beyond the residential area of new Hatta is a gravel road that continues to the **Hatta Pools** (water catchment areas in the wadis) and the Omani villages of **Al Fay** and **Rayy**. This is definitely four-wheel-drive terrain that is best explored with assistance. The luxurious **Hatta Fort Hotel**, with its lovely gardens, offers tours with experienced drivers and guides. It is also a good place to lunch and swim after an adventure into the mountains and wadis.

BELOW: garden pots for sale on the road to Hatta.

Tax-Free Bonanza

Of all the Gulf states, the UAE is clearly ahead in the tourist stakes, and of the seven emirates, swashbuckling Dubai is number one.

To get tourists to stop in the country in the first place meant getting the long-haul flights from Europe to stop over in Dubai on their way to the Far East or Australia. Stopovers mean lucrative airport fees for the host country – a lesson that Singapore learnt many years ago.

A major stepping stone to this aim is tax-free outlets at international airports. Shannon, in Ireland, had led the way, and it is Irish management that took Dubai International Airport from nothing in 1983 to one of the most popular tax-free shopping centres in the world, competing on equal terms with Amsterdam and Singapore, and sometimes beating them. Turnover rose sevenfold in the first 10 years, as businessmen and tourists found it worthwhile to route their journeys through Dubai. The duty-free complex is seen more as a service to passengers than as a money-making operation for the authorities, who waive concession fees, a factor that elsewhere can add 50–60 percent to prices charged to travellers.

Abu Dhabi gradually joined in the competition and has now approached Dubai's reputation in the tax-free stakes. Arriving, departing or in transit makes no difference: the same facilities are available to all comers. Passengers can even browse in a display shop in Abu Dhabi city and have their purchases delivered to the airport for collection.

For those bringing goods into the country, the UAE has the most generous tax-free limits in the world. Dubai allows 2,000 cigarettes, 400 cigars, 2 kg of tobacco, 2 litres of wine or 2 litres of spirits and a reasonable quantity of perfume. Abu Dhabi has responded with "more than" Dubai's allowances of cigarettes, cigars, tobacco, wine and spirits and a reasonable quantity of perfume. Alcohol allowances are for non-Muslims only.

Tax-free does not only mean the great array of shops at Dubai and Abu Dhabi airports. The UAE levies no income tax, purchase tax or value-added tax. It is a tax-free country. Shoppers have been known to travel all the way from Europe just to shop for anything from Iranian caviar to a Mercedes.

The concentration on tax-free shopping no doubt pays handsome dividends to other aspects of UAE tourism – from Emirates, the national airline, to local hotels. To keep the words tax-free in the public mind, Dubai Duty Free has entered sports sponsorship in a big way. The $US1 million World Series event ATP Tour Dubai Tennis Open, owned and organised by Dubai Duty Free, has attracted the world's best players, while power-boat racing and pop concerts also pull in tourists under the Duty Free banner. Vigorous marketing has taken the name overseas with sponsorship of horse races at Newmarket and Longchamps and show-jumping at Hickstead, as well as at snooker, golf and water-ski competitions.

Generations of trading traditions in the Gulf have raised the tax-free/duty-free concept and the successes won by Abu Dhabi and Dubai to the level of national status symbols. With such competition, tourists can only benefit.

RIGHT: luxury cars are won in Dubai Duty Free's $US139-a-ticket "Finest Surprise Raffle".

SHARJAH

In the shadow of Dubai, Sharjah is often overlooked by visitors, but it has some fine old architecture and atmospheric souqs. At one time it was the leading Trucial State

Map, pages 242–3

t's Sharjah's good fortune to have been included in Sir Wilfred Thesiger's 1959 book *Arabian Sands*. It's just a shame that Thesiger, respected chronicler of the Arab world, didn't like it.

"We approached a small Arab town on an open beach," he wrote, "it was as drab and tumble-down as Abu Dhabi, but infinitely more squalid, for it was littered with discarded rubbish which had been mass-produced elsewhere."

It's indicative of the amazing pace of change in the UAE that less than 50 years later "drab", "tumble-down", "squalid" Sharjah is regarded as the UAE's heritage centre, famed for its architecture and *souqs*.

Its ruler, Sheikh Dr Sultan bin Mohammed Al Qasimi, instigated the restoration and reconstruction of buildings in the Al Marija and Al Souq Al Shuheen districts in the early 1990s. The resulting clusters of coral-stone museums, with their cool, high-sided alleyways and attractive windtowers, offer glimpses of what life was like here 100 years before Thesiger arrived.

Although the city, capital of the country's third largest emirate, is now overshadowed by Abu Dhabi and Dubai, it's older than both. Recorded references to Sharjah, which means "Eastern" in Arabic, date back to at least 1490, when the Arab navigator Ahmad ibn Majid wrote that ships could find it if they followed the stars from the island of Tunb. On a map of 1669, the city is called Quixmi, after the Qasimi family, ancestors of the present ruler. In the 18th century, the Dutch knew Sharjah as Scharge.

By the time British interests developed in the late 18th century, the city was a stronghold from which the seafaring Qasimis, known as the Qawasim or Joasmees, dominated the Arabian Gulf. In 1819 the British, alarmed by the power of the Qawasim, attacked and destroyed its fleet and bases at Sharjah and Ras Al Khaimah. Sharjah's standing did not diminish, however. Throughout the 19th century it remained the leading city on the Trucial Coast and the second most important port in the Gulf after Kuwait. The Sheikh of the Qawasim, Sultan bin Saqr – great-great grandfather to the present ruler – chose Sharjah as his headquarters. From 1823, Britain's resident political agent for the Trucial States and Oman lived here (the political agency didn't move to Dubai until 1954).

The British built the Trucial States' first airport on Sharjah's outskirts in 1932 and maintained a military presence there until independence in 1971. Sharjah was the headquarters of the British-sponsored Trucial Oman Scouts and in 1970 the staging post for Special Air Service (SAS) operations in Oman.

The city's fortunes waned in the 1940s when Khalid Creek silted up and sea trade was diverted to Dubai. Fortunes improved with the discovery of offshore oil in

PRECEDING PAGES: Sharjah's Central Souq, depicted on the Dhs5 banknote. **LEFT:** by the Book. **BELOW:** modern communication.

1972 and the dredging of the creek, but the oil price crash of 1985 left Sharjah in debt. In 1992, major new natural gas and condensate discoveries improved the economy to the extent that the city's motto "Smile You Are In Sharjah" has never seemed more appropriate.

City sights

Al Arsa Souq, a good place to browse for antique daggers.

Most sights are within walking distance of **Arouba Road**, Sharjah's main street which runs northeast from Khalid Lagoon through the city centre. The surrounding streets, crammed with textile and perfume shops, come alive after dark. To the west of the road lie the old districts of Al Marija and Al Souq Al Shuheen, with **Al Borj Avenue** (Bank Street) cutting between them. **Al Marija**, south of Al Borj, is a delight to explore. **Al Arsa Souq Ⓐ**, made from coralstone, lime and plaster and topped with palm fronds, is lined with small antique and souvenir shops that are open during normal trading hours. Here a few pearl traders still buy and sell, the last participants in an industry that in the 19th century sent more boats to the pearl banks than Dubai. In the evening the *souq's* coffee house is where elderly local men, dressed in traditional robes, while away the hours between prayers at one of the district's three mosques.

The rooftops here are dotted with minarets and windtowers, early forms of air-conditioning designed to catch and circulate breezes (*see page 231*). The most distinctive tower is the round one above **Majlis of Ibrahim Mohammed Al Madfa Ⓑ** (Saturday to Thursday 8.30am–1pm and 5–8pm; Friday 5–8pm), the only one of its kind in the Trucial States. In addition to founding the region's first newspaper, *Oman*, in 1927, Ibrahim Mohammed Al Madfa acted as adviser to the ruling Al Qasimi family. His *majlis*, where he would receive business

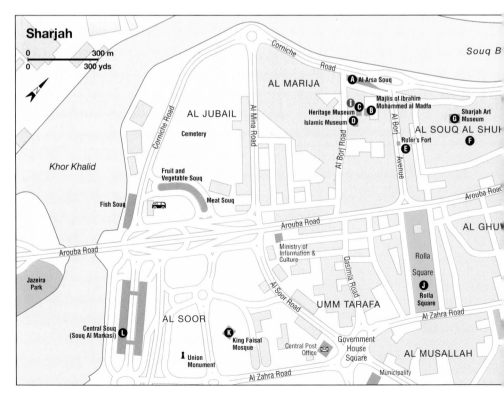

guests, is now a small **museum** (open daily; Friday, evening only) housing some of his personal effects.

The nearby home of wealthy trading family Al Naboodah, an atmospheric two-storey collection of rooms around a colonnaded courtyard, has become **Sharjah Heritage Museum** (Saturday to Thursday 8.30am–1pm and 5–8pm; Friday 5–8pm). A tour of its colourful displays of regional costumes, jewellery and restored bedrooms is invariably followed by an invitation to recline on Bedu cushions and enjoy a cardamom-flavoured coffee with one of the guides.

Behind the Naboodah residence, the house of another wealthy inhabitant, Said bin Mohammed Al Shamsi, is now Sharjah's **Islamic Museum** (Saturday to Thursday 7.30am–1.30pm and 4.30–7.30pm; Friday 4.30–7.30pm). Don't expect to find out much about the religion here; the museum is more a showcase for artefacts from Islamic countries.

On Borj Avenue, the **Ruler's Fort** , demolished before the possibilities of tourism were envisaged, has been painstakingly rebuilt. To the west of it, on the far side of **Khalid Creek**, the skeletal frames of oil rigs in **Port Khalid** contrast with the masts of more traditional wooden vessels moored at the **dhow wharf** parallel to **Corniche Road**. The Corniche, a short walk from the fort, is a hive of activity in the cooler mornings and evenings, when goods from Iran, India and Pakistan are unloaded onto the quayside.

Inland from the Corniche, to the north of Al Borj Avenue, is **Al Souq Al Shuheen** district, the trading centre of old Sharjah, where women dressed in flowing black robes and wearing traditional *burqa* face masks are still a common sight. Several old storefronts on the Corniche mark the beginning of the

Map, pages 242–3

Following Dubai's success in attracting international sporting events, Sharjah has become a venue for world-class cricket and now hosts the Sharjah Cup.

BELOW: in the Sharjah sun.

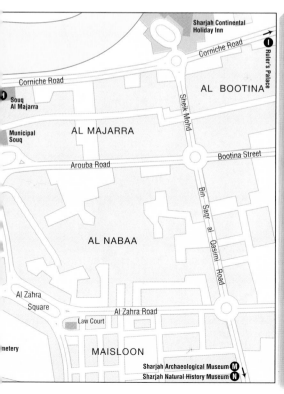

souq, but in the main it is now a jumble of fluorescent lighting and plastic, topped with corrugated zinc.

Narrow alleyways connect the souq with the former home of Eisa bin Abdul Letif Al Rurkai, British resident agent from 1919–1935. In the 1960s the 150-year-old building became an American missionary hospital specialising in gynaecology. In early 1997 its collection of artworks, by the the likes of the well known 18th-century orientalist David Roberts, and oils, watercolours and lithographs from the personal collection of the ruler of Sharjah, moved across the road into the purpose-built **Sharjah Art Museum**  (Saturday to Thursday 9.30am–1pm and 5–8pm; Friday 5–8pm), an imposing modern building that nonetheless remains in keeping with others in the area, one of which is the restored **Ad Dalil Mosque**, next to the museum and said to be the oldest mosque in Sharjah.

Further north along Corniche Road is **Souq Al Majarra**. Golden-domed with an attractive terracotta and grey stone finish, it opened in 1987. To the north stands the imposing **Sharjah Continental Holiday Inn**, which dominates the entrance to the creek and has its own sandy beach. Behind it stands the modern **Ruler's Palace**.

To the east of Arouba Road is **Rolla Square**, which is such a popular meeting place for the large Indian Keralite community that each village has its own particular banyan tree. The original banyan is remembered by a sculpture with a hollow centre in the shape of a tree. Fountains at each end of the park are guarded by cannons. Stone columns brought from India in 1926 are dotted around the edges.

Rolla is a popular meeting place on Thursday evenings, Fridays and on

BELOW: Rolla Square.

National Day (December 2), but Emiratis prefer to picnic in **Al Majaz Park** near the banks of **Khalid Lagoon**, in the newer Buhaira district to the south. The lagoon boasts the world's third-largest water fountain, after Geneva and Jeddah. The 100-metre (330-ft) fountain can be best enjoyed at sunset from a traditional *barasti* (palm frond) public coffee house near the park on the lagoon's northeastern shore.

At the eastern end of Rolla Park lies Al Zahra Road, which connects the Al Zahra Roundabout (**Clocktower Roundabout**) with **Government House Square**. Despite the grand title, the square, which also has Sharjah's main post office, is bland.

Al Ittihad Square is verdant in comparison. At the lagoon end of Arouba Road, it boasts **Al Ittihad Monument**, unveiled in 1989, whose seven pearl branches symbolise the unity of the seven emirates. **King Faisal Mosque ⓚ**, with room for 3,000 worshippers and the largest mosque in the UAE, is on one side of the square in what was once the turning circle for aircraft using the original Sharjah airport. The runway is now King Abd Al Aziz Street and the original fortress-resthouse, built in 1932 when Sharjah was a stopover on Imperial Airways' London to India and Australia routes, can still be seen to the north of the road.

At the lagoon end of Al Ittihad Square stands the superb **Central Souq ⓛ** (Souq Al Markasi), a landmark building depicted on the country's Dhs5 banknote and pictured on pages 238–9 of this book. The first floor antique and carpet shops are particularly interesting and attract souvenir-hunting visitors staying in other emirates. Persian carpets are a speciality.

Nearby, water taxis (*abra*) offer enjoyable excursions around the lagoon and

Map, pages 242–3

Map, pages 242–3

TIP

In 1985 Sharjah's Sheikh banned the sale of alcohol. To offset a subsequent loss of business among expats, restaurateurs have kept prices much lower than their counterparts in Dubai, a short distance away.

BELOW: Khalid Lagoon at dusk.

Maps,
pp 242–3,
208

Songbirds, a popular home accessory, for sale in Sharjah's animal market

BELOW: Khor Kalba.
OPPOSITE: Sharjah's fish market.

to the mouth of the creek. A pleasant and moderately priced **Dhow Restaurant** is just a short walk away, as is the 10-square-km (4-square-mile) **Jazeira Park**, on an island but connected to the city centre by Sharjah Bridge.

On the lagoon-end of Al Arouba, but on the opposite side of a road flyover from Central Souq, is the **fish market**. The best time to watch restaurateurs bidding for sharks' fins and the like is early in the morning. The nearby **fruit and vegetable market** is a riot of colour during the day, but is especially pleasant to visit in the evening, when its outdoor stalls are lit by hissing kerosene lamps. The **meat market** next to it is not for the squeamish. A live **animal market**, which sells everything from falcons to cows, is tucked behind shops and restaurants on the south side of nearby Al Mina Road. Most of the falcons here are imported from India or Pakistan.

Sharjah Archaeological Museum Ⓜ (Saturday to Thursday 8.30am–12.30pm and 5–8pm; Friday 5–8pm) stands near the Ruler's Office and an impressive Qur'an monument at Cultural Roundabout in the northern suburbs of the city, on the road to the modern international airport and the town of Dhaid. Completed in 1992, the purpose-built museum has two storeys of exhibition rooms showcasing objects from Sharjah's past – from finds at the ancient town of Mileiha (*see below*) to the 1930s and more recent times, as well as Islamic antiquities.

Sharjah Natural History Museum Ⓝ (Saturday to Thursday 9am–7pm; Friday 10am–8pm; closed Sunday), the headquarters for the Arabian Leopard Trust dedicated to saving the animal from extinction (*see page 203*), is beyond the airport on the left side of the Sharjah-Dhaid highway. The museum has five exhibition halls featuring displays on UAE geology (including a section documenting the story of oil), ecology, flora and fauna and marine life.

Outside the city

Dhaid ❹ an ancient inland oasis 50 km (30 miles) east of the city and roughly halfway between Sharjah's Arabian Gulf coast and Gulf of Oman coast (it's the only emirate to have two such coasts) is worth visiting if only to see that parts of Arabia can be incredibly fertile. Irrigation in Dhaid is based on ancient *falaj* water courses (*see page 156*) that run from the foot of the Hajar Mountains, but the supply is now a trickle and is topped up with mains water.

To the south of Dhaid are the 4th-century BC ruins at **Mileiha** ❺, where excavations have revealed a necropolis of large, monumental tombs, a large fort and graves containing sacrificed camels and horses (*see page 25*), while on the Gulf of Oman coast, **Khor Kalba** ❻ is home to a 2,000-year-old mangrove swamp and one of the world's most famous shell beaches. Such sites were attractive to early settlers, as the mangrove swamps were a rich source of easily obtainable food such as shellfish and birds.

In 1936 Britain recognised Kalba as independent from Sharjah, in an attempt to persuade the local sheikh, Said bin Hamad, to grant landing rights for British planes. However, Kalba eventually rejoined the state of Sharjah in 1951.

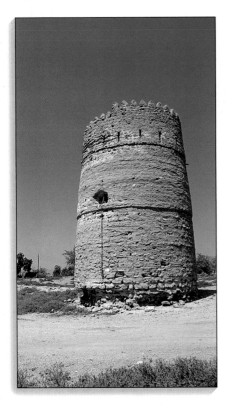

AJMAN

The smallest of the seven emirates, Ajman is almost a suburb of Sharjah. Its chief attraction for visitors is its traditional dhow-building yards

Map, page 252

At 259 square km (100 square miles), Ajman is the smallest of the UAE's seven emirates. Its main territory, surrounded by Sharjah, basks along the sun-scorched beaches of the Arabian Gulf coast. But there are also two inland enclaves, the fertile mountain villages of Masfut and Manama, to the southeast and east of the modest port town that passes for the emirate's capital.

Ajman town, 8 km (5 miles) north of Sharjah, is known for its dhow-building heritage. Pearling dhows sailed from its shores from the 3rd century BC until the 1930s, when the stiff easterly winds of competition, from Japanese cultured pearls, swept them – and the men who worked on them – into the history books. Fishing dhows are still made on Ajman's sheltered creek, though today most are made of fibreglass.

Ajman hasn't experienced the oil and gas bonanzas enjoyed by other emirates, but it has cashed in on them by updating its boatyard tradition: its port now houses one of the UAE's largest ship repair companies, which maintains oilfield supply boats along more than 5 km (3 miles) of creekside wharfage.

The town has a proud media heritage, too. In 1961, the Public Radio Station, the UAE's first, was established here by Rashid Abdullah Ali bin Hamdha. Powered with dry batteries and supported by public donations, the station broadcast readings from the Qur'an, speeches of the Prophet Mohammed, poems and songs until it closed in 1965. Today, Ajman's television channel, Channel 4, competes for viewers with global satellite networks. But it still maintains its predecessor's tradition of readings from the holy book.

Apart from Ajman's dhow-building yards, the biggest draw for visitors is its excellent fortress museum, which, with its sand-plastered round-towers, deliberate parapets and lack of windows, looks like a magnificent sandcastle.

Ajman's sights

It's possible to see Ajman in a day; at the widest point of its tapered north-facing promontory, just 2.5 km (1½ miles) of streets and sandy lanes separate the Gulf from the creek.

For visitors arriving from Sharjah on the coastal Arabian Gulf Street, the first of the town's rather limited number of sights is a crumbling **watchtower** that stands guard over a long sandy beach. Most of the UAE's defensive watchtowers are round, but, unusually, this one is square. Created from dirt, sand and stone, it looks as if it was constructed by a colony of African ants working from a blueprint of the squat parapeted tower of an English Norman church.

For visitors in the summer, when the temperatures soar into the high 40's C (over 110–120°F) with high

PRECEDING PAGES: shadows in the boatyards. **LEFT:** the fortress housing Ajman Museum. **BELOW:** school's out.

humidity, nearby **juice shops** offer a variety of thirst-quenching fruit concoctions which will reinvigorate them for the 3 km (2-mile) walk through the town centre to the fort.

From the coast road, Khalid bin Al Waleed Street leads to the **Ruler's Palace Ⓐ**, which stands on the south side of the junction with Kasr Az Zahr Street and Sheikh Rashid Street. The palace, home to Sheikh Humaid bin Rashid Al Nuaimi, who succeeded his father in 1981, is not open to the public, but it's possible to peer into the leafy compound from its main gate.

Sheikh Rashid Street, a tree-lined road of carpet and tricycle shops, runs north from the palace. Together with **Hamad bin Abdul Aziz Street**, a street of banks and ubiquitous camera shops that continues northwards, it forms Ajman's main thoroughfare.

Windtower at Ajman Museum

The must-see fortress, which has housed **Ajman Museum Ⓑ** (Sunday to Wednesday 9am–1pm and 4–7pm; Thursday 9am–noon; Friday 4–7pm; closed Saturday) since the 1980s, is just off Clocktower Roundabout and Central Square. Built around 1775, this building was the ruler's residence until 1970 and the police headquarters from 1970–78. The museum showcases life in the region from ancient times to the modern era with *barasti* houses and dhows just beyond the entrance and, in the old fort proper, displays on policing (practised since the days of the Prophet Mohammed in the 7th century), the bedroom of Sheikh Rashid bin Humaid Al Nuaimi (1928–81), and a market tableau – a more recent addition beyond the site of the now demolished east wall of the original fortress.

BELOW: in the shadows.

The museum's Traditional Medicine Hall has bottles of medicinal red mud, mercury and coconut oil, amongst others, and a fascinating section on Qur'anic

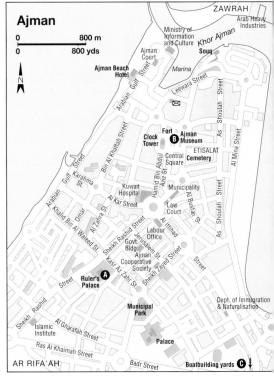

treatments. In one, a pious elder would write verses from the holy book on a white china bowl using a mix of saffron and rose water for ink. The inscription was then washed with rosewater and the collected solution given to the patient to drink or rub on the affected part of his body.

The museum also has an excellent example of a windtower (*Al Barjeel*) open on four sides to catch breezes and disperse rising hot air. Benches have been placed under it for visitors to sit in the *majlis* with the cooing pigeons that congregate in its rafters.

Beyond the fort, off Leewara Street and alongside a marina where wooden dhows jostle with modern leisure craft, are Ajman's bustling *souqs*, selling bric-a-brac, vegetables, meat and fish.

On the other side of the marina, at the northern end of Arabian Gulf Street, hotels will let you soak up the sun on their **beaches** for a small fee. They serve alcohol to non-Muslims, except during Ramadan.

Ajman's **boatbuilding yards ◉** are on the creek, a taxi ride from the town centre. Two of the most accessible are on **Tareq bin Ziyad Street** in the Mushairef district. Typically, a primitive production line of fishing dhow hulls are propped up on oil drums. Although most boats are made of fibreglass now, the deck rails that rise toward the stern are still made of wood.

Away from the coast, **Masfut ❼** is at the foot of the Hajar Mountains near the Dubai enclave of Hatta, 100 km (62 miles) southeast of Ajman town. It's known for its tobacco.

The date palms, citrus trees and reputedly haunted fort of more accessible **Manama ❻**, "the sleeping place", are near Dhaid, 60 km (37 miles) east of Ajman town.

Maps, pages 252, 208

BELOW: building boats.

UMM AL QAIWAIN

The second-smallest emirate and the least populated, UAQ is something of a backwater. Its main activity is fishing, and there is a strong flavour of the Subcontinent

Map, page 257

Umm Al Qaiwain may be known locally as UAQ, after the letters on its car licence plates, but it's no LA or KL – initials do not a city make. The northern Emirates town is a sleepy backwater of low buildings and backyard palm trees on a sandy spit well off the main highway that links Ajman, some 20 km (12 miles) southwest, with Ras Al Khaimah.

It may not be the smallest Emirate in terms of land area (Ajman is) but it's the least populous. UAQ's 40,000 residents would be pushed to fill Abu Dhabi's Sheikh Zayed sports stadium, and in the heat of the day there are more animals than people on its streets: scrawny cats that dart down back alleys in big-eyed alarm; goats that munch discarded tea bags at its roadsides; and cows that graze on patchy scrub around three defensive watchtowers that stand at the neck of the old town promontory like fortified links in a chain.

The emirate belongs as much to animals as anything. The island of **As Siniyyah ⑨**, visible from the old town's Corniche Road and site of the original settlement until sweetwater supplies ran out, is a wildlife haven. Herons nest among the mangrove trees at the water's edge; cormorants, turtles and seasnakes are not uncommon; dugong, or sea cows, swim in its shallows. With an estimated dugong population of 1,000, the UAE is the world's second-largest sanctuary for the curious-looking mammal, known in Arabic as *arus al bahar* (sea-bride). Archaeological excavations on the island of Akab revealed that inhabitants were hunting dugong 5,000 years ago.

Permission is needed to visit As Siniyyah, but along the coast to the south and east of UAQ town, **Khor Al Beidah ⑩** holds further delights for naturalists – birdwatchers, in particular. It hosts the country's largest wintering flock of Crab Plover, the rare Great Knot (previously thought to winter only in the Far East and Australasia), the Greater Sand Plover, Whimbrel and Terek Sandpiper. Its intertidal mudflats, islands and mangroves are bounded inland by *sabkha* (salt flats) and dunes that host breeding larks. In winter Isabelline and Desert Wheatear, Desert Warbler and Tawny Pipit are as common in these parts as coffee and dates.

City sights

It takes little more than a day to see Umm Al Qaiwain ("mother of the powers" in Arabic) – a name that reflects a long seafaring tradition that is today maintained by Indian and Bangladeshi fishermen and, in a less dignified way, by those who take to its coastal waters on rental jet skis, windsurfing boards and catamarans. The three defensive **watchtowers ❹** off Al Soor Road, to the west of King Faisal Road, are a good place to begin a walking tour of the old town. Round and of differing sizes, they were once joined by a wall.

PRECEDING PAGES: the ultimate accessory, a red Cadillac.
LEFT: a stitch in time.

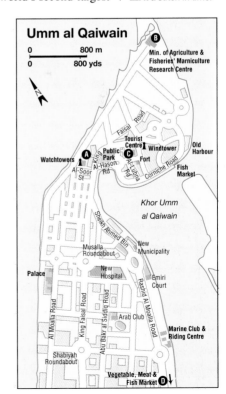

Umm al Qaiwain

The Ministry of Agriculture and Fisheries' Marniculture and Research Centre (Saturday to Wednesday 7.30am–1.30pm; Thursday 7.30am–noon; closed Friday) can be reached by following Al Soor Road west, to the Arabian Gulf, and then turning right. The centre, which is open to the public every morning except Friday, is working to increase sea-based food production and has an aquarium and research laboratory devoted to marine fauna.

On the creek side of Al Soor Road, Al Hason Road passes a small but surprisingly lush **public park** on its way to UAQ's **fortress**, which stands at the junction with Al Lubna Road. A former police headquarters, it's awaiting restoration. Policed now by goats, it's not open to the public. A tumbledown coralstone **merchant's house** behind it provides an interesting dissection of traditional architecture.

South along Al Lubna Road lies **Corniche Road**, where UAQ's main activity, fishing, is much in evidence. **Umm Al Qaiwain Tourist Centre** is within net-casting distance of the old harbour. If a cruise ship is docked in the seaport next to it, an incongruous sight in such a small place, it fills the skyline.

There is a strong Subcontinental feel to the old town: an open-air cinema near the seaport shows Hindi films, its restaurants sell *biriyani*, its pavements are stained red with beteljuice, and its dusty roads are home to boxy Padmini cars, imported from India.

Corniche Road loops around the old town to become King Faisal Road. In the streets in the centre of the loop are flour mills, small general stores and textile traders. Minarets are taller than the houses here, and cast long shadows in the sandy back lanes. On the rooftops, three old **windtowers** (*see page 231*) mingle with satellite dishes.

TIP

Umm al Qaiwain Tourist Centre boasts one of the capital's three bars (the others are in the Pearl Hotel and Beach Hotel).

BELOW: a cruise ship docks.

Further down King Faisal Road, in the new town, a seven-storey apartment block at **Musalla Roundabout** can probably lay claim to being the UAQ's tallest building. West of it, on Al Moalla Road, are the emirate's most ostentatious buildings, the beachside homes of UAQ ruler Sheikh Rashid bin Ahmad Al Mualla's family. From the junction of Al Moalla Road and Aqba bin Nafa Road, it's a short walk to the modest **vegetable, meat and fish market** ⓓ on Sheikh Ahmed bin Rashid Al Moalla Road.

Outside the city

The archaeological site of **Ad Door** ⑪ is opposite Khor Al Beidah, off the coastal highway that passes about 10 km (6 miles) south of the town centre. The 2,000-year-old remains of the settlement, which means "the houses" in Arabic, were exposed by archaeologists from Belgium, France, Australia and Britain. Ad Door, separated from the road by undulating dunes, is thought to have been "Omana", noted by classical geographers as an important trading emporium and one of the largest towns in Arabia. *The Periplus of the Erythraean Sea*, a description of trade around the coast of the Indian Ocean written by a Greek sailor in the employ of the Roman Navy in the 1st century AD, mentions Omana. Archaeological evidence confirms that Ad Door had commercial links with India and the eastern Mediterranean.

The oasis of **Falaj Al Mualla** ⑫ is 50 km (30 miles) inland from UAQ town. Watered by *falaj* (*see page 156*), it is known for date cultivation and now has one of the country's largest poultry farms. A **camel racing track** on the road there, on the banks of a wadi at the foot of high dunes, is probably the most picturesque in the country.

Maps, pages 257, 208

Smart address, Al Moalla Road

BELOW: the fortress.

RAS AL KHAIMAH

*The base of the Qawasim "pirates" in the 19th century,
Ras al Khaimah was once a powerful maritime state.
Today RAK is known for its restful beauty*

Map,
page 263

Abu Dhabi
UNITED ARAB
EMIRATES

F or centuries **Ras al Khaimah** has been renowned as a place "where dwell persons of great wealth, great navigators and traders" (Duarte Barbosa, *circa* 1510). It is a fertile area rich in resources with extensive date palm groves, grazing plains for sheep and cattle, and abundant sea life. The natural beauty of the high mountains, coastal sand dunes and native plants and animals have made it a favoured place for both residents and visitors to the UAE.

The ruling family of Ras Al Khaimah are Al Qawasim (plural of Qasimi), who claim to be *sharifs*, descendants of the Prophet Mohammed. In 711 the General Mohammed (born Al Qasim Al Thaqafi) lay the foundations of the Muslim colony of Sind by converting all who lived between Fars Province, Persia and the mouth of Indus south of Karachi. The Hawala, the parent clan of the Qawasim, have inhabited both sides of the Arabian Gulf for millennia.

During maritime conflicts with the British in the early 1800s the Qawasim were referred to as "pirates" (*see page 34*). At the time the British had aligned themselves with the sultan of Oman and disliked the trading strength of the Qawasim in India. The Qasimi considered the British intrusion unsustainable and a fierce naval campaign resulted. In 1806 Sheikh Sultan bin Saqr signed a treaty with the British agreeing "not to molest English ships in the future". The piratical reputation of the people of Ras al Khaimah has been corrected by recent history books.

PRECEDING PAGES:
abstract-patterned
house gates
LEFT: calm waters,
Ras al Khaimah.

City sights

The Old Town of Ras al Khaimah, first settled in around 1500, is right on the sea, bordering the mouth of the *khor* (creek) and is easily discovered on foot. From Ras al Khaimah Museum, on Al Hosn Road, walk along the small street lined with tailors and fabric shops, with the long, white-sanded beach and the Corniche straight ahead. Turn right at the Corniche and walk towards the boatbuilding yards at the far end. A beautiful crenellated mud-brick mosque stands out on a small rise overlooking the sea. The road continues around to the right and follows the shore of the *khor*. The shops here have quaint wooden shutters and sell grain, fabric, household items and camel sticks.

Take the first left-hand turn to visit **Al Abrah Market**, a small group of stalls set up on the shore of the creek. On a gravel area opposite this market fish nets are prepared daily by local fishermen, and large rolls of *barasti* (palm fronds) are stored for sale to local farmers. On the same road, under the impressively long Khor Bridge, is Ras al Khaimah's colourful fruit and vegetable market, with its extensive range of fresh produce.

The **Ras al Khaimah Museum Ⓐ** (8am– 12noon and 4–7pm; closed Tuesday, and closed Friday during Ramadan) is housed in a 19th-century fort. Until the

Ras al Khaimah

0   800 m
0   800 yds

early 1960s it was the home of Sheikh Saqr bin Mohammed Al Qasimi, Ruler of the emirate since 1948, and then used as a prison until it was developed as a museum in the 1980s. The impressive building includes several styles of construction, a defensive staggered entrance and a magnificent windtower.

Inside, displays include ancient manuscripts, coins minted in Samarkand, Tashkent, Baghdad and Sohar during the 10th century, finds made by archaeologists in the region, local jewellery, costumes, furniture and displays relating to natural history.

Beyond the Old Town, modern Ras al Khaimah expands. Houses and commercial buildings spread from the shore of the creek to the edge of the majestic Hajar Mountains, a range formed about 200 million years ago and running from the Musandam into northern Oman. The Hajar are Eastern Arabia's oldest mountain group.

TIP

The Musandam Peninsula (Ruus al Jebel – the Mountain Peaks), an Omani enclave north of Ras al Khaimah, is easily reached by road, but an Omani visa is required at the Ash Sham border post.

Ancient Julfar

The predecessor of modern-day Ras al Khaimah was **Julfar ❸**, a flourishing trading port dating back to around AD 200 but which had disappeared by the mid-1600s. Streets, houses, a fort and a mosque of the city were excavated during the 1980s, but evidence pre-AD 300 has yet to be found. Like Ubar in the Dhofar, ancient Julfar was always considered a mythical place, but archaeological evidence and records show that it is located north of Ras al Khaimah.

To reach Julfar from Ras al Khaimah, cross the bridge to Al Nakheel and turn left at the first set of trafficlights. After two more sets of lights turn right at the T-junction, and take the U-turn back to the left. Take the first right, continue for about 2 km (1 mile), then turn left about 50 metres/yards after the only service station on this road, with the sea directly ahead. An abandoned house standing alone marks the entrance to the site.

BELOW: in Ras al Khaimah museum.

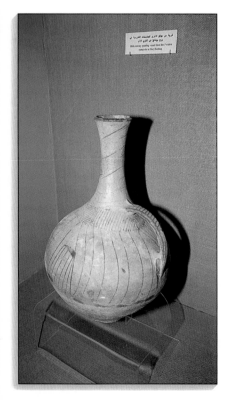

From about AD 900 Julfar was a rival to Sohar in Oman, reputedly the home of Sindbad the Sailor and cornerstone of trade from Asia into medieval Europe. Arab geographers such as Al Idrisi (writing in AD 1154) and a Yaqut Al Hamawi (*circa* 1250) described how fertile the region was, how at Sharm there was "a sizeable river that flowed out to the sea close to Julfar". It is believed that Ahmed bin Majid, one of the great Arab navigators, was born in Julfar during the 1430s.

Sited so close to the Strait of Hormuz it was inevitable that this prosperous city should attract attention. From about 1400 much of Julfar was controlled by the island of Hormuz. The Arab dynasty that controlled the island also mastered the pearl trade stretching from Julfar to Bahrain. By 1500 the Portuguese coveted this Arabian jewel, and for almost a century they occupied the coastal city, building a fort from which they maintained their powerful trading position throughout the Gulf.

In 1621 the Portuguese lost Hormuz to the Persians and British, the new force in the region. In retaliation a Portuguese captain set up his cannons in a local mosque and bombarded the seized fort. The Portuguese continued their hold on Julfar until 1633, when they were eventually overthrown by local forces.

Around Ras al Khaimah

There are a number of interesting places to visit around Ras al Khaimah. The coastal village of **Jazirah Al Hamra** ⓭ (the Red Island) was originally built on a small promontory which at high tide became an island (it is also believed that the earliest Julfar settlement was on this site). The old village and fort still stand but are abandoned, for the new village is on the mainland.

Travelling along the coast by road from Sharjah, you will see two large watchtowers set high on a right-hand sand dune. These mark the entrance to Jazirat Al Hamra, even thought the village is another 2 km (1 mile) away. The towers gave advanced warning of intruders approaching the village from the desert.

The **Ras al Khaimah Camel Racing Track** is about 6 miles (10 km) out of town in the village of **Digdagga** ⓮. Claimed to be the most exciting venue for camel racing in the UAE it offers an entertaining way to spend a Friday morning in winter. Locals enjoy the excitement and thrill of following the camels in 4WDs, so watch out for vehicles as well as unwieldly camels.

The village of **Khatt** ⓯ is about 800 metres/yards away from the **Khatt Hot Springs** (5am–11pm). From Ras al Khaimah drive towards the airport and take an easy-to-miss left turn to the village about 10 km (6 miles) from the *khor* (creek) bridge. Since 1985 the bathing areas have been developed into segregated enclosures that provide both privacy and comfort. Prior to this development the bathing area was open and shaded by a palm tree oasis.

Shimmel ⓰ is the site of an archaeological dig that has discovered remnants of a settlement dating from about 3000 BC. Located in the foothills north of Wadi Bih, about 5 km (3 miles) north of Ras al Khaimah, Shimmel has extensive palm groves that once fed the entire region. A large circular, divided burial tomb, like

Map, page 208

BELOW: Iranian market.

the one discovered at Umm an-Nar island in Abu Dhabi and dating to about 2500 BC was excavated here during the late 1980s. Prior to 1986 it was believed that the Umm an-Nar-type tomb was restricted to the Abu Dhabi region but a similar find in Ajman altered archaeological perceptions of the Emirates. The Shimmel tomb is one of the largest of its type to be found to date and has the most northerly location.

At Shimmel too is the famed **Queen of Sheba's Palace**, or *Hisn Shimmel*. The stony ruins of the "palace" are believed to have been part of a large fortified hill settlement that existed from about 1300–1800, and have little connection with the 10th-century Yemeni queen. The view towards Ras al Khaimah and the sea is wonderful. To reach this unaltered, ancient place turn right about 4.5 km (3 miles) out of RAK on the Oman Road heading towards Rams, and after 1.5 km (1 mile) take the first right turn off the roundabout and continue for about 2.3 km (1 mile). Turn left at a fort-like building, continue straight ahead on a dirt track and take the right track at a fork just after a small mosque. A hill surrounded by a fence appears straight ahead. Keep the hill to the right and after less than 1 km park. Continue on foot through a hole in the fence and climb the hill via a rough track. The villagers are not fond of visitors so the site must be approached with care.

The small, quiet villages of **Rams** ⓱ and **Dhayah** ⓲, north of Ras al Khaimah, are worth exploring on foot. Old watchtowers, Dhayah Fort and other coral and mudbrick buildings nestle amongst palm groves. British forces chose Rams as a stategic landing site for their invasion of the southern Gulf in 1819. The people of Rams fled to Dhayah fort, where they surrendered after four days of intensive fighting.

Ras al Khaimah is able to supply fresh milk daily to its citizens thanks to air-conditioned barns and a constantly watered green pasture that its herd of specially imported Friesians enjoy

BELOW: fresh milk supplied at Digdagga.

Wadi Bih

One of the most thrilling adventures in the UAE is to cross the Hajar Mountains from Ras al Khaimah to Dibba via the Wadi Bih. In the past, to avoid the treacherous waters of the Strait of Hormuz, **Wadi Bih** was used as a trade route linking the Arabian Gulf with the Gulf of Oman, a journey that would take up to three weeks to complete.

Map, page 208

Today this journey can be achieved in a day with a four-wheel-drive. To find Wadi Bih cross the Khor Bridge in Ras al Khaimah, turn right at the second set of lights, and then turn left at the lights after the Emirates petrol station. Go straight over the Palm Tree and Coffee Pot roundabouts and continue to a group of small shops on the right. At this junction turn right, keeping the shops on the left. Continue straight on, then turn left after the military camp. Take the first road on the right, then go straight towards a T-intersection and turn right again. Follow the new tarmac road as it sweeps back towards the left around the back of Wadi Bih's large dam wall.

The road climbs into the mountains through a natural cut and ends in a stony wadi (from here it is impossible to continue without a 4WD). After a further 20 minutes of driving the track forks on a gravel plain. Keep right as the heavily used track on the left goes into Wadi Khab Shamsi. At the Omani Police Post, more than an hour into the journey, turn right along the fenceline and begin the 1,500-metre (4,900-ft) climb to the "top of the world". The track to Dibba is often impassable after heavy rains as the road becomes dangerous and covered with boulders from landslides.

As with all wadi trips caution should be heeded during the winter months as flash floods may occur.

BELOW: Dhayah Fort.

FUJAIRAH AND THE EAST COAST

Map, page 272

Hemmed in by the Hajar Mountains, Fujairah is a beautiful emirate, with deserted beaches and dramatic wadis. Within this region are several enclaves belonging to Sharjah

Abu Dhabi
UNITED ARAB EMIRATES

The pace of life in Fujairah is relaxed. The city faces the Indian Ocean and is protected from the rest of the Arabian Peninsula by the Hajar mountain range. It is the only emirate of the UAE not located on the Arabian Gulf. The Arabs of the east coast are Sharqiyyin, who trace their origins back to ⸱men, and the great Hinawi-Ghafiri tribes that divided southeastern Arabia ⸱uring the 17th century. They are of the Azdite group of Arab tribes, descended ⸱om Fahm bin Malik. Their arrival in the area around 570, followed the col-⸱pse of Saba's Great Dam of Marib. Their cousins are the Shihuh, an impor-⸱nt tribe that continues to populate the Musandam Peninsula north of Dibba ⸱d Ras Al Khaimah.

The strength of the Sharqiyyin lay in their control of Wadi Ham, which runs ⸱om Fujairah past Bitnah and Masafi to link with Wadi Siji where it continues ⸱t onto desert plains. Wadi Ham has been the site of many battles down the ⸱nturies. Apart from the trade route from Ras Al Khaimah to Dibba it was the ⸱ly means of access to the Gulf of Oman from the western regions.

Although the Persians, Portuguese and Dutch had a presence on the east coast, ⸱e remoteness of the mountains has enabled the peo-⸱e of Fujairah to protect themselves against foreign rule ⸱d outside tribal influences. Sheikh Abdulla bin ⸱ohammed Al Sharqi is considered to be the emirate's ⸱under. He united the four sub-tribes of the Sharqiyyin ⸱ their fight to maintain independence during the 19th ⸱ntury. In 1888 he was succeeded by his son Sheikh ⸱amad, grandfather of today's ruler Sheikh Hamad bin ⸱ohammed Al Sharqi.

Until his death in 1932, Sheikh Hamad struggled for ⸱cognition of Fujairah's independence from Sharjah ⸱e British maintained the area was part of the Trucial ⸱ate of Sharjah). In a clash with the British Royal Navy ⸱ 20 April 1925, the ruler refused to comply with the ⸱ms of the ultimatum from the Political Resident, Lt ⸱lonel Prideaux, and British ships were ordered to ⸱mbard Fujairah castle for 90 minutes, resulting in ⸱mage to the towers and walls that can still be seen ⸱lay. It was not until 1952 that Fujairah was acknowl-⸱ged by Britain as the seventh Trucial State.

⸱jairah city

⸱jairah is a small city. A large green belt of date palms ⸱parates the old fort and town from the coast. The eas-⸱t route to the old town is from Al Njaimat Road in ⸱ Al Mudhannab area – turn right at Madab Road and ⸱low the signs to the Fujairah Museum; the fort and ⸱w mudbrick houses of the old town come into view

PRECEDING PAGES: Asian workers dry sardines for winter feeding of livestock. **LEFT:** Masafi road from Dibba. **BELOW:** bringing it all back home.

Date palms flourish

on the left. To reach the designated heritage area continue straight ahead to the Coffee Pot Roundabout, make a U-turn back down the opposite side of the road and, leaving the bitumen road, turn right onto a sandy track leading to the old village.

The **fort** 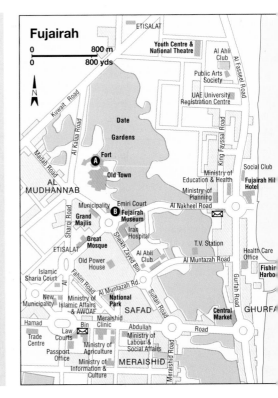 stands majestically on a rocky hill with the Hajar Mountains looming in the background. Although in disrepair, with both square and round towers awkwardly repaired with concrete bricks, the high solid walls give the impression of a once impenetrable structure. Built in the late 18th century, the fort was the residence of Fujairah's ruler and his extended family.

Many of the mudbrick village houses that surrounded the fort still stand. Some have been reduced to low walls, but others show signs of being inhabited – air conditioners protrude from windows and old cars are parked in make-shift car ports. A mosque below the fort has been well maintained. It has small, decorative wooden windows and doors typical of the area.

Fujairah Museum (Sunday to Thursday 9am–1pm and 4–6pm; Friday 2–6pm; Saturday closed) is at the intersection of Al Nakheel and Sheikh Zayed bin Sultan roads, in a low, walled building. It houses archaeological and ethnographic exhibits from the area, mostly from sites discovered at Bitnah, Qidfa and Bidiyah. The exterior of the museum is slightly uninviting and run-down but exhibits inside more than compensate.

The **Corniche** is a short paved walking area beginning at the Fujairah Hilton across from the Al Nakheel Road/Coffee Pot Roundabout. It is possible to walk along the beach from Fujairah to Kalba, but the five-minute taxi ride is more relaxing. **Kalba** (part of Sharjah emirate) is a long and narrow fishing village. Large holiday homes dominate its Corniche, but many small older buildings

BULLFIGHTING

Traditional Arab sports such as falconry and camel racing are not suited to the terrain of the east coast. As a result, the large Brahmin bull, which has worked for centuries in the area's palm groves, is bred to compete in a contest of strength. The contest is between two large, pampered bulls, each weighing a tonne (ton) or more and fed on a diet of milk, honey and meal. The bulls try to force each other to the ground. Winners are also declared if an opposing bull turns and flees. The sport was possibly introduced in the 16th century by the Portuguese. An almost identical competition between bulls take place in parts of western India, and Barka and Seeb in Oman, both under Portuguese influence from 1500–1650. However, the sport may pre-date Islam with its source in Persia, where the bull was once worshipped. The Fujairah contests are held on Friday in winter from 4–5.30pm, near the palm groves off the Kalba/Oman road.

ings show that it hasn't changed that much since the 1960s. Halfway along the Corniche several old buildings have been incorporated into a roundabout, and a renovated fort with cream stone walls is visible on the right. Fifty metres/yards further down the road is the colourful Kalba fish and vegetable *souq*.

Continue the drive out of Kalba towards **Khor Kalba** to see the mangroves at the *khor* (creek) entrance (*also see page 246*). At sunset the blue water of the Gulf highlights their rich green, emphasising the natural beauty of this region.

From Khor Kalba the road leads into Oman at the **Khatmat Malahah** checkpoint. A visa is required for the coastline journey to Muscat, but the view along the Batinah Coast makes it worth the effort. **Wahlah ㉕** (Awhalla), a one-hour drive on a rough track southwest of Khatmat Malahah, is the site of an on-going archaeological dig. A 4WD is imperative for this journey, especially if the track is followed all the way to Hatta, a mountain oasis in Dubai (*see page 235*).

Outside Fujairah city

The two main routes to Fujairah from the western emirates begin at Masafi, where the roads divides at a large roundabout. **Masafi ㉑** itself is a small rural village surrounded by deep wadis and the Hajar Mountains. A water-bottling factory has made the town a familiar place name throughout the emirates. The **Friday Market**, 5 km (3 miles) outside Masafi on the road leading to Dhaid and Sharjah, is a wonderful place to browse for local pottery, inexpensive machine-made carpets, fruit and vegetables.

The left-hand route to Fujairah quickly ascends into the mountains, passes the Masafi Water Factory, then plunges down through the wadis towards the coastal city of Dibba. **Dibba ㉒** divides into three sections, each governed by

Map, page 208

BELOW: bulls lock horns at a bullfight.

Clocktower in Dibba. Clocktowers have become popular city decorations throughout the UAE and Oman.

Fujairah, Sharjah and Oman respectively. It is a beautiful coastal place untouched by tourism. Located on a wide bay it is home to families of fishermen and farmers. From the main road from Masafi, turn left at the Dolphin Roundabout, continue straight through the Tower Roundabout and turn right at the small Sharjah Police Box. From here the road goes into the old village then curves left along the Corniche. A small **fort** (closed to visitors) and harbour *souq* are part of Sharjah emirate. Omani Dibba is marked by a sign saying Welcome to Oman, but there is no border post, and no visa is required unless travel to Khasab in the Musandam is intended. The further north the village spreads along the coast the stronger the Omani influence becomes. Houses are mostly one-storey with colourful gates, and the men who can often be seen playing cards on the white sandy beach, wear typical Omani dress. A distinguishing feature of Dibba is the magnificent backdrop created by the Musandam mountains.

From Dibba the main road follows the coastline. The impressive view is often interrupted by sudden and dramatic passes that have been cut through the mountains running parallel to the sea. Fishermen can be spotted on the beaches in this area hauling large nets full of sardines onto the shore. The fish are left to dry and the catch is later bagged as fertiliser.

Aqqa ㉓ near Sharm is best known for the Sandy Beach Motel, which is part of Dubai emirate. 'Snoopy Rock', named after a small offshore island that looks like the well-known cartoon character lying on his kennel, has become a renowned snorkelling and diving site. The Dive Centre provides good hire equipment and organises one-day and weekend diving trips. Many colourful and exotic fish feed from the coral reef that surrounds the island. At low tide you can walk across a sand bar to the island. The individual chalets and other

BELOW: snorkelling among the coral off Sandy Beach Motel.

amenities at Sandy Beach make it a comfortable and convenient base for exploring the east coast.

Five minutes drive from **Sharm** is the tiny village of **Bidiyah ㉔**. Two small **watchtowers**, that may have been Portuguese fortifications, mark the entrance. Below them is the small white **Ottoman Mosque**, named after its architect Othman, not the empire. The mosque is built from alabaster and stone, has two flattened cupolas supported by a single internal pillar and has no minaret. It is the oldest mosque still in use in the UAE, and possibly dates to a time when Islam had not yet been fully accepted in the area. As it continues to be used for prayers non-Muslims are asked not to enter.

The walk up the hill to the watchtowers is recommended, especially at sunset when the elevation presents a glorious view across to the mountains and the reds and purples of the sky are beautifully juxtaposed against a floor of green date palms. The opposite view is also worth the climb – hundreds of banana trees and date palms set against a blue sea.

Behind the row of shops opposite Bidiyah's colourful fruit and vegetable *souq* are the foundations of a stone-built round tower that archaeologists believe is almost identical to the plan and construction of the one at Hili, in Al Ain (*see page 217*). This tower dates settlement in Bidiyah to well over 4,000 years. Another important archaeological site in the area includes a massive 30-metre (98-ft) long covered tomb similar to the type excavated at Shimmel in Ras Al Khaimah, and dating to approximately 1000 BC.

Fifteen kilometres (9 miles) south of Bidiyah and 20 km (12 miles) away from Fujairah, is the Sharjah enclave of **Khor Fakkan ㉕**. A spur of the Hajar Mountains sweeps down onto the coast and forms a natural defence for the picturesque

Map, page 208

BELOW: roundabout in Dibba.

township. The defences are reinforced by a watchtower perched high on the spur. Khor Fakkan's horseshoe-shaped harbour is constantly busy with trading dhows and tankers. To reach the small fish *souq* and the port follow the Corniche to the far right-hand side: the road gets a bit rough, but once there the area offers myriad sights, smells and sounds.

The **Oceanic Hotel** is an architectural landmark of Khor Fakkan. It is the town's tallest building and the rooms feature a porthole effect with enormous round windows. The hotel's white sandy beach is ideal for swimming, wind surfing, sailing and snorkelling. A dive centre provides tuition and regular diving trips into the Gulf of Oman.

In 1985 an archaeologist's dream came true when an untouched ancient burial was discovered in the palm groves of the village of **Qidfah** ㉖, 5 km (3 miles) south of Khor Fakkan. The 3,000-year-old horseshoe-shaped tomb was uncovered by a local farmer while he was using a bulldozer to level a mound of earth. The site yielded an enormous collection of different artefacts, including bronze vessels, swords, daggers, axes, bracelets and pottery, and is believed to be the most important Iron Age (1500–500 BC) burial to be found in the whole Arabian Peninsula.

A small Omani neutral zone can be visited inland from the villages of **Qidfah** and **Murbah**. The main village is **Madha** ㉗, which is well known for its mineral spring (*ain*). The village's small hilltop fort is not open to the public but the two watchtowers highlight the Omani architectural style.

From Murbah the coastal road leads back into Fujairah. To complete the loop back to Masafi turn right at Al Nakheel Road (Coffee Pot Roundabout in front of the Fujairah Hilton) and travel inland through the mountains along Wadi Ham.

BELOW: the oldest mosque in the UAE at Khor Fakkan.

About 2 km (1 mile) after Fujairah's last roundabout there is a left turn, opposite a small police post, into **Wadi Hail**, a rough 4WD trip to the site of the summer palace of the Fujairah sheikhs. The old village of **Hail** ㉘ was for centuries a summer retreat enjoyed for its cool altitude and lush fertility. From the new village of Hail a rough stony track rises into the mountains and ends at an impressive fortified castle and large square watchtower. The buildings are in good repair and clearly demonstrate how important this mountain oasis was to the ruling family. An abundance of flora and fauna can be seen on any one of the many mountain and wadi walks in the area.

Bitnah ㉙ is about 12 km (7 miles) from Fujairah on the right-hand side of the Wadi Ham road, approximately 30 km (19 miles) from Masafi. Nestled amongst a series of lush palm groves, and high above the water course of Wadi Ham is the village **fort**. Look for the UAE flag that proudly flies from the top of the round tower. The best way to explore the oasis and fort is to walk along the wadi, and follow the *falaj* high on the left wall. By car, from the main road turn right onto the tarmac side road leading to the Etisalat communications tower, after about 500 metres/yards turn left onto a gravel track, then keep right where the track forks. Head towards an unused bridge, leave the car under a tree for shade and walk down into the wadi.

Bitnah has been settled since about 1000 BC, and is the site of a massive T-shaped burial tomb. This tomb and others in the area were used over successive centuries and have yielded finds showing Greek influence in the Gulf from about 325 BC. A Greek designed ceramic glazed vessel from the Hellenistic period (300 BC–AD 200) found at Bitnah in the early 1990s shows that the Greek world influenced the Shumayliyah coast before the acceptance of Islam.

Map, page 208

BELOW: Friday drumming near Dibba.

INSIGHT GUIDES
TRAVEL TIPS

See the World with a different eye

The world's leading series
of full-colour travel guides

★ More than 300 titles

★ Three distinct formats
tailored for individual needs

★ Spectacular photography
and award-winning writing

APA INSIGHT GUIDES

CONTENTS

Getting Acquainted

The Place

Area 310,000 sq. km (119,690 sq. miles) with 1,700 km (1,056 miles) of coastline.
Capital Muscat.
Highest Mountain Jebel Shams at 3,000 metres (9,840 ft).
Population 2 million.
Language Arabic is the national language but English is spoken by many Omanis.
Religion Islam, but other religions (mainly followed by the expatriates) are tolerated.
Time Zone GMT + 4 hours, BST + 3 hours.
Currency Rial/baiza.
Weights and Measures Metric.
Electricity 220/240 volts AC with three-pin plugs. Many appliances have two-pin plugs so adaptors are used.
International Dialling Code 00 968.
The best time to visit Oman is from **October to April**. The coolest months in Muscat are

Five Facts on Oman

- Muscat is one of the hottest capital cities in the world
- There are only two Sultanates in the world – Oman and Brunei.
- Over 50 percent of Omanis are under 15 years of age.
- McDonalds, the burger chain, made its first home delivery in Oman.
- Oman has its own Grand Canyon in the Jebel Akhdar, with vertical drops of 1,000 metres (3,280ft).

December and January when nights are cool and daytime temperatures rarely go above 30°C (86°F). From **May to September** it is hot and humid except in Dhofar where it rains during the monsoon. Rainfall in the Muscat region is rare, but torrential when it occurs – often causing flash floods. **July and August** are the hottest months with temperatures sometimes hitting 50°C (122°F).

The Economy

Oman's economy is oil-based, and since 1970 the country has blossomed into a modern state with an impressive infrastructure. Discoveries of gas are now being exploited to maintain a good standard of living for most people.

The Government

The ruler, Sultan Qaboos bin Said, has total control of the running of the country. In 1992, a consultative council was set up and the members discuss topics put forward to them by the Sultan. There is no heir to the Sultan, although secret measures have been made for any eventuality.

Etiquette

Generally, Oman is still very traditional. Shorts are fine on the beach, but not in the shops. Women should wear garments that cover their upper arms and their legs to the knee.

When taking photographs of any of the locals, especially the women, always ask their permission first. Photographing military establishments is not allowed.

Non-Muslims are not allowed to enter mosques, and during Ramadan, it is important not to eat, smoke or drink in public. Do not drink and drive as penalties are severe.

Planning the Trip

What to Bring

Light, cotton clothes are ideal to cope with the heat. In public, visitors are expected to cover up, so pack accordingly.

Sunglasses and sun cream are essential. If you want to explore, walking boots would be wise. Do not bring video films which contain erotic scenes as these will be confiscated and edited

Health

Check with your doctor, as inoculation advice changes. But expect several jabs for your visit to Oman. Malaria is still a problem in the country areas. Tap water is drinkable but most people drink bottled.

Visas & Passports

A valid passport is required to enter Oman, plus a visa. The type of visa issued depends, in part, on your nationality, as does its cost. British citizens are issued a single-entry visa for 21 days only. For a longer-stay, apply for a long-stay visa, which must be sponsored by an organisation in Oman.

Different rules apply to US citizens , who are issued with a multi-entry visa valid for two years.

For further information in the **UK**, tel: 0891 600567. For further information in the **USA**, tel: (202) 387 1980 and ask for the visa dept.

Money

Credit cards are widely accepted in shops, restaurants and hotels. Traveller's cheques are acceptable too.

Getting There

BY AIR
Major airlines are Gulf Air, Emirates Airlines, British Airways, Swissair, KLM and Air France. Contact your local office for details. The national carrier, Oman Air, is expanding its network but this does not yet extend to Europe or the USA.
Gulf Air:
10 Albermarle St, London W1. Tel: 0171-408 1717
Central number for USA: 1-888 359 4853
Emirates:
125 Pall Mall, London SW1. Tel: 0171-930371
405 Park Avenue, Suite 1002, New York, NY 10022, USA. Tel: 212-758 2786

BY SHIP
There are no scheduled passenger services into Oman, although some cruise ships do occasionally stop off at Muscat.

BY TRAIN OR BUS
Oman has no railways. Bus services into the country are available from the UAE.

Public Holidays

For most people Friday is a weekly holiday. National Day is a fixed holiday on 18 November.
Religious holidays, which are not on fixed dates, are the Islamic New Year, the Prophet's birthday, ascension of the Prophet, Eid Al Fitr (four days at the end of Ramadan), and Eid Al Ahda (five days at the end of the month of the pilgrimage to Mecca, or Haj).
Christian expatriates are normally allowed Christmas Day as a holiday.

Website

Oman Studies Centre for Documentation and Research on Oman and the Arabian Gulf promotes research on Oman. Its Internet websites, hhtp://www.oman.org and http://ourworld.compuserve.com/homepages/oman provides a range of information on Oman, including info for tourists.

By Car If you are driving from the UAE, a road permit is required from the Omani Embassy there. Road development is taking place all the time, and road conditions are excellent in town.

Accommodation

It is worth booking hotels in advance (*see page 283*).

Tour Operators

The number of companies operating to Oman is still small.
UK
Abercrombie & Kent, Sloane Square House, Holbein Place, London SW1. Tel: 0171-7309600. High quality tailor-made tours, self-drive or chauffeur-driven.
Cox & Kings, 4th Floor, Gordon House, 10 Greencoat Place, London SW1. Tel: 0171-873 5000. Offers one-week group tours as well as tailor-made.
Jasmin Tours, High Street, Cookham, Maidenhead, Berks SL6 9SQ. Tel: 016285-31121. Offers an interesting nine-day tour of the north and its coast, plus a possible five-day extension in Salalah.
Kuoni Travel Limited, Kuoni House, Dorking, Surrey RG5 4AZ. Tel: 01306-740888. Offers an 'Arabian Adventure', which includes a visit to Oman on a whirlwind tour of the Middle East, as well as tailor-made tours.

Practical Tips

Business Hours

Government offices are open Saturday to Wednesday 7am–2pm. Hours of private sector businesses vary widely between 8am–5pm days, and 8am–1pm and 4–7pm days. Most businesses are closed on Friday. Shopping centres are open 9am–1pm and 4–9pm. Smaller shops and supermarkets are open throughout the day.

Tipping

A tip of 10 percent is considered the norm at hotels and restaurants. It is not usual to tip custodians of museums, forts and such like, who are usually Omani citizens rather than immigrant workers. Fares for taxis should be agreed before you get into the car – always barter, it's expected.

Religious Services

Catholic Church of St Peter and St Paul, Ruwi. Tel: 701893.
The Protestant Church in Oman, Ruwi. Tel: 702372.
Salalah Christian Centre, Salalah. Tel: 235727.

Media

Print There are two daily English language newspapers in the country – the *Oman Observer* and the *Times of Oman*. Both are mediocre but do carry the latest world news and sports results. Gulf papers such as the *Khaleej Times* are more comprehensive.

Tourist Offices

Tourist Information Offices do not exist in Oman. It is best to try the nearest travel agency, which will be able to give you information about tours, etc (*see page 283 for listing*). For advance information, contact: **The Department of Tourism, Ministry of Commerce and Industry**, PO Box 550, Muscat 113. tel: 968 791921, fax: 968 794239
Ministry of Information, PO Box 600, Muscat 113. Tel: 968 600591 fax: 968 698430.
You an also try contacting the **Oman embassy** before leaving for Oman. It can provide basic brochures.

Newspapers from other countries are available at shops and cafés about two days after publication. *Oman Today*, a bi-monthly English magazine aimed at expats and visitors, is worth buying. Along with feature articles (often including some on exploring Oman independently), it contains a comprehensive dining guide and information on the latest happenings and events. If there isn't a complimentary copy in your hotel room, ask for it at the bookshop. **Broadcast Media** Oman TV has an English news segment but generally there is nothing worth watching. Satellite TV is widely available featuring BBC and CNN reports.

Post & Telecoms

Post Offices are dotted all over but the most central one in Muscat is at Al Harthy Shopping Complex. Phone cards, available from supermarkets for both local and international calls, avoid the expensive alternative of calling from the hotel. DHL and TNT have offices in Muscat.

Embassies

Your embassy cannot give you money in an emergency, but it will contact relatives who can on your behalf and, if necessary, put you in touch with lawyers.
Bahrain Tel: 605075; fax: 605072
France Tel: 604266; fax: 604300
Germany Tel: 702482; fax: 705690
Italy Tel: 564832; fax: 564846
Netherlands Tel: 705410; fax: 799020
New Zealand Tel: 795726, fax: 706443, E-mail: tecodev@gto.net.om
Saudi Arabia Tel: 601744, fax: 603540
UAE Tel: 600988, fax: 602584
UK Tel: 693077, fax: 693088
USA Tel: 698989, fax: 699778; E-mail: aemctoco@gto.net.om.

Getting Around

On Arrival

Seeb International Airport at Muscat is a small airport and procedures do not take long. Car hire is available from the airport or you can catch a taxi. Taxis are not metered so your bartering technique will be put to the test. The drive to the city centre takes about 20 minutes, and around 30 minutes if you are heading for Al Bustan Hotel.

Public Transport

Bus services are available between the major towns and there is also a service between Dubai and Muscat. But generally, if you have not hired a car, you will opt for taxis. They are numerous and should not be too expensive once you have perfected your bartering technique.
A cheaper alternative to car taxis are bus taxis – 12-seater buses which swarm all over the country picking people up from

Emergencies

By most standards, Oman is a safe place to visit, but crime does exist even though it is rarely reported in the newspapers. It is sensible to take the same sort of precautions as you would at home. In particular, remember to lock your vehicle
Pharmacies are open 9am–1pm and 4–9pm.

Emergency services
Muscat
Fire, tel: 999
Royal Oman Police, tel:560099
Al Hahdha Hospital, tel: 707800
Khoula Hospital, tel: 563625
Royal Hospital, tel: 592888
Salalah
Fire, tel: 999
Royal Oman Police, tel: 290099

Medical and Dental Centres
Al Massaraa, tel: 566435
Al Shatti Hospital, tel: 604263
Gulf Medical Centre, tel:564639
Harub Dental Clinic, tel: 563814
Hatat Polyclinic, tel: 563641.
Medident, tel: 600668
These all have English-speaking staff.

the side of the road. You have to hope that they are going in your general direction (so ask) or else you must wait until everyone else has been dropped off first before you get to your destination. Muscat's main bus terminal is in Ruwi, just down from the Sheraton Hotel.

There is no railway in Oman.

Private Transport

Omanis drive on the right-hand side of the road. Watch out for the bus taxis (*see above*) which stop or pull out with very little notice. One off-putting habit of many drivers is to travel very close to the car in front. Driving standards generaly are not as good as in the West, so be on your guard for some bizarre manoeuvres.

If you do have the misfortune to have an accident, you must not move the vehicles until a policeman arrives. It does not matter if this is at the busiest junction in the city, you must wait until you have police authority to move on.

Dual carriageways exist in Muscat and between Muscat and Dubai, and Muscat and Nizwa. The speed limits go up to 120 kph on the dual carriageways. Other speed limits vary from 60 to 100 kph depending on the type of road and where it is. Keep an eye out for speed-limit changes. Signs are in both Arabic and English. Traffic is never too heavy and driving in Oman is usually an enjoyable experience. If you are driving across desert plains be wary of wandering camels – they can be lethal.

To really appreciate the country you need to go off-road in a four-wheel-drive, but this is not really for the inexperienced as you'll have to navigate steep and dangerous roads to get to some of the most scenic parts of Oman.

If you do decide to drive

yourself, make sure that you go with another vehicle driven by someone who has experience because it is easy to find yourself in difficulties. You must be properly prepared before you head-off into the Interior. Alternatively, tour companies can organise wadi-bashing trips for you (*see below*).

CAR HIRE

Hiring either saloon cars or four-wheel-drives is not too costly and can be done by the day or the week. It is certainly worth it for a three or four-day period. One bonus of driving in Oman is the low cost of petrol which means that a four-wheel-drive does not cost you the fortune in fuel that it might elsewhere in the world. Most hotels have a car-hire desk.

CAR HIRE FIRMS

Avis, tel: 607235
Budget, tel: 704244
Europcar, tel: 700190
Hertz, tel: 566208
Mark Rent-a-Car, tel: 562444
Suwatco, tel: 707840
Thrifty, tel: 604248
Toyota, tel: 561427

Specialist Tours

Oman offers a wide variety of exciting tours, including wadi-bashing, dhow trips, diving courses, wildlife excursions, camping in the desert, and visits to historic sites:

- **Arabian Sea Safaris**, tel: 782112. Professional game fishing trips.
- **Empty Quarter Tours**, tel: 957093. Trips to the Wahiba Sands.
- **Gulf Explorers**, tel: 704739. Sunrise balloon trips from various locations.
- **Oman Dive Centre**, tel: 950261. Complete diving packages.
- **Orient Tours**, tel: 605066. Offers well-organised wadi-bashing trips.

Where to Stay

Booking a Hotel

The choice of accommodation for those visiting Oman is not extensive but the facilities that do exist are generally good. During the tourist season – between October and April – the hotels are fully booked, so make sure that you make your reservations in advance.

Out of season, the hotels are not that busy and cheap packages can be easily negotiated. Plans for a number of new hotels are in the offing and these should help solve the shortage of rooms during the peak season. Prices, as in other countries in the Middle East, are quite high. Bed and breakfast establishments do not exist in Oman.

Although there are no campgrounds in the country, camping is a favourite with many of the expatriates living here, so for those who want to save money and rough it for a few nights, equipment is readily available.

Hotels

MUSCAT
Al Bustan Palace Hotel£££ +
Tel: 799666, fax: 799600,
E-mail: albustan@interconti.com
Regularly voted one of the top hotels in the world. Located in its own bay just outside the city, it has a resort feel to it. Prettily tiled rooms have an Andalusian flavour. Facilities include eight restaurants, tennis village, pool, squash courts, gym, diving and watersports.

Price Categories

- Luxurious £££ + = OR100/head.
- Expensive £££ = OR40+/head.
- Moderate ££ = OR15–40/head.
- Inexpensive £ = up to OR15/head.

Gulf Hotel£££ Tel: 560100, fax: 560650, E-mail: gulfotl@gto.net.om
Perched on a cliff overlooking Qurm beach, this hotel has the best views in the city. A new extension has boosted facilities and room numbers.
Muscat Holiday Inn£££ Tel: 697123, fax: 697789.
Located in Al Khuwair, providing the normal Holiday Inn standards. This hotel has everything you want and although it doesn't have the luxury of the Al Bustan Palace Hotel or the Inter-Continental, the prices are not so steep.
Muscat Inter-Continental Hotel£££ Tel: 600500, fax: 600012.
Next to the beach in the Shati Al Qurm district of the city, this large resort hotel attracts both businesspeople and holidaymakers. High standards of food and accommodation. New executive floor.
Oman Sheraton Hotel£££ Tel: 799899, fax: 795791.
In the business district of Ruwi, this hotel offers an ideal location and good services for people on business, but its position makes it less attractive for tourists.
Mercure Al Falaj Hotel££ Tel: 702311, fax: 795853.
One of the oldest hotels in the country with good sporting facilities. Located in Ruwi.
Muttrah Hotel££ Tel: 798401, fax: 790953.
Sad-looking place in Muttrah High Street.
Ruwi Novotel££ Tel: 704244, fax: 704248

Hotel in the Ruwi district giving standard accommodation.
Seeb Novotel££ Tel: 510300, fax: 510055.
Large, dull hotel next to the airport. Twenty minutes' drive from the city, so not convenient if you're on business.
Qurm Beach House£ Tel: 564070, fax: 560761.
Tucked away at the bottom of the hill leading to the Gulf Hotel. Small establishment close to Qurm beach.
Majan Hotel£ Tel: 592900, fax: 592979.
Medium-sized hotel in Al Khuwair with several restaurants.
Mina Hotel£ Tel: 711828, fax: 714981.
Great location on the Muttrah Corniche but not blessed with the highest of standards.

THE NORTH AND THE BATTINAH
Al Buraimi Hotel££ Tel: 652010, fax: 652011.
Situated in Buraimi on the Oman/UAE border, this hotel provides a convenient stopping-off point.
Al Sawadi Beach Resort££ Tel: 895545, fax: 895535, E-mail gulfotl@gto.net.om
About 45 minutes drive from Muscat, this secluded hotel is popular for weekend breaks.
Sohar Beach Hotel££ Tel: 843701 fax: 843766.
A good resort hotel half-way between Muscat and Dubai. Two hours' drive from Muscat.
Al Wadi Hotel, Sohar£ Tel: 840058, fax: 841997.
Basic accommodation in the centre of Sohar.

THE INTERIOR
Falaj Daris Hotel££ Tel: 410500, fax: 410537.
This hotel in the centre of Nizwa is a little run down but it has tidy rooms around an attractive swimming pool.
Nizwa Hotel££ Tel: 431616, fax: 431619.
Quiet, modern hotel about 10 minutes' drive from Nizwa.

Pleasant rooms, high standards, good value.
Bahla Motel£ Tel: 420211, fax: 420212.
Strangely shaped building with good rooms in the village of Bahla. Ideally located for touring one of the country's most interesting regions.
Ghaba Motel, Al Ghaftain Motel, Wadi Quitbit Motel£ Tel: 951385.
All positioned on the Muscat to Salalah road, providing basic accommodation for those making the long drive between Oman's two biggest cities.

SUR AND THE EAST
Sur Resort Beach Motel££ Tel: 442031, fax: 442228.
Resort hotel in the old town of Sur, famous for its dhow building. The hotel is nothing special but always busy, and the restaurant quite good.
Al Qabil Motel£ Tel: 481243, fax: 481119.
Basic accommodation on the Muscat to Sur road.

THE SOUTH
Salalah Holiday Inn£££Tel: 235333, fax: 235137.
Provides all the usual Holiday Inn facilities with a location on the beach.
Haffa House, Salalah££ Tel: 294755, fax: 294873.
Friendly establishment with comfortable accommodation.
Hamdan Plaza Hotel, Salalah££ Tel: 211025, fax: 211187.
Large, dull place just outside the centre of the town.

MUSANDAM
Khasab Hotel£ Tel. 830267.
Adequate small hotel in Khasab, and there's no other choice if you want to explore this isolated part of the country and don't fancy camping

Where to Eat

Where to Eat

Oman is a great place for eating out. A lot of the restaurants are in the hotels but there are many which are independent and quite a few in the shopping centres. Muscat offers the best choice of restaurants, with a wide range of food to choose from.

For those into Indian cuisine, there is a vast array of restaurants. The Indian coffee shops are ideal for take-away snacks such as samosas and Indian potato balls. You also have the opportunity to dine at one of the finest hotels in the world – the Al Bustan Palace Hotel – where, in comparison with prices at a similar standard of establishment in the West, you can eat like a king for relatively little. The Al Khiran Terrace theme nights at the Al Bustan are highly recommended.

Oman is catching up with the rest of the world and fast-food joints are spread across its capital. Coffee shops in the shopping areas of Qurm are also popular with locals who spend hours chatting and observing.

The local Arabic cuisine is hard to find unless you are invited for a meal at someone's house. A couple of restaurants have tried to run special Omani theme nights but they haven't proved to be too popular. The closest you may get is Lebanese food, and there is a good choice of that in Muscat. The hotels contain the majority of the better restaurants while Ruwi High Street offers a good choice of inexpensive Indian food.

Restaurant Listings

MUSCAT

Al Marjan£££ Tel: 799666. Al Bustan Palace Hotel. A luxurious French restaurant with prices to match. Only for special occasions or for those not on a budget. A magical experience.

Beach Pavilion£££ Tel: 799666. Al Bustan Palace Hotel. A fine seafood eatery on the beach next to the hotel. Live music.

Golden Oryx£££ Tel: 702266. Opposite Bank of Oman, Bahrain and Kuwait in Muscat Business District. Large restaurant featuring Chinese and Thai with a Mongolian barbecue upstairs.

Il Giardino£££ Tel: 799666. Another of the restaurants at Al Bustan Palace Hotel. Fancy Italian eatery with high quality cuisine.

Price Categories

Expensive£££ = OR10+/head excluding alcohol
Moderate££ = OR5–10/head excluding alcohol
Inexpensive£ = up to OR5/head excluding alcohol

La Terrazza£££ Tel: 564252. Behind Hatat House, Wattayeh. Brilliant restaurant. Superb Italian food. Good value for money.

Mumtaz Mahal£££ Tel: 563850. Next to Capital Stores, Qurm shopping area. Upmarket Indian restaurant serving high quality cuisine in good surroundings.

O Sole Mio£££ Tel: 601343. Jawaharat A'Shati Complex. Upmarket Italian eatery. Lacks lively atmosphere.

Qurm Restaurant£££ Tel: 600500. Muscat Inter·Continental Hotel. French restaurant – one of the top venues in Oman. Food, atmosphere and service difficult to match.

Tokyo Taro£££ Tel: 702311.

Mercure Al Falaj Hotel. Popular Japanese restaurant.

Al Khiran Terrace££ Tel: 799666. Al Bustan Palace Hotel. Eat on the terrace of one of the world's finest hotels and indulge in one of their superb theme nights. Very popular. Excellent value for money. Live music. Moves indoors during the hot summer months.

Al Inshirah££ Tel: 713061. Muttrah Corniche. Seafood restaurant which features a dhow cruise around Muscat followed by a buffet.

Al Pasha££ Tel: 708132. Behind Copper Chimney Restaurant in Muscat Business District. Good Lebanese food at reasonable prices. Small and friendly.

Come Prima££ Tel: 560100. Gulf Hotel. Superb Italian food in small venue overlooking Qurm Beach. Ask for window table.

Copper Chimney££ Tel:706420. Opposite British Bank in Muscat Business District. Reasonably priced Indian dishes.

Cork's Bistro££ Tel: 702311. Mercure Al Falaj Hotel. French bistro with good lunchtime offers.

Glacier££ Tel: 560974. CCC Shopping Complex. Busy café serving continental dishes. Western newspapers available. Popular with expatriate women.

Golden Dragon££ Tel: 697374. Behind Al Fair Supermarket in Medinat Qaboos. Chinese and Thai food in a large restuarant with a good mix of customers.

Green Mountain££ Tel: 799899. Sheraton Hotel. Continental restaurant with special theme nights. Good value.

Just Jazz££ Tel: ~~607123~~. 687123 Muscat Holiday Inn. Creole cuisine served in smart surroundings with live jazz music.

La Mamma££ Tel: 799899. Sheraton Hotel. Small restaurant with good Italian food.

Mijana££ Tel: 601730. Medinat Qaboos shopping area. For

those who want to try Lebanese food. Excellent mezze starters.
Musandam Café and Terrace££ Tel: 600500. Muscat Inter-Continental Hotel. Excellent buffets in a delightful restaurant.
OK Corral££ Tel: 600500. Muscat Inter-Continental Hotel. Live country-and-western music at this winter season outdoor venue which specialises in steaks and seafood.
Pavo Real££ Tel: 602603. MQ shopping area. One of the most popular restaurants in Muscat, mainly for the atmosphere and not for the basic but plentiful Mexican food. Good live bands.
Pegasus Thai Orchid££ Tel: 786352. Next to the Family Bookshop in Muscat Business District. The best Thai food available. Small friendly venue.
Rodeo Ranch££ Tel: 711292. Al Inshiral Restaurant Complex. Steaks and seafood in a Western-style bar with live music. Excellent decor and friendly staff.
Shangri-La££ Tel: 791095. Muttrah High Street. Large Chinese restaurant with Mongolian barbecue.
Shiraz££ Tel: 560100. Gulf Hotel. Iranian food, small eating area, popular with Omanis.
Al Akhtam£ Tel: 603292. Behind OIB Bank HQ in Al Khuwair. Indian, Chinese and Filipino food in a small, narrow but very friendly restaurant.
Alauddin Restaurant£ Tel: 600667. Al Khuwair/ Medinat Qaboos Crossroads. Cheap and

Drinking

The majority of restaurants are licensed although wine is generally very expensive. Most hotels have bars, many trying to take on a British style. Duke's Bar at the Gulf Hotel and the Al Ghazal at the Inter-Continental Hotel are the most popular. Live music is generally included.

cheerful, serving big portions of Indian and Chinese food. Popular with expatriates.
Atrium Tea Lounge£ Tel: 799666. Al Bustan Palace Hotel. Enjoy the beauty of this fine hotel while indulging in a cream tea.
Curry House£ Tel: 564033. Opposite car showrooms in Wattayeh. Simple restaurant serving a vast array of Indian dishes at good prices.
Epicure Café£ Tel: 601305. Jawaharat A'Shati Complex, Shati Al Qurm. Quiet cafe offering superb value snacks.
Ofair£ Tel: 693965. Behind Muscat Holiday Inn. Strange place with individual rooms serving Arabic food. Each room has its own TV set.
Our Beaches£ Tel: 954815. Gubrah Boat Roundabout. Chinese, Indian and Continental food served in clean, basic restaurant. Good fish dishes.
Woodlands£ Tel: 700192. Europcar Building in Muscat Business District. Spicy Indian cuisine with a lot of vegetarian dishes. Pleasant decor.

OUTSIDE MUSCAT

Al Zafran, Sohar££ Tel:843701. Sohar Beach Hotel. Seafood grill between Dubai and Muscat.
Barka Restaurant, A'Sawadi££ Tel: 895545. A'Sawadi Beach Resort. Continental buffets, 45 minutes' drive from Muscat on the way to Dubai.
Birkat Al Mauz, Nizwa££ Tel: 431616. Nizwa Hotel. Quiet, pleasant restaurant.
Tropicana, Buraimi££ Tel: 652010. Buraimi Hotel. Continental buffets on the Oman/UAE border.
Al Kharif Coffee Shop, Salalah££ Tel: 235333. Salalah Holiday Inn.
Al Luban, Salalah££ Tel: 235333. Salalah Holiday Inn.
Bin Atique, Salalah£ Tel: 292384. 23rd July Street. Simple, inexpensive Arabic food.

Culture

Music & Dance

A few special musical entertainments may take place at the **Al Bustan Palace Hotel Auditorium** (Tel: 799666) or at some of the other hotels.

If you want traditional music or dancing you may be lucky and see a display during a festival. A new auditorium at the Qurm Park is expected to be a focal point for cultural events. Check the local press when you arrive.

Art Galleries

Jabreen Art Gallery at the Al Araimi Shopping Complex, and Yiti Art Gallery, close to the Sheraton Hotel in the Muscat Business District, are both commercial galleries that stock the work of local artists.

Theatre & Cinema

A few travelling shows stop at the **Muscat Inter-Continental Hotel** (Tel: 600500). They have about three productions a year by the British Airways Theatre Company. Check local press.
Star Cinema (Tel: 791641), next to the British Bank in Muscat Business District, shows Western and Hindi films.

Nightlife

Nightlife is very sedate in Oman. But discos exist in Muscat's hotels. **Saba Nightclub** at the Sheraton Hotel (Tel: 799899) and **Sur Nightclub** at Muscat Inter-Continental Hotel (Tel: 600500) are the best.

Sport

Watersports

The coastline provides unspoilt beaches and superb diving opportunities. **Jet-skiing, windsurfing** and **waterskiing** are all available. There are also a number of dive centres which offer a range of packages.

For a good selection of watersports try the Marina Bander Al Rowdha (Tel: 737288), which is in the next bay up from the Al Bustan Palace Hotel. Or try the Capital Area Yacht Club (tel: 604897).

Hotel Facilities

Tennis, **squash** and **swimming** are available at all the big hotels (*see Where to Stay, page 283*). Membership fees are required, although daily passes can be arranged.

A number of the hotels also have **gyms**. Contact the Al Bustan Palace Hotel (tel: 799666), The Gulf Hotel (tel: 560100), or the Muscat Inter.Continental (tel: 600500) for details.

Golf

Oman does not have grass golf courses but courses do exist where the greens are known as browns. Contact Ghala Wentworth (tel: 591248).

Sports Clubs

Muscat also has its own **rugby** club (tel: 604890), **go-karting** circuit (tel: 510239), and **softball** league (tel: 602961).

Spectator Sports

Although Oman features a number of sports stadia, there are few high-profile events. The national football team normally plays at the stadium in Wattayeh. Powerboat racing takes place at the new marina.

Shopping

The main shopping malls are in **Qurm**, where all the usual designer goods can be purchased. For more unusual gifts, take a trip to **Muttrah Souq** where you'll find a wide variety of silver items. **Ruwi High Street** offers cheap clothing.

You are expected to barter. Simply asking, "What's your best price?" will usually provide you with an automatic discount on the initial asking price.

The malls are open 9am–1pm and 4–9pm. Except for Muttrah, the souqs are not open on Friday morning.

Silver

Oman is famous for its silver and you can get both old and new items in the shopping malls and Muttrah Souq. Buying antique silverware is not for the inexperienced and you may be taken for a ride by the vendor. In some of the souqs you may be lucky enough to come across a Omani silversmith.

Gold

Oman is one of the cheapest places to buy gold and you can find it in both the souqs and the shopping centres. The price is according to the weight of the article and you will not get anything less than 18 carat. Muttrah Souq has a huge section of gold outlets and all the shopping centres contain stores specialising in gold.

Khanjars

These are the curved daggers worn by Omani men. The scabbard is made of silver. They have intricate designs and the handles can be made from a variety of materials. The best place to get these is in the souqs, try Muttrah Souq or the one at Nizwa.

Pottery

If you visit the town of Bahla you'll get the chance to buy some Omani pots. They're very cheap but obviously difficult to transport. If you're travelling on the road to Nizwa you'll see pottery for sale on the side of the road at the town of Fanja.

Carpets

Expensive Persian carpets are available from the large shopping centres. In the same shops you'll see chests and tables with brass detail from Pakistan and India.

Frankincense

As soon as you enter the souqs you'll smell the frankincense that's being burnt. The normal method of use is to place the perfume on charcoal in an incense burner. The smoke is laced with perfume and smells fantastic. There are hundreds of different blends and mixtures, including substances such as sandalwood. Make sure you buy a burner as well as the frankincense. The powdered blends are available in the souqs and shopping malls.

Getting Acquainted

The Place

Area 83,600 sq. km (32,280 sq. miles).
Capital Abu Dhabi in Abu Dhabi Emirate.
Highest Mountain The Hajar Mountains lie inland to the north, rising to 2,000 metres (6.560 ft). They form a barrier between Fujairah in the east and the other emirates.
Population Approximately 2.3 million.
Language Arabic.
Religion Islam is the official religion. UAE nationals are Sunni Muslims. Other religions are tolerated.
Time Zone GMT + 4 hours, BST + 3 hours.
Currency 1 UAE Dirham (Dh) = 100 fils. Value is linked with the US$.
Weights and Measures Metric.
Electricity 220/240 volts.
International Dialling Code 00 971 followed by city code and number.
City Codes Abu Dhabi: 02; Al Ain: 03; Dubai: 04; Fujairah: 09; Ras Al Khaimah: 07; Sharjah: 06.

The Climate

Summers are very hot. From **May to September** daytime temperatures are rarely below 40°C (104°F), with humidity up to 90 percent.

From **October to April** there is very good weather (sunny and warm) with temperatures ranging from as low as 10°C (50°F) inland to 30°C (mid-80°sF, but strong winds sometimes bring sandstorms, and it occasionally rains very heavily. The rain usually comes sometime from **January to March**, and can result in large areas of flooding. The desert inland gets much colder than the coastal regions at night and during the winter months.

The Economy

The UAE's economy is based on oil and gas extraction, which brings in the vast majority of the government's revenue and forms about 40 percent of GDP. Abu Dhabi generates about two-thirds of the total GDP and Dubai, the main port of the UAE, about a quarter. Over the past 10 years, oil refining and non-oil industries have begun to play a more substantial part in the economy, and in Dubai trade is now a very important part of the economy.

The Government

The UAE is a federation of seven emirates, all of which are ruled by sheikhs. The president of the UAE is the Sheikh of Abu Dhabi, the largest and richest emirate. The federal government runs a major part of the country's infrastructure and affairs, while the individual emirates retain considerable autonomy which they exercise to a greater or lesser degree.

Etiquette

Although the UAE is a very liberal country compared with other states in the Gulf region, it is still a conservative Muslim country and visitors should respect this. Women especially should remember that clothing that is acceptable in a nightclub is not right to wear on the street during the day.

Outside the cities, dress more conservatively. Everyone should cover their upper arms and women should wear longer skirts or trousers. Don't photograph people without asking first, especially women. Men should not wear shorts in a business situation. Jackets and ties are often required in the evenings. During the holy month of Ramadan don't eat, smoke or drink in public. Never drink and drive as the penalties are severe.

If visiting the home of a UAE citizen it is customary to remove shoes before venturing on the carpets (a measure originally introduced when conditions were considerably dustier than they are today) and avoid showing the soles of your feet when sitting down. If you wish to take a present, a box of pastries or sweetmeats is a safe option,

Five Facts About the UAE

- When oil production first began in Abu Dhabi in 1962, there was not a kilometre of tarmac road in the whole country.
- A healthy yearling camel of good racing stock costs about Dhs3,000 (US$800) in one of the UAE's camel markets.
- When the UAE was formed in 1971, the population was approximately 180,000. Now it is in the region of 2.23 million.
- Just over 80 percent of the population of the UAE is expatriate.
- The equivalent of 25 percent of the world's annual gold production is traded every year in Dubai, one the world's largest gold markets.

Planning the Trip

What to Bring

You can buy most items in the UAE but if you're taking certain medicines then you should bring a supply with you. Film is readily available and cheap. Same-day developing is easy to find.

In the summer months it is extremely hot, so bring a sun hat, sunblock and wear cool cotton clothes. Women are advised to wear modest clothes in the streets, particularly in the souqs, but on the beaches swimsuits, shorts or bikinis are fine. For business a light suit is useful, and men are expected to wear a jacket and tie in some hotel restaurants.

Books and magazines are expensive so it's wise to bring some paperbacks to read, avoiding any that may cause offence. Do not bring in videos as they'll be confiscated at customs to be censored. If they are confiscated they are usually returned after editing.

Visas & Passports

Visas are required by all nationalities except GCC members. British nationals get an automatic 30-day visa upon entry and can then renew this stamp for a further two months, after which time they must leave the country. This visa does not permit the holder to work.

Other nationalities can obtain business, tourist or transit visas through UAE embassies abroad or through some larger UAE hotels as a routine part of booking a room. If a hotel obtains a tourist visa for you, you enter the country on their sponsorship for the duration of your stay. You generally have to stay with them for a few nights and you can then travel freely within the UAE for the rest of your stay. It is very important to keep copies of all paperwork, and of your visa, and useful to carry photocopies of your passport with you.

It is essential to sort out your visa before travelling to the UAE. They vary between a single-entry visa valid for use within three months to a 10-year multiple-entry visa. Periods of stay can vary from two weeks to three months. Entry regulations change from time to time so check before your trip.

As well as a valid visa you will need proof of sponsorship from within the UAE. This can be a letter from a friend, a hotel reservation or a company letter, to indicate that there is someone to contact in the UAE.

Duty-Free Goods

Duty-free goods can be brought into the country:
- 1,000 cigarettes, 400 cigars or 2 kg loose tobacco.
- No limits on perfume.
- Non-Muslims can bring in 2 litres of wine or spirits, unless you are arriving in Sharjah where alcohol is prohibited. You are not allowed to bring in alcohol if arriving overland. Check these allowances have not changed when you travel.)

Health

Travel insurance is advisable as healthcare can be expensive, although there are good government hospitals as well as numerous private clinics.

No special injections are required for the UAE. Cholera and yellow fever certificates are only necessary if you arrive from an infected area. It is sensible to take precautions against malaria and meningitis. It is wise to drink bottled water. The drinking water is safe but your system may not have time to acclimatise.

Money

Any currency can be exchanged at one of the many banks or at money exchanges. Money changers offer varying rates and are sometimes better value than banks. They are mainly located in the souq area.

Traveller's cheques are sometimes accepted in major shops and are easily exchanged at banks. It is best to have the purchase receipt with you. Credit cards are widely accepted and banks also have globally linked ATM points. Money transfers can also be made through any bank.

Public Holidays

Religious holidays follow the Islamic calendar and are not fixed dates. The main holidays are the Eid Al Fitr (the end of Ramadan), Eid Al Adha (during the month of the Haj, or pilgrimage to Mecca), the ascension of the Prophet, the Prophet's birthday, and the Islamic New Year. Other holidays include New Year's Day (1 January) and National Day (2 December). Some emirates honour their rulers, as in Abu Dhabi where 6 August is a holiday to mark the accession of Sheikh Zayed

Getting There

BY AIR
The main international airports are:
- **Abu Dhabi**. Tel: 02-757500.
- **Dubai**. Tel: 04-245555.
- **Sharjah**. Tel: 06-581111.
There are smaller airports at:

● **Ras Al Khaimah**. Tel: 07-448111.
● **Fujairah**. Tel: 09-226222.
● **Al Ain**. Tel: 03-855555.
Most major airlines operate in and out of the main airports, and smaller airlines and charter flights are also available. Dubai offers the largest choice of airlines operating in and out of the country.

BY SHIP

Arrival by ship is not as common as by plane and it is important to make sure you have the correct paperwork for port entry. It is essential to have the paperwork clarified before leaving your own country and to check these procedures carefully. Visas can be obtained from some entry ports on arrival in the country.

BY TRAIN OR BUS

There are no trains in the UAE but there are bus services from Oman.

BY CAR

The city and inter-emirate roads are well-planned and well-maintained, and are mainly dual carriageways. If you are arriving by road from outside the UAE, as with other means of entry you will need to obtain a visa beforehand.

Useful Addresses

UAE Embassy in London,
30 Princes Gate, London SW7 tel: 0171-581 1281. Consular section: 0171-589 3434
UAE Embassy in Washington
1255 22nd St Northwest, Suite 700, Washington DC. Tel: (202) 955 6238; fax: (202) 337 7029; fax for consulate: (202) 333 3246.
Emirates Airlines
125 Pall Mall, London SW1, tel: 0171-930 5356.
405 Park Avenue, Suite 1002, New York, NY 10022. Tel: (212) 758 2786.

Accommodation

All the emirates now have hotels ranging from deluxe to medium-class but there are no very cheap hotels. Most cater for business travellers or offer rates linked to package holidays (*see* Where to Stay, *page 295 for details*). Apartments and self-service flats can also be rented for longer stays, usually of a month or more. There are beach chalets available in some emirates, for rent on a nightly or daily basis. These often offer weekend packages.

On Departure

There is no airport departure tax. The UAE's duty-free shops are some of the best in the world so it's worth getting to the airport early. The UAE is an excellent point of transit for other destinations. Many airlines and tour operators transit through Dubai.
There are many cargo ships leaving all the main ports and some take passengers. Phone an agent and ask for details.
In Abu Dhabi try:
● **National Shipping Gulf Agency**. Tel: 02-730500.
● **Mazroui International Cargo Company (MICCO)**. Tel: 02-776096).
In Dubai:
● **Inchcape Shipping Services**. Tel: 04-262222.
● **The Kanoo Group** Tel: 04-521525.
● **Linkage International**. Tel: 04-278844.
● **Orient Shipping Services**. Tel: 04-522626.
In Sharjah:
● **Oasis Freight Company**. Tel: 06-596325.
In Fujairah:
● **Fujairah National Shipping Company**. Tel: 09-228151.

To Oman Flying is one way to get to Muscat in Oman, and it is also possible by bus from Dubai. You must have a visa but this is relatively easy to obtain through a hotel or directly from the Omani Consulate. It is easy to leave the UAE this way, but problems may arise if you want to return, when you will receive a transit visa valid for 48 hours only. You must also obtain an entry visa to go to Oman by car from the UAE. Residents of GCC countries do not require a visa to go to Oman.
To obtain a visa, go to the **Omani Consulate** in Bur Dubai, behind the Indian Consulate, behind the Strand Cinema on Khalid bin Waleed Street (Tel: 04-515000; PO Box 1898) to get a visa.

Airlines

ABU DHABI
● **Air India**. Tel: 02-334766
● **British Airways**. Tel: 02-225777
● **Emirates Airlines**. Tel: 02-315777
● **Gulf Air**. Tel: 02-332600
DUBAI
● **Emirates Airlines**. Tel: 04-215544
● **Air India**. Tel: 04-276787
● **British Airways**. Tel: 04-075555
● **Cathay Pacific**. Tel: 04-283126

Practical Tips

Business Hours

Government offices work 7/7.30am–1.30pm Saturday to Wednesday. On Thursday offices tend to close at noon.

Banks, private companies and shops are open 8/9am–1/1.30pm and 4/4.30–8pm Saturday to Wednesday, and 8/9am–1/1.30pm Thursday. All these times vary, so check.

Increasingly, the large shopping malls remain open all day until 10pm, Saturday to Thursday. They are closed on Friday during the day, but may open in the evening.

In the northern emirates some small shops may close during prayer time although you will always find some shops open. Prayer times usually only mean a delay of about half an hour while the proprietor goes to pray. Most shops are closed during religious holidays.

Religious Services

ABU DHABI
St Andrew's. Tel: 02–461631. Next to the Al Khubairat School.
St George Orthodox Church. Tel: 02–464565. Behind Old Airport Road, behind the Immigration Office.
St Joseph Catholic Church. Tel: 02–461929. Near new Immigration Office, near Airport Road.

AL AIN
St Mary's Church. Tel: 03–663417
DUBAI
All the churches are in the same location, near the law courts, on the road underneath the Maktoum Bridge.
Holy Trinity Church. Tel: 04-370247.
International Christian Church. Tel: 04-440828.
St Mary's Church. Tel: 04-370087.
St Thomas Orthodox Church. Tel: 04-371122.
SHARJAH
St Gregorius Orthodox Church. Tel: 06-358765.
St Martin's Church. Tel: 06-357530.
St Michael's Catholic Church. Tel: 06-355049.

Tipping

It is not compulsory to tip, but most people do. It is usual to tip waiters in restaurants, although service charges are also added to your bill. Supermarket employees who carry bags to your car are usually tipped, as are petrol attendants who wash your windscreens.

Media

Print The main English-language newspapers in the UAE are: *Gulf News*, *Khaleej Times*, *Gulf Today* and *Emirates News*. Emirates News is based in Abu Dhabi, *Gulf News* and *Khaleej Times* in Dubai, and *Gulf Today* in Sharjah. Most of these newspapers have a daily tabloid section, film and TV listings, and a features magazine published once a week.

The main source of information on events, concerts and hotel functions in the UAE is *What's On*, a monthly listings magazine, published in Dubai, available at most bookshops and hotel newsagents. A good women's magazine is *Emirates Woman*. A useful local guide aimed at the expatriate is *Connector* magazine, free in shops.

Broadcast media The main English-language TV stations are Abu Dhabi channel 2, Dubai channel 33, Sharjah channel and Ajman TV. These show imported serials, English-language films and news in English. Picture reception varies from emirate to emirate and the time of year.

There are also many satellite TV stations available, which include CNN and BBC services. Listings are in the local English press.

There are English FM radio stations in both Abu Dhabi and Dubai, playing largely pop music with hourly news bulletins. Abu Dhabi FM is at 100.5, Dubai FM is 92.

The BBC and Voice of America are also available on short- and medium-wave radio, and through PAS4 satellite service. The best wavelengths change, and best results are gained by using either a good outdoor shortwave aerial or an indoor telescopic one. BBC World Service details are available in *Gulfwide* magazine.

Post & Telecoms

Poste restante facilities are not available in the UAE. The American Express office will hold mail for card holders, or you can receive mail at your hotel. Mail is usually delivered to a PO box number, not directly to a residence. The main **Abu Dhabi Post Office** is located on East Road, between Al Falah Street and Zayed the Second Street. The main **Dubai Post Office** is located on Zabeel Road, Al Karama.

Direct international telephone dialling is available from all phones. Local calls within the same city are free from a subscriber's phone. There are card- and coin-operated public phones on the streets, although increasingly more card- than coin-operated ones. Cards can be purchased from local shops and are available at values of Dh25, Dh50 and Dh100. Some phones also use credit cards, and in many hotels you can make a call and pay for it at the reception desk.

Faxes can also be sent from many shops, offices or the main ETISALAT offices. The big hotels can usually send a fax for you.

Tourist Information

There are no actual tourist offices in the UAE. Hotels or travel agents can give you advice, and in Dubai there is the **Dubai Commerce and Tourism Promotion Board**, PO Box 594, tel: 04-511600, near ABN Bank Building, by the Bur Juman Shopping Mall.

Embassies

ABU DHABI
UK, Khalid bin Al Waleed Street (near the Corniche) , tel: 02-326600
US, Sudan Street (near Al Nahayan Street), tel: 02-436691

DUBAI (CONSULATES)
Australia, World Trade Centre, tel: 04-313444.
Kuwait, Beniyas Road (opposite Sheraton Hotel), tel: 04-284111.
UK, Al Seef Road (Dubai side of creek), tel: 04-521070.
US, World Trade Centre Tel: 04-313115.

Emergencies

Security and Crime The UAE is generally a safe country for both men and women. The crime rate is low, and although petty theft is as common as in most countries, major crimes are relatively rare. The level of personal security is also high, but for women to avoid personal

harassment it is recommended not to walk around alone at night, although there is no real physical danger.

Taxis are safe to take during the day, or at night within towns as long as a woman is wearing demure clothing and knows her route so that she can avoid being taken on a "detour". Fares should be agreed in advance, to avoid arguments at the end of the journey. Inter-emirate registered taxis are fine and taxi shares are safe for women in the day. At night, women alone are advised not to get a taxi out of town into desert areas, or for a long inter-emirate drive.

Medical Services There are good government hospitals where treatment is free to health-card holders (only available with residence visas).

Emergency treatment is available to everyone but it is often easier for visitors to visit a private clinic and make a health insurance claim rather than spend time queueing in the government hospitals.

Emergency Numbers

Ambulance. Tel: 998.
Fire. Tel: 997.
Police. Tel: 999.

ABU DHABI HOSPITALS
Central Hospital, Al Manhal Street, tel: 02-214666. 24-hour emergency.
Corniche Hospital, Corniche Road, Tel: 02-724900. Obstetrics and 24-hour emergency.

DUBAI HOSPITALS
Al Wasl Hospital, Oud Metha Road (opposite Wafi Shopping Mall), tel: 04-341111. Primarily paediatric hospital.
American Hospital Dubai (In front of Al Nasr Leisureland), tel: 04-367777. Private hospital operating to American standards.

Rashid Hospital (Bur Dubai side of Al Maktoum Bridge near the British Council), tel: 04-374000 24-hour casualty.

SHARJAH HOSPITALS
Al Zahra Private Hospital, Al Zahra Square (Clocktower Roundabout). tel: 06-378866. Private general hospital. All medical, surgical and dental specialities. 24-hour emergency. Takes insurance plans.

ABU DHABI PRIVATE CLINICS
American Clinic, Salam Street (opposite Corniche Pharmacy), tel: 02-771310.
Medicare Centre, Salam Street, (Corniche Pharmacy Building), tel: 02-743375.
New Medical Centre, Electra Road (Hamad Centre Building), tel: 02-332255.

DUBAI PRIVATE CLINICS
Al Borj Medical Centre, Al Diyafah Street, Satwa, tel: 04-454666.
Dubai London Clinic, Al Wasl Road, Jumeira, tel: 04-446663.
General Medical Centre, Beach Road, Jumeira, Magrudy Centre, tel: 04-495959.
Manchester Clinic, Beach Road, Jumeira, tel: 04-440300.

ABU DHABI DENTISTS
British Dental Clinic, Hamdan Street (Bin Ham Building), tel: 02-773308.
Swedish Dental Clinic, Salam Street (American Clinic Building), tel: 02-722666.

DUBAI DENTISTS
American Dental Clinic, Trade Centre Apartment, Block A, tel: 04-313668.
Swedish Dental Clinic, Al Maktoum Street, (Nasr Building), tel: 04-231297

SHARJAH DENTISTS
Al Zahra Private Hospita,l Al Zahra Square (Clocktower Roundabout), tel: 06-378866.

Getting Around

Public Transport

There are no trains in the UAE. Details of bus services are available from all main bus stations. For journeys from one emirate to another, service (shared) taxis provide a frequent and cheap service, with the exception of the Dubai/Sharjah route on which the taxis were banned following the start in October 1997 of a new bus service for Dhs5 per trip. These buses leave from the central taxi stands in both Sharjah and Dubai.

Generally, taxis are cheap although if not metered it is always best to agree the fare in advance. There are taxi companies which can be telephoned to collect you, as well as metered taxis on the street. Women should always sit in the back of a taxi.

ABU DHABI

Bus The main bus terminal is on East Road. It is often easier to get a taxi than a bus for local trips, as the bus routes cater for those living in outer suburbs and workers' camps outside the city. It is not a particularly recommended mode of transport in Abu Dhabi city.
Service Taxi This is located adjacent to the main bus station on East Road. From here you can get to Dubai, Sharjah and Al Ain.
Taxi Taxis have meters but it is still wise to agree the fare before setting off. You can phone **Al Ghazal Taxi Service**, tel: 02-447787.

On Arrival

There are buses and taxis available from the airports, or you can hire a car. If you are with a tour group or being met by a hotel, they will provide a free bus to your hotel.
● **Abu Dhabi** Bus No. 901 runs between the airport and the main bus station, 24 hours. Airport and ordinary taxis are also available. Check the fare in advance. The airport is just outside the city, but the journey can take up to an hour, depending on detours and traffic jams.
● **Al Ain** The airport is on the Abu Dhabi Road, approximately 20 km (12$\frac{1}{2}$ miles) from the centre. Bus No. 500 runs every 30 minutes, 24 hours a day. Bus No. 130 is another option. Both take approximately one hour. Airport taxis are more expensive than ordinary metered taxis.
● **Dubai** The airport is approximately 20 minutes from the city centre. Buses No. 4 and 11 run between the airport and Deira. Airport taxis are more expensive than ordinary metered taxis, and taxi fares are higher to Bur Dubai across the creek.
● **Sharjah** The airport is approx. 15 km (9$\frac{1}{4}$ miles) from the centre. There are no buses, so get a metered taxi to the town centre or to nearby Dubai.
● **Ras Al Khaimah** The airport is 23 km (14$\frac{1}{4}$ miles) from the centre. Take a taxi.
● **Fujairah** The airport is located south of the city. Metered taxis only.

AL AIN

Bus Buses run regularly to Abu Dhabi from the bus station behind the Al Ain Co-operative Society Supermarket. ONAT bus company also runs a service to Ruwi bus station in Muscat from outside Hotel Al Buraimi. Visitors must have an Omani visa before setting off. Expatriates resident in Oman need a road permit.
Service Taxi These are located in the large parking area behind the Grand Mosque near to Abu Baker Al Siddiq Street, near the Coffeepot Roundabout. Service taxis are easy to get to Dubai and Abu Dhabi.
Taxi Taxis have meters, although it is always best to agree a fare before setting off.

DUBAI

Bus Local buses run from Deira bus station, behind the gold souq, and the Dubai service taxi and bus station on Al Ghubaida Road.

The No. 16 bus goes to Hatta from the Deira bus station near to the gold souq. It returns to Dubai from near the Hatta Palace Grocery Store.

The bus to **Muscat, Oman**, goes from next to the Airline Centre on Al Maktoum Road. Tickets can be bought from the Biman Bangladesh Airlines desk at **Airline Centre**, tel: 04-228151 for information.
Service Taxi There are two stations for these, one on each side of the creek. The Deira taxi station – which is for taxis going to Sharjah, Ajman, Umm Al Qaiwain, Ras Al Khaimah and Fujairah, where you change to go to Khor Fakkan – is near the intersection of Umar ibn Al Khattab Road and Al Rigga Road. For taxis to Al Ain and Abu Dhabi, go to the Dubai taxi and bus station, on Al Ghubaiba Road, on the Dubai side of the creek, near the Plaza Cinema.
Taxi Most taxis are not metered, except for the cream-coloured **Dubai Transport** taxis. Hotel taxis are more expensive but are reliable.
Dubai Transport taxis, tel: 04-313131, are reliable, safe and metered. You can phone and ask them to pick you up.

Water Taxi or Abra Dubai is split in two by the creek, use an abra or water taxi to get across. This is an atmospheric short journey of about five minutes. The abra stands on the Deira side are opposite the gold souq and near the Inter-Continental Hotel. On the Bur Dubai side, go from the quay near to the Captain's Stores next to the British Bank. Abras can also be hired for up to an hour for a personal trip up and down the creek.

SHARJAH

Bus No bus service.
Service Taxi There are two stations. From Al Arouba Road opposite Al Hamra Cinema they go to Umm Al Qaiwain and Ras Al Khaimah. The other station is next to the vegetable souq near Khalid Lagoon near the amusement park. To reach the nearby emirates of Ajman or Dubai it is often easier to get an ordinary taxi.
Taxi Non-metered taxis only.

AJMAN

There is no bus service or taxi stand. It is easy to get a Sharjah taxi to or from here.

UMM AL QAIWAIN

Taxis only, from the stand on King Faisal Street across from Al Salam Hotel.

RAS AL KHAIMAH

Bus No bus service.
Service taxi The station is located on King Faisal Street near the Bin Majid Beach Hotel. Taxis go from here to Dubai, passing Umm Al Qaiwain, Ajman and Sharjah on the way. Change in Dubai for Abu Dhabi, Al Ain and the east coast.
Taxi Non-metered taxis only.

FUJAIRAH

Bus No bus service.
Service taxi The stand is on the edge of town, west of the airport on the road to Sharjahi.
Taxi Non-metered taxisonly.

Private Transport

The UAE has very efficient traffic systems and is generally a safe place to drive, but it's advisable to try and get into lane early as trying to cross fast-moving four-lane traffic is not for the faint-hearted! Speed limits are generally adhered to on the residential roads. However, once out on the main highways cars do travel fast. Roads are mainly dual-carriageway, well-signposted and in good condition.

Any accident, however minor, must be reported to the police. In most of the emirates you must not move the car until the police arrive. In Dubai, cars can be moved to the side of the road if they are blocking traffic and if the accident is not serious. Always wait with the car for the police.

Rules of the Road

- Drive on the right-hand side of the road.
- No right turns at lights.
- Speed limits are normally 60 kph in town and 100 kph on highways.
- Speeding tickets are often issued automatically by camera, without the driver knowing. Car rental agencies claim these from you.
- Always carry your driving licence with you.

Inter-emirate Travel This is unrestricted and easy by road. There are no check-points or passport controls to go through between emirates. Sometimes the police do spot checks on the road for illegal immigrants or alcohol, although this is relatively rare. It is advisable to carry your papers on you while travelling in the UAE.
Car Hire Hiring a car makes travelling around much easierespecially in the very hot summer. Most car-hire companies will accept foreign licences if you have a visit or transit visa. Hire costs are relatively low, and there is fierce competition between companies so a good bargain can be found.

ABU DHABI

Avis, Al Nasr Street (near British Embassy), tel: 02-323760.
Budget (behind British Embassy), tel: 02-334200.
Europcar, Istiqlal Street (behind Abu Dhabi Chamber of Commerce), tel: 02-319922.

DUBAI

Avis, Deira (near the Emirates petrol station, near the Clocktower Roundabout), tel: 04-282121.
Budget, Airport Road (opposite Federal Express International), tel: 04-823030.
Europcar, Bur Dubai (opposite Ramada Hotel in Al Rais Building), tel: 04-520033.

SHARJAH

Autorent, Al Wahda Street (opposite Wonderworld shop), tel: 06-590333.
Avis, King Faisal Street (opposite British Bank of Middle East), tel: 06-280437.
Budget, King Faisal Street (opposite Nova Park Hotel), tel: 06-373600.

RAS AL KHAIMAH

Gulf Rent-a-Car, tel: 07-222674.

FUJAIRAH

Avis, tel: 09-222021.

Specialist Tours

The main areas of interest to the tourist are exploring all the emirates and discovering the desert, the wadis and the mountains. It is dangerous to go off-road with only one vehicle, or in a group with no desert experience. You may feel safer contacting one of the tour groups operating in the emirates and tours on offer range from day trips to overnight stays.

ABU DHABI

Adventures Unlimited, tel: 03-687458. Al Ain Inter·Continental Hotel. Ex SAS-run, offers dune-bashing, rock-climbing, hang-gliding and other pursuits.
Al Ain Camel Safari, tel: 03-688006. Al Ain Inter·Continental Hotel. Camel safaris with overnight stays in the desert.
Blue Dolphin, tel: 02-669392. Le Meridien Hotel. Dhow trips with barbecues, fishing and diving.
Falcon Tours, tel: 02-776775. Electra Street, opposite Salem Studio. Desert and mountain safaris. Dhow cruises.
Net Tours and Travels, tel: 02-794656. Khalifa Street, next to TNT, near to Sheraton Hotel. Desert safaris, golf packages, half- and full-day tours.
Sunshine Tours, tel: 02-449914. Next to Gulf Hotel near Mercedes showroom. Four-wheel-drives, sand-skiing, camel rides and inter-emirate tours.

DUBAI

Arabian Adventures, tel: 04-317373. Sheikh Zayed Street, Al Moosa Tower. City tours, east coast safaris, desert dinners.
Coastline Leisure, tel: 04-450867. From Deira docks opposite Sheraton Hotel. Dhow trips and dinner on board.
Desert Rangers, tel: 04-453091/460808. Satwa High Street, Dune Centre. Canoe, mountain bikes, outward bound.
Net Tours, tel: 04-666655. Deira, near DNATA centre. Dhow trips, desert barbecues and trips to the other emirates.

SHARJAH

Emirates Tours, tel: 06-351411. Opposite Sharjah Cinema.
Orient Tours, tel: 06-549333. Al Aruba Street. Dune surfing.
SNTTA, tel: 06-548296. Al Aruba Street, opposite Sharjah Cinema. All types of tours.

Where to Stay

Booking a Hotel

Generally, hotels in the UAE are not cheap and cater for business travellers and tour groups rather than individual budget travellers. If you are travelling independently, it is possible to find cheaper hotels, although they are still expensive compared with cheap accommodation in other countries.

At the time of writing, single women cannot book a hotel room unless they are part of a group or on business and can produce a company letter to prove it. Women would be advised to check on this before arrival as it is subject to change.

In the price guides below, the lower figure gives an indication of the rates charged for a single room, and the higher figure for a double. However, these prices do vary according to season and length of stay. An extra charge of 15–20 percent (tax/service) is sometimes added, so it's worth checking whether this has been included or not.

Abu Dhabi

Al Ain Palace Hotel£££ Tel: 02-794777, fax: 02-795713. Located on the Corniche, the first hotel built in Abu Dhabi. There are chalets around the pool as well as other rooms, suites and a health club. Access to nearby Lulu Island resort.
Baynunah Hilton Tower£££ Tel: 02-32777, fax: 02-216777. On the Corniche, near the British Embassy. Of soaring blue glass, this is the tallest and most striking building in Abu Dhabi. Has luxurious self-catering rooms and apartments. World-class hotel catering for the longer-term guest. It also has a very good shopping centre, business and fitness centres, and one of the best conference venues in town.
Beach Hotel Abu Dhabi£££ Tel: 02-743000, fax: 02-742111. Next to ADMA-OPCO offices in the Tourist Club area. Set on its own beach in the centre of town. All rooms are sea-facing with their own balcony. Has excellent restaurants and business centre.
Forte Grand Hotel£££ Tel: 02-742020, fax: 02-7050434. On Khalifa Street near the Corniche. Smart five-star hotel, of spectacular height, overlooking the Corniche and surroundings. Wonderful views especially from the revolving rooftop restaurant, Al Fanar. The hotel shares an excellent pool and sun-lounging area with the Al Ain Palace. Has indoor gymnasium and access to offshore Lulu Island beach via boat transfer.
Hilton International Hotel£££ Tel: 02-661900, fax: 02-669696. Beside ADNOC offices on the Corniche, next to the Inter.Continental Hotel. One of Abu Dhabi's oldest five-star hotels, and much improved after a dramatic expansion a few years ago. The Jazz Bar, Hemingways, is one of the most popular gathering spots in town. The hotel is opposite one of the best areas of beach in Abu

Price Categories

For Abu Dhabi Hotels:
● Expensive£££ = Dhs500-850/room.
● Moderate££ = Dhs350-600/room.
● Inexpensive£ = Dhs200-400/room.

Dhabi and has easy access to the beach club.

Hotel Inter·Continental£££ Tel: 02-666888, fax: 02-669153. On the Corniche. Has one of the best sea locations in town, at the western end of the Corniche. All rooms have sea views and the hotel is surrounded by gardens. It has a beach resort with a wide range of water sports. Has been a regular venue for the GCC summit meetings. Excellent facilities.

Le Meridien£££ Tel: 02-776666, fax: 02-729315. Near the Tourist Club and Co-operative Society at the end of Electra Road. The Meridien underwent a major overhaul in 1997, and is now one of Abu Dhabi's top hotels. The Waka Tau cocktail bar and restaurant, overlooking the sea channels to the north of Abu Dhabi island, is one of Abu Dhabi's meeting places. Has its own beach and leisure resort.

Sheraton Abu Dhabi Resort and Tower£££ Tel: 02-773333, fax: 02-725149. On the Corniche, next to the Corniche Hospital. Efficient and business-like, with renowned business centre. For the non-businessperson it also has the well-established Its Tavern is a major hub of social life. Near the city centre, with a beach resort, shopping arcade and one of the biggest ballrooms in town.

Al Hamra Plaza Residence££ Tel: 02-725000, fax: 02-766338. On Electra Street opposite Eldorado Cinema. Centrally located, with apartments available to let as well as rooms.

Price Categories

For Abu Dhabi Hotels:
- Expensive£££ = Dhs500-850/room
- Moderate££ = Dhs350-600/room
- Inexpensive£ = Dhs200-400/room

Holiday Apartments

Estate agents often have apartments for short lets.

ABU DHABI

Corniche Residence Tel: 02-276000, fax: 02-270099. Corniche Road opposite large water fountain.

Dalma Centre Tel: 02-32100, fax: 02-329228. Hamdan Street, same building as British Bank of the Middle East.

Habara House Tel: 02-431010, fax: 02-432885. Old Airport Road, opposite Akai building.

DUBAI

Asteco Property Management Tel: 04-693155, fax: 04-692548. Office in Deira on Abu Baker Al Siddiq Street, in The Centre.

Corniche Residence Hilton££ Tel: 02-276000, fax: 02-270099. On the Corniche near to the Volcano Fountain. All rooms have cooking facilities which make this a good place for the long-term visitor. A rooftop restaurant offers wonderful views and the Café Cappuccino is a good meeting place.

Holiday Inn Crowne Plaza££ Tel: 02-210000, fax: 02-217444. In the middle of town on Sheikh Hamdan Street. Rooms for non-smokers and disabled, and also a special Japanese floor. Three floors of executive rooms with business facilities. Sports facilities include a rooftop pool and access to beach.

Novotel Centre Hotel££ Tel: 02-333555, fax: 02-343633. On Sheikh Hamdan Street in the middle of town. It has a French feel, with many bars and bistros. Outdoor pool and fitness centre.

Airport Hotel£ Tel: 02-757377, fax: 02-757458. At Abu Dhabi airport. Ideal for those making a short stopover. Fitness centre and children's playroom.

Golden Sands c/o Arenco Estate Agents Tel: 04-72402/514732, fax: 04-375335/516832. Arenco have offices in Karama (on Al Zabeel Road, next to the General Post Office) and in Golden Sands Building No. 3.

Property Shop Tel: 04-494214, fax: 04-449553. Office is in Merkaz Al Jumeira Plaza on the Beach Road, Jumeira.

Royal Plaza Tel: 04-236444, fax: 04-218326. Al Rigga Street, behind Abu Dhabi Commercial Bank.

Trade Centre Apartments Tel: 04-314555, fax: 04-313800. Next to the Hilton Hotel on the Abu Dhabi/Dubai Rood.

Khalidiya Palace Hotel£ Tel: 02-662470, fax: 02-660411. Between the Inter·Continental Hotel and the Ladies Beach. Lovely beachfront location. Water sports and a swimming pool. Excellent oriental restaurants.

Zakher Hotel£ Tel: 02-275940, fax: 02-272270. In the middle of town. Very lively hotel full of good restaurants and late-night discos.

Federal Hotel£ Tel: 02-789000, fax: 02-794728. Khalifa Street, in front of Forte Grand Hotel. A small hotel with only 18 rooms, conveniently located in the middle of town.

Al Ain

Al Ain Hilton£££ Tel: 03-686666, fax: 03-686888. Al Sarooj Street, near the Museum. An oasis of lush gardens with a backdrop of mountains. A luxury hotel with all sports facilities. Ideal base for exploring the area. Tour groups operate from this hotel for camel-trekking and wadi-bashing.

Inter·Continental Al Ain£££ Tel: 03-686686, fax: 03-686766. Niadat Street, near the Mazead Roundabout. Luxury hotel with huge landscaped gardens and all sports facilities.

Dubai

Forte Grand Airport£££ Tel: 04-824040, fax: 04-825540. Situated opposite Dubai International Airport. Lush gardens and a shaded swimming pool. Good sports facilities.
Forte Grand Jumeira Beach£££ Tel: 04-845555, fax: 04-846999. Dubai/Abu Dhabi Highway interchange No. 5. In Jumeira area, away from the city centre. Facilities include its own beach, landscaped gardens and swimming pool.
Hilton Hotel£££ Tel: 04-314000, fax: 04-313383. Next to the World Trade Centre. Business-oriented hotel, with usual Hilton facilities plus a popular coffee shop. The lobby makes a pleasant meeting place for tea. Excellent chocolate and cake shop, as well as a good pub.
Hyatt Regency Hotel£££ Tel: 04-731234, fax: 04-713868. On the Corniche Road, Deira. Adjoins a shopping mall, with cinema and fitness centre. Lively place with revolving rooftop restaurant and a popular pub.
Inter·Continental Hotel£££ Tel: 04-227171, fax: 04-284777. In Deira, on Baniyas Street. Overlooking the creek near the centre of Deira, with a fish restaurant and a popular jazz club. Excellent Italian terrace restaurant.
Jebel Ali Hotel£££ Tel: 04-835252, fax: 04-835543. Beyond Jebel Ali freezone area. A spectacular hotel next to the sea. Enormous gardens, palm trees on the beach, marina and wonderful restaurants. One of the most attractive hotels in Dubai, 40 minutes' drive from the city centre.

Price Categories

For Dubai Hotels:
● Expensive£££ = Dhs500–850/room
● Moderate££ = Dhs350–600/room
● Inexpensive£ = Dhs250–400/room

J.W. Marriott£££ Tel: 04-624444, fax: 04-626264. Abu Baker Al Siddiq Road in Deira, opposite Dubai Cinema. Huge lobby and a very good American bar. Restaurants include steak house and Italian restaurant.
Metropolitan Hotel£££ Tel: 04-440000, fax: 04-441146. On the Abu Dhabi Road near the World Trade Centre. Business hotel with cinemas and good restaurants.
Royal Abjar£££ Tel: 04-625555, fax: 04-697358. Deira, on Salahadin Street. Hosts many shows and is a major meeting place.
Sheraton Hotel£££ Tel: 04-281111, fax: 04-213468. Opposite Etisalat Building on Deira creekside. Interesting building with attractive atrium and a waterfall running through the lobby. The dhows are moored close by.
Chicago Beach Hotel££ Tel: 04-480000, fax: 04-482273. Beach Road, Umm Sequiem. Spectacular new building, with wonderful location on the beach. Has become popular with tour groups. Has sports facilities, swimming pools and restaurants. Out of town.
Dubai Marine Hotel££ Tel: 04-520900,fax: 04-521035. Bur Dubai, between Ramada Hotel and Falcon Roundabout on Khalid bin Waleed Street. Central location but with access to a beach club in Jumeira. Has a popular English-style pub called Thatchers.
Ramada Hotel££ Tel: 04-521010, fax: 04-521033. Bur Dubai, Al Mankhool Street near

Spinneys Supermarket. Particularly convenient for the souq. Has one of the largest stained glass windows in the Middle East as a design feature in the lobby.
Airport Hotel£ Tel: 04-823464, fax: 04-823781. Near the airport, opposite cargo village. Excellent value. Has a popular Italian restaurant with terrace, lively pub and good sports facilities.
Al Khaleej Hotel£ Tel: 04-211144, fax: 04-237140. Deira, Al Nasr Square beside Emirates Bank International.
Ambassador Hotel£ Tel: 04-531000, fax: 04-534751. Al Falah Street, Bur Dubai, near British Bank. Right in the heart of Dubai, near the souq and convenient for the abras.
Astoria£ Tel: 04-534300, fax: 04-535665. In the middle of the Bur Dubai souq area. Has lively nightlife at Panchos, a Tex-Mex restaurant with band.
Baisan Residence£ Tel: 04-554545, fax: 04-551707. Behind Ramada Hotel, Bur Dubai. Used as a hotel and as holiday apartments. A long-stay option. Swimming pool. Restaurant, no bar. Bus to beach.
Carlton Tower Hotel£ Tel: 04-227111, fax: 04-228249. Deira, Baniyas Road, after Dubai Intercontinental Hotel.
Deira Park Hotel£ Tel: 04-239922, fax: 04-239893. Near Fish Roundabout. Has a courtesy bus to take visitors to the Jumeira public beach. Restaurant but no bar.
Dubai Park Hotel£ Tel: 04-487111, fax: 04-487222. Dubai/Abu Dhabi Road opposite Emirates Golf Club. Good value. Has popular Irish pub.
Palm Beach£ Tel: 04-525550, fax: 04-528320. Khalid bin Waleed Street in Bur Dubai. Offers value for money.
Rimal Residence£ Tel: 04-688000, fax: 04-688777.

On Muraghabat Road near the Marriott Hotel. Has a bus shuttle into town. Doesn's serve alcohol but has a restaurant and self-catering facilities. Recommended simple hotel.

HATTA

Hatta Fort Hotel££/£££ Tel: 085-23211, fax: 085-23561. Hatta is in Dubai emirate 105 km (65 miles) from Dubai city, near the Hajar Mountains. This hotel is clearly signposted at the town's main roundabout. A wonderful resort hotel offering peace and quiet. Bar and dining area overlook the pool, with spectacular views of the surrounding mountains. Chalet-style rooms with huge views. Many sports including archery, golf and safaris.

Sharjah

There are many reasonably priced beach-side hotels in Sharjah. The city is only 30 minutes' drive from Dubai and it is well-located for the northern and eastern emirates. Alcohol is not sold in any of Sharjah's hotels.

Continental Hotel£££ Tel: 06-371111, fax: 06-524090. On the Corniche. One of the best hotels in town. Near the dhows and the souq area. Good coffee shop.

Hotel Holiday International£££ Tel: 06-357357, fax: 06-372254. Located onBouhara Corniche beside Marbella Club.

Sharjah Carlton Hotel££ Tel: 06-283711, fax: 06-284962. In Al Khan, Port Road near Grand Hotel.

Price Categories

For Sharjah Hotels:
● Expensive£££ = Dhs400-650/room
● Moderate££ = Dhs300–450/room
● Inexpensive£ = Dhs200–300/room.

Beach Hotel£ Tel: 06-358311, fax: 06-525422. Port Road, Al Khan area.
Coral Beach Hotel£ Tel: 06-221011, fax: 06-274101. Corniche Road towards Ajman. Beside Ajman Roundabout.

Summerland Apartments£ Tel: 06-281321, fax: 06-280745. Al Khan area, Port Road opposite the Beach Hotel. Used as a hotel and as holiday apartments. A long-stay option.

Ajman

Ajman Beach Hotel£ Tel: 06-423333, fax: 06-423363. On the Creek Road. Has a casino.

Ras Al Khalmah

Ras Al Khaimah Hotel£/££ Tel: 07-362999, fax: 07-362990. Located in the Khozan area, close to the Corniche. 4 km (2¹/₂ miles) from Clocktower Roundabout.

East Coast

The east coast with its beautiful beaches and mountainous backdrop is a wonderful place to spend a few quiet, relaxing days beside the sea.

Price Categories

For East Coast Hotels:
● Expensive£££ = Dhs350-500/room
● Moderate££ = Dhs300-490/chalet

Hilton International Fujairah£££ Tel: 09-222411, fax: 09-226541. Enjoys good position right on the beach. An excellent fish barbecue is held on Fridays. A lovely garden surrounds the swimming pool.

Oceanic Hotel, Khor Fakkan£££ Tel: 09-385111, fax: 09-387716. Corniche Road, Khor

Camping

There are no official campsites in the UAE, but it's possible to camp almost anywhere in the desert and mountain areas. It's better not to camp too close to a village or town, and to beware of camping or driving in wadi beds during the rainy season.

Hire a four-wheel-drive but it's safer not to go alone. It's also wise to tell someone where you're going and when you're planning to come back, and take lots of water, spare petrol and a map. There are various books on sale in larger supermarkets advising routes to follow (*see Armchair Traveller, page 311*).

Camping equipment is widely available in the shops, and it's a sensible idea to add a rope and a shovel to the usual list – to get you out of deep sand should you suddenly sink up to your axles!

Fakkan. Diving centre for the area.

Sandy Beach Motel££ Tel: 09-445354, fax: 09-445207. On the beach in front of an island, between Dibba and Khor Fakkan. Quiet un-glitzy chalets on the beach. Self-catering with a good restaurant. Barbecues are provided but you take your own charcoal or buy it locally. Take towels. Very good for diving, and expeditions can be organised. Offshore island that you can walk to at low tide. Backdrop of high mountains.

Where to Eat

What to Eat

The eating-out choice is huge in the UAE. You can find dishes from almost anywhere in the world, either in small, sometimes quite basic, unlicensed eating houses or in larger, more lavish, licensed hotel restaurants. Standards of hygiene are high and even the simple restaurants are clean as inspections are frequent and the penalties severe.

The Arabic convenience foods such as *shawarmas* (meat cooked on a vertical spit, then sliced, topped with tahini or yogurt and salad, served in pitta bread and eaten like a sandwich), or *falafel* (deep-fried chick-pea balls, served in paper bags from street vendors), make cheap and delicious snacks on the move.

Lebanese and Arabic food is delicious. The meal usually begins with an array of small dishes, the *mezze*, followed by a main course of grilled meat or fish. These restaurants often offer good-value lunchtime specials, and the quantities are usually very generous. Puddings often include nuts, syrup and fresh cream. Finish with Arabic coffee or peppermint tea.

Freshly squeezed fruit and vegetable juices or sodas accompany meals in unlicensed premises. If you do want to drink alcohol with your meal, there are plenty of hotel restaurants to choose from but the prices are higher. These restaurants are often luxuriously decorated and have first-class chefs. There are

often specials for a short while, which can offer memorable tastes and sometimes include special entertainment. Look out for details in the local press.

Price Categories

For Abu Dhabi Restaurants (per head):
- Expensive£££L= Dhs100–150 (licensed).
- Moderate££L = Dhs50–100 (licensed).
- Moderate££U = Dhs50–100 (unlicensed).
- Inexpensive£U = Dhs30–50 (unlicensed)
- Cafés CU (unlicensed).

Abu Dhabi

Alamo Bar and Restaurant£££L Abu Dhabi Marina Club Tel: 02-721300. Live entertainment and music while you eat. Very popular.

Al Fanar£££L Forte Grand Hotel Tel: 02-742020. A revolving rooftop restaurant with good views – seafood and grills.

Al Mansouri Dhow£££L Forte Grand Hotel Tel: 02-742020. A romantic dinner cruise.

Amalfi£££L Forte Grand Hotel Tel: 02-742020. Good Italian.

The Fish Market£££L Inter-Continental Hotel Tel: 02-666888. Memorable restaurant. Designed to be like a fish market on the beach. Select your fish and specify how you want it cooked.

King Creole£££L Sheraton Hotel Tel: 02-773333. New Orleans Cajun. Beside the beach.

The Pearl£££L Hilton Hotel Tel: 02-661900. Elegant and sophisticated, and specialising in French cuisine.

The Spice Garden£££L Sheraton Hotel Tel: 02-773333. Far Eastern bistro serving spicy Asian food. Terrace overlooking the sea.

Trader Vic's£££L Beach Hotel. Tel: 02-743000. French

Polynesian. One of the city's favourite places. Exotic menu with oriental and South-Sea-Island specialities. Inside, but overlooking the beach.

Waka Tau£££L Le Meridien Tel: 02-776666. Polynesian cuisine. Beside the sea. Outside terrace as well as inside. Excellent cocktails.

Hotel Coffee Shops£££L All the main hotels have licensed coffee shops.

Abu Shakra££U Tel: 02-313400. Istiqal Street (opposite Europcar); Electra Road (near Holiday Inn). Arabic cuisine, including kebabs, grills and good selection of *mezze*.

Abu Tafish Floating Restaurant££U Tel: 02-666331. Bateen area, dhow harbour. Dhow restaurant serving delicious grilled fish.

Al Dhafra Restaurant££U Tel: 02-732266. Mina Free-Port area. Dhow restaurant with good grilled fish and meats.

Al Safina Dhow Restaurant££U Tel: 02-662085. Corniche breakwater. Good food and atmosphere.

Al Sofon Dhow Restaurant££U Tel: 02-655135. Corniche breakwater. Another of Abu Dhabi's recommended dhow eateries.

Golden Fish££U Tel: 02-661091. Khalidia Street (next to Mothercare). Long-established and excellent fish restaurant. Also does good grills and Arabic food.

Istanbouli££U Tel: 02-333874. Old Passport Road. Grills, fish and Arabic mezze.

Tarbouche££U Tel: 02-216828. Hamdan Street (near the City Centre Shopping Mall, opposite British Home Stores). Arabic food.

Anand's Vegetarian Restaurant£U Tel: 02-775599. Hamdan Street (near Automatic Restaurant).

Kwality Restaurant£U Tel: 02-727337. On Salam Street.

Royal Arab Udupi£U
Tel: 02-743485.
Hamdan Street (behind Shakeys
Pizza).
Woodside Restaurant£U Tel: 02-
792419. Tourist Club. South
Indian vegetarian. Dhosas and
rice dishes.
Al Ajami CU Khalidia Street (next
to Abela Supermarket).
La Brioche CUCorniche Road
(near ZADCO).
La Chaumine CU Khalifa Street.
Seaside Patisserie CU Salam
Street.

<u>AL AIN</u>
Al Khayam££L Hilton Hotel Tel:
03-686666. Persian.
**Thai Fish Market
Restaurant**££L Inter-Continental
Hotel Tel: 03-686686. The fish
is laid out on ice. You choose
your own and the type of sauce,
and it's cooked to order.
Golden Gate Restaurant£U
Chinese and Filipino.

Price Catagories

**For Al Ain Restaurants
(per head):**
● Moderate££L= Dhs50–100
(licensed in hotels).
● Inexpensive£U = Dhs30–50
(unlicensed).

Dubai

Le Ciel£££L Inter-Continental
Tel: 04-227171 French–
excellent. Pick an alcove in the
window for a panorama of the
creek.
Ciros Pizza Pomodoro£££L
Royal Abjar Hotel Tel: 04-
625555. Live music and packed
every night. A fun place to go.
Cucina£££L J.W. Marriott Tel:
04-624444. Italian. Light and
fresh food.
Dynasty£££L Ramada Hotel Tel:
04-521010.
Quality Chinese restaurant.
Cantonese and Szechuan food.
The Fish Market£££L
Inter-Continental Tel: 04-

227171. Choose your fish and
the way you want it cooked.
Huge windows give a view across
the creek. Restaurant has
interesting aquariums and a
glass panelled kitchen so you
can see the chefs in action.
JW's Steakhouse£££L J.W.
Marriott Tel: 04-624444. Grills
with an American slant. Cooked
under a flame and prepared
exactly as you like. Very good
wine list. Clubby decor: lots of
panelled wood and huge deep
leather chairs.
Lou Lou's£££L Sheraton Hotel
Tel: 04-2071717. French.
Window seats with views over
the creek. A very plush
restaurant. Cordon bleu food
using lots of cream and rich
sauces.
Summer Palace£££L
Metropolitan Hotel Tel: 04-
84500. Chinese. Lovely room
and delicious food. Aromatic
duck is a house speciality. Can
cater for large parties.
Boardwalk££L Creek Golf Club
Tel: 04-821000. On the creek.
Sit outside under an umbrella
and watch the yachts, dhows
and abras go by. Salads and
oriental dishes, Mexican tastes
and toasted sandwiches. Lovely
place to watch the sun go down.
Café Insigna££L Ramada Hotel
Tel: 04-521010. Continental
style wine bar with interesting
food. Walls are hung with local
art, all of which is for sale. If you
feel so inclined you can scribble
on the table cloths and you may
win a prize. Reminiscent of a
Parisian café with wrought-iron
tables and many potted trees.
Coconut Grove££L Plaza Hotel.
Tel: 04-454545. Delicious food
in a room full of Indian artefacts.
Spicy curries from south India,
with Goan influences.
Da Vinci's££L
Airport Hotel Tel: 04-823464.
Homely Italian restaurant. Very
popular. Reasonable prices and
friendly staff. Trattoria decor.
Has an outside patio which is
enclosed in the summer. The

Fish Bazaar££L Metropolitan
Hotel Tel: 04-8450000. Choose
your fish and have it cooked to
taste. Pleasant room, windows
overlooking the main highway to
Abu Dhabi and further across Al
Safa Park. Very pleasant
Shahjahan££L Metropolitan

Price Catagories

**For Dubai Restaurants
(per head):**
● Expensive#£££L=
Dhs100–200 (licensed).
● Moderate££L = Dhs50–100
(licensed).
● Moderate££U = Dhs50–100
(unlicensed).
● Inexpensive£U = Dhs30–50
(unlicensed).
● Cafés CU (unlicensed).

Hotel Tel: 04-8450000. North
Indian cuisine, served in a light
and airy room. Live Indian music
in the evening.
TGI Thursdays££L Astoria Hotel
Tel: 04-534300. Emphasis on
burgers and steaks. Young and
fun.
Wok Night££L Sheraton Hotel
Tel: 04-281111. Japanese.
Choose your ingredients from a
huge display and watch them
being cooked in front of you. Fun
and delicious.
Hotel Coffee Shops££L All the
main hotels have licensed
coffee shops.
Automatic££U Tel: 04-277824
(Rigga Street); 04-494888 (The
Beach Centre in Jumeira).
Delicious Lebanese food. Both
branches are always full of
people enjoying these
unpretentious but very good
restaurants. Great value and
huge helpings.
China Garden££U Tel: 04-
440253. Next to Spinneys
Supermarket in Jumeira. Good
Chinese food in a small friendly
restaurant.
Pars Iranian Kitchen££U Tel: 04-
452222. Satwa Roundabout.
Excellent choice of authentic
Iranian dishes.

Drinking

You cannot buy alcohol for home consumption in the UAE unless you hold an alcohol licence. These are only issued to non-Muslims with residence visas. However, alcohol is served in hotel bars and restaurants in most of the emirates, apart from Sharjah. There are many excellent pubs, bars and discos (*see Nightlife, page 303*).

Chappan Bhog£U Tel: 04-364176. Trade Centre Road. Traditional vegetarian Indian food is served upstairs. Indian sweet shop downstairs.
Johnny Rockets£U Tel: 04-447859. Opposite Magrudy Shopping Mall in Jumeira. 1950s-style American diner. Rock'n'roll and hamburgers.
Mini Chinese£U
Tel: 04-459976.
Satwa High Street. Busy with good food to eat in or take away. Clean and quick service.
Pizza Corner£U
Tel: 04-222671.
Creek Road. One of the first pizza restaurants in Dubai. On the creek in Deira. Huge choice friendly service. A good place to go before shopping around Al Nasr Square and the souq.
Ravis£U
Tel: 04 -15353. Satwa. Delicious *dal*, *chappattis* and tandoori chicken. Excellent value.
The Kitchen£U
Tel: 04-453043.
Satwa (turn down alley near Hardees). A huge menu including Indian and Chinese. Small, heavily decorated restaurant, with bread oven downstairs.
Woodlands£U
Tel: 04-370253.Karama. Specialities include south Indian *dhosas* and rice dishes. Huge amounts of food for amazing low prices. Basic decor and tin crockery. Clean surroundings and delicious food.
Café de Paris CU

Tel: 04-451418.
Satwa High Street. Very popular people-watching place. Delicious croissants and cappuccino.
Café des Pyramids CU
Tel: 04-346866.
Wafi Shopping Mall.
On the upper level, with light flooding down from the atrium roof. A quiet retreat from the designer shoppers.
Café Wein CU
Tel: 04-448001.
Beach Centre Mall, Jumeira. Fountains splash among the trees that surround this quiet oasis serving Austrian dishes.

Price Catagories

For Dubai Restaurants (per head):
● Expensive#£££L= Dhs100–200 (licensed).
● Moderate££L = Dhs50–100 (licensed).
● Moderate££U = Dhs50–100 (unlicensed).
● Inexpensive£U = Dhs30–50 (unlicensed).
● CafésCU (unlicensed).

Gelato CU
Tel: 04-451685.
Dune Centre, Satwa High Street. Attracts a young clientèle and stays open late. Outside tables.
Gerrards CU
Tel: 04-228637 (Al Ghurair Centre); 04-443327 (Magrudy Shopping Mall).
Very popular cafés to stop at for a croissant and a cappuccino. The one at Magrudy has an outside area which is pleasant in the cooler months.

Sharjah

Al Khaima£££U
Lou Lou Hotel Tel: 06-285000. Arabic tent setting with live music in the evenings.
Caesar's Palace£££U
Marbella Resort Tel: 06-357123.
Stylish setting. Good pizzas.

Le Petit Suisse£££U
Beach Hotel Tel: 06-281311. View over the Gulf. International cuisine.
Al Fawar££U
Tel: 06-593739.
King Faisal Street. Excellent Lebanese restaurant with good *mezze*. Has a good-value buffet on Friday.
Arous Al Bahar££U
Tel: 06-727335.
Khalid Lagoon. Arabic atmospere and pleasant setting next to the water. Traditional Iranian and Lebanese dishes.
The Dhow££U
Tel: 06-730222.
Khalid Lagoon. Two-tier floating restaurant with Lebanese cuisine.
The Mandarin££U
Tel: 06-355284.
Mina Street. Excellent Chinese food. Has some private rooms.
The Peking££U
Tel: 06-545666.
Al Qassimia Roundabout. An intimate candlelit restaurant serving excellent seafood specialities.
Sanobar££U
Tel: 06-593739.
Al Khan Road. Family-run seafood restaurant.
Fresh Chicken£U
Tel: 06-357800.
Al Estiqlal Road. Simple take-away ofering grilled chicken and salad.
Deeva Leena£U
Tel: 06-357161.
Al Zahra Road. Indian.
Al Arsah Public Coffee Shop CU
Tel: 06-540903.

Price Catagories

For Sharjah Restaurants (per head):
● Expensive£££U = Dhs75+ (unlicensed).
● Moderate££U= Dhs25–75 (unlicensed).
● Inexpensive£U = Dhs25 (unlicensed).
● CafésCU (unlicensed).

Heritage Souq. Authentic Arabian coffee shop. Ask for menu details and advice. Excellent location.
Al Gahwa Al Shaabiya CU
Tel: 06-723788.
Khalid Lagoon. *Barasti* (palm-frond) setting with open section on waterfront. No sign at the front. Soak up the traditional atmosphere and sample the local dishes.
Café Internet CU
Tel: 06-534238.
Khalid Lagoon. If you want (or need) to cruise the Internet, you can do it here. Appropriately located under the computer school.
GerrardsCU
Tel: 06-722045.
Khalid Lagoon. Come here in the morning for delicious croissants and coffee.

East Coast

The main places to eat are the hotel restaurants.
Fujairah Hilton (Tel: 09-222411) serves a Friday seafood buffet in the gardens by the sea.
Oceanic Hotel at Khor Fakkan (Tel: 09-385111) has an international buffet restaurant with wonderful sea views.

Culture

Music & Dance

There are not many concerts or dance performances in the UAE although performers do come and give concerts in the larger hotels. Also, many bands and groups perform in night clubs and bars. Concerts and public performances are advertised in the local press and on local FM radio stations.

Art Galleries

ABU DHABI
The Cultural Foundation, tel: 02-215300.
Often has exhibitions. Look in the local newspapers for details.
DUBAI
Al Abbar Art Gallery, tel: 04-449207.
Beach Centre Shopping Mall. Sells prints and originals.
Creative Arts Centre, tel: 04-442303.
Jumeira. Runs art classes and sells local artists' work.
Dubai International Arts Centre, tel: 04-444398.
Jumeira. Runs art classes and sells local artists' work.
Green Art Gallery, tel: 04-449888. Off Jumeira Beach Road. Exhibits and sells quality paintings.

Theatre

There are seasonal visits by travelling groups who put on dinner theatre in the major hotels and advertise in the local press. There are also very active amateur dramatic groups who stage productions.

London Frameworks, tel: 04-526639.
Bur Juman Shopping Mall. Sells mainly prints.
Majlis Gallery, tel: 04-536233.
Bastikyia area in Bur Dubai. In a beautifully restored Arab house in the oldest part of Dubai. Sells original art by well-known artists.
Profile Gallery, tel: 04-491147.
Has som interesting prints. Sells good quality Omani silver and antique furniture.
World Trade Centre, tel: 04-3054083. Host to many exhibitions.
SHARJAH
Sharjah Cultural Foundation, tel: 06-241238.
Qur'an Roundabout. Exhibitions, plays, films.
Sharjah Museum, tel: 06-366466.
Holds exhibitions.
Sharjah Women's Club, tel: 06-355511. Art classes and exhibitions.

Cinema

Films in English (censored) can be seen. Programme details are found in the English press.

ABU DHABI
Al Jazira, tel: 02-431116.
Old Airport Road.
Eldorado, tel: 02-763555.
Electra Road (behind Wimpy).
National, tel: 02-711700.
Electra Road.
DUBAI
Al Massa, tel: 04 -43244.
Dubai Metropolitan Hotel on Abu Dhabi Highway.
Al Nasr, tel: 04-374353.
Near Al Nasr Leisureland.
Galleria, tel: 04-2064094.
Hyatt Regency Hotel Shopping Mall.
Lamcy Plaza, tel: 04-368808.
Opposite American Hospital off Al Qutaiet Road.

SHARJAH
Al Hamra, tel: 06-523953.
Rolla Square.

Nightlife

Pubs and Bars

ABU DHABI

Ally Pally, Al Ain Hotel, tel: 02-794777.
Long-established pub. Holds quiz nights and has a special curry lunch on Thursday.
Columbia Café, Beach Hotel, tel: 02-743000.
Pianist.
Finnegans, Forte Grand, tel: 02-742020.
Irish pub with live entertainment.
The Tavern, Sheraton Hotel, tel: 02-773333. English style, good food. Has theme nights. A very popular meeting place.
Waka Taua, Le Meridien, tel: 02-776666.
Polynesian beach-front cocktail bar and restaurant.

AL AIN

Horse and Jockey, Inter-Continental Hotel, tel: 03-686686.
Lively pub. Holds quiz nights.
Pacos, Hilton Hotel, tel: 03-686666.
Pub with food, mainly burgers. Special nights with music, as advertised on the noticeboard.

DUBAI

Biggles, Airport Hotel, tel: 04-823464.
English-style pub decorated with aviation memorabilia. Good food and a popular meeting place.
Billy Blues, Plaza Hotel, tel: 04-454545.
A cowboy bar, very lively and fun with rhythm-and-blues-music. Young and friendly. Serves Tex-Mex food and steaks. Open late.
Carpenters, Hyatt Regency Hotel, tel: 04-221234.
English-type pub with food served in the evening. Friendly and lively. Filipino band.
Cheers, The Lodge, Near Al Nasr Leisureland, tel: 04-379470.
English pub with pictures of hunting scenes. Good for a quiet drink before the nearby club opens. Then it becomes very busy.
Chelsea Arms, Sheraton Hotel, tel: 04-2071721. Pleasant pub run with Irish flair. Dark panelled room with stained glass. Jazz and blues appeal to the slightly older crowd. Quality pub food.
Dubliners, Forte Grand Airport. tel: 04-824040. Irish pub with excellent music and food. Tables outside and inside.
Harvesters, Holiday Inn, tel: 04-311111. Large busy family pub with outside balcony.
Humphrey's Tavern, Hilton Hotel, tel: 04-314000.
Lunchtime pub catering for clientele from the neighbouring Trade Centre offices. Lively and popular, serving pub food.
Thatchers, Dubai Marine Hotel, tel: 04 -20900. Pub food with oriental dishes and a set meal of the day. Especially popular with business crowd.
The Pub, Inter-Continental Hotel, tel: 04-227171. Traditional English fayre. Always busy.

Nightclubs & Discos

ABU DHABI

Al Sahara, International Hotel, tel: 02-779900. Belly dancing.
Beachcombers, Abu Dhabi Marina, tel: 02-721300. Disco and barbecue.
El Paso, Inter-Continental Hotel, tel: 02-666888. Live band.
Hemingways, Holiday Inn,tel: 02-661900. Jazz club. Popular.
Odyssey Disco, Khalidiya Hotel, tel: 02-662470. DJ every night.
Scorpio Disco, International Hotel, tel: 02-779900. Live entertainment every night.
Zeno, Le Meridien, tel: 02-776666. Disco.

AL AIN

La Bamba, Inter-Continental Hotel, tel: 03-686686.
Entertainment from live Filipino band and dancers.
Samantha's, Inter-Continental Hotel, tel: 03-686686. Disco.

DUBAI

Al Mushref, St George Hotel,tel: 04-251122. Excellent late-night downtown feel. Good belly dancer. Strict door code is enforced. Pleasant atmosphere.
Al Sarab, Forte Grand Jumeira Beach, tel: 04-845555. Patrons are announced at the door. Get near the stage to see the cabaret acts including a very good belly dancer. Very Arabic feel.
Al Tannour, Holiday Inn Crowne Plaza, tel: 04-311111. Authentic Lebanese hospitality here. Traditional decor. Go late in the evening, around 11pm.
A Palmeiras, Metropolitan Hotel, tel: 04-440000. Live band.
Charlie Brown's, Plaza Hotel, tel: 04-454545. Open until 3am.
Chequers, Inter-Continental Hotel, tel: 04-227171. Resident DJ. Monthly theme evenings.
Cyclone, Al Nasr Leisureland, tel: 04-369991. Large dance area. Strict dress code enforced. Men must wear jacket and tie on the balcony. Trendy music and open very late. Packed.
Escoba, Al Khaleej Palace, tel: 04-231000. Good Lebanese cuisine and excellent belly dancer.
Hakuna Matata, Maredias Hotel, tel: 04-289393. Great

Nightlife

There is a lively nightlife in the UAE. See current listings in *What's On* magazine. Dubai is the main place for clubbing, followed by Abu Dhabi. Except in Sharjah, all the main hotels have bars and some also have entertainment. There are no bars outside hotels.

African music. Comes to life at
11pm. Wild atmosphere.
Rumours, Ramada Hotel, tel: 04-
521010. Lively, friendly,
atmospheric club.
The Lodge, Near Al Nasr
Leisureland, tel: 04-379470.
Five different bar areas merge at
midnight, with an additional
outside dance floor in the cooler
weather. Very good breakfasts.
Up On the 10th, Inter-
Continental Hotel, tel: 04-
227171. Good live jazz
performers. Downtown city feel.

Attractions

Parks and Gardens

Contrary to expectations of a
desert region, there are many
parks in the UAE. The cities are
very green with well-kept flower
beds and lawns throughout. They
are all immaculately clean and
litter is collected daily. Dogs are
not allowed in the parks or on
many beaches.
Check for ladies- and children-
only days. There are boards put
up outside the parks when it is
ladies' day. Boys usually have to
be under 10 years old.

ABU DHABI:
The Corniche
A long stretch of promenade in
the city, beside the beach and
lined with gardens. Another
corniche, with shades and
gardens, is developing along
Channel Street.
Umm Al Nar Beach Park
A short drive out of the city, next
to the Dubai Road. 10 km (6
miles) of quiet and clean beach
with grass and trees.
**Khalidiya Ladies' and Children's
Park**
Beyond the breakwater close to
the Presidential Palace,
enclosed by a high wall.
Beautiful beach.
Khalidiya Park for Families
Khalidiya Street, next to French
Gallery building, with facilities
for children.

DUBAI:
Al Khazzan Park
Between first interchange on
Sheikh Zayed Road and Al Wasl
Road. Small family park with
children's play area .

Al Mamzar Park
5 km (3 miles) after the turn-off
to Al Hamriyah Port. Has
barbecue sites, private chalets
to hire, a pool, food kiosks and a
beach with a safe swimming
area and many children's play
areas. Piped music is played
during the day and there are
grassy picnic spots.
Al Wasl Park
Off Al Wasl Road behind Iranian
Hospital. A small shaded family
park with seating and children's
play area.
Creekside Park
Bur Dubai creekside between Al
Maktoum and Al Garhoud
bridges. Entry behind Dubai
Courts. A very large park
extending for 2.5 km (1 $\frac{1}{2}$
miles) along the creek shore
with stunning views of the city
across the water. Has children's
play area, jogging paths,
barbecue sites, 18-hole mini-golf
course, fishing jetties. Well
cultivated and plenty of shade.
Jumeira Beach Park
On the Beach Road in Jumeira
next to the Hilton Beach Club.
Lush park next to clean and wide
beach. Barbecue sites,
children's play areas and food
kiosks. Lifeguard on duty. It does
get quite crowded as tourists
staying in beachless Deira-side
hotels get bused in for the day.
There's also a public bus stop
outside – No. 8 and No. 20 (ask
the driver before setting off).
Jumeira Corniche Public Beach
Off Beach Road in Jumaira, next
to Dubai Marine Beach Club.
Promenade of 800 metres (875
yards) along the seashore.
Picnic sites and playground
areas for children. Showers.
Mushrif Park
Al Awir Road past Dubai
International Airport. Large park
with separate pools for men and
women; fountain and lakes;
children's play area; train, pony
and camel rides. There is an
international area exhibiting
miniature houses from different
countries.

Safa Park
Between second interchange on Sheikh Zayed Road and Al Wasl Road, opposite Metropolitan Hotel. A large, well-established park with duck pond and many facilities for families including a huge ferris wheel, a train ride, bicycles, tennis courts, volleyball and football. Lake fed from a waterfall, with a man-made hill. Barbecue sites and individual ornamental gardens.
Umm Suqeim Park
Next to Chicago Beach Hotel in Umm Suqeim. Ladies and children only. Excellent for children, with different equipment for different age groups. An Arabic-style cafeteria and lush garden areas with tables and chairs. Opposite a wide, clean public beach.

<u>SHARJAH:</u>
Al Majaz Park. Tel: 06-446706. Between Khalid Lagoon and Jamal Abdul Nasser Street.
Jazeira Park. Tel: 06-723101. On the island in Khalid Lagoon opposite the Blue Souq. Has a train and landscaped gardens.
Sharjah National Park. At the intersection of No. 5 Sharjah/Al Dhaid Highway. Sharjah's largest park. Giant slide, duck pond, picnic and play areas.

Leisure Facilities

<u>ABU DHABI:</u>
Abu Dhabi Ice Rink. Tel: 02-448498. Off Airport Road near Zayed Sports City. Olympic-size rink with teachers on hand.

<u>AL AIN:</u>
Hili Fun Park. Tel: 03-845542 8 km (5 miles) north of Al Ain, near Hili gardens. Contains ice rink and amusement park.

<u>DUBAI:</u>
Al Boom Heritage Village. Tel: 04-523330. Complex of dhows and restaurants, including Al Boom fish restaurant, beside the creek. Replica of a traditional

building. Boat trips from here along the creek.
WonderWorld. Tel: 04-41222. Next to Al Garhoud Bridge adjoining the Creek Park. Rides and amusements for children including Waterworld, a fantastic area of water rides and pools next to the creek.
Al Nasr Leisureland. Tel: 04-371234. Near Zabeel Road. Ice rink, bowling, water slides.
Galleria Ice Skating Rink. Tel: 04-720222. Hyatt Hotel Mall.
Magic Planet. Tel: 04-284333. Deira City Centre Shopping Mall. Huge indoor area filled with rides, a soft playball park and carousel. Many fast-food restaurants around the perimeter. Great for kids.
Uncle Toby's. Tel: 04-552868. Bur Juman Shopping Mall. Indoor soft play area and ball park. Cafeteria. Separate play areas for small toddlers and for older children.
Al Khaleej Fun Corner. Tel: 04-558862. Al Khaleej Centre opposite Ramada Hotel, Bur Dubai, and at large Spinneys Supermarket on Al Wasl Road in Umm Suqeim. Indoor safe play area with castle.

<u>UMM AL QAIWAIN:</u>
Dreamland. Ras Al Khaimah Road, 17 km (10 ½ miles) past Umm Al Quwain. One of the largest water parks in the world. Fantastic rides and scenic walks for all ages. Cafés and shops.

Cruises

There are many dhow cruises available. Details from hotels or tour operators.

Zoos

<u>AL AIN:</u>
Al Ain Zoo and Aquarium. Tel: 03-828188. South of town.

<u>DUBAI:</u>
Dubai Zoo. Tel: 04-40462. On Beach Road in Jumeira.

Sport

What Sport?

There are long, deserted beaches open to the public throughout the UAE, the desert and mountains to explore, and in the cities numerous pools, sports facilities and clubs. Many independent sports clubs and hotels have gymnasiums, swimming pools and tennis courts where daily entrance rates are usually available.

Other sports available include abseiling, aquabiking, deep-sea fishing, dune-buggy driving, fishing, golf, horse racing, polo, ice skating, go-karting, sailing, sand skiing, water sports of all kinds and many many more. Horse and camel races usually take place on Thursday and Friday during the cooler winter months, and are open to everyone. Dhow sailing and racing are memorable sights – look for details in the press.

Major tournaments that attract world-class players, including golf, tennis, powerboat racing and horse racing, are also held throughout the winter months. Dates of these events and ticket office locations are advertised in the local press.

Sports Facilities

Contact the following hotels and clubs to arrange using their sports facilities for a daily fee:

<u>ABU DHABI:</u>
Abu Dhabi Beach Hotel
Tel: 02-743000.Floodlit tennis, swimming pools, water-skiing, windsurfing, boating and fishing.

Al Ain Palace Hotel.Tel: 02-794777.Health club, swimming pool.
British Club.Tel: 02-731111. Tennis and squash, private beach and swimming pool.
Forte Grand.Tel: 02-742020. Indoor pool and access to Lulu Island. Uses the facilities of the Al Ain Palace Hotel next door.
Gulf Hotel.Tel: 02-414777. Good beach with water sports. Pools, squash and a health club.
Hilton Hotel. Tel: 02-669043 Beach setting. Four interconnecting pools, water sports and fitness centre.
Hotel Inter-Continental. Tel: 02-666888. New club open in 1997. Wonderful beach, water sports and all facilities.
Sheraton Resort and Towers. Tel: 02 773232. Water sports and lovely beach. Boat excursions and scuba diving.

DUBAI:
Chicago Beach Resort. Tel: 04-480000. Beach with all water sports. Tennis courts, children's playground.
Dubai Country Club. Tel: 04-331155.Golf, pool, gym.
Dubai International Marine Club. Tel: 04-846111. Marina, scuba diving, swimming pool and squash courts.
Forte Grand Jumeira Beach. Tel: 04 -45555.Water-skiing, jetskiing, scuba-diving, swimming pools.
SAS Radisson. Tel: 04-845533. Gym, jetskiing, windsurfing, tennis and beach.

AL AIN:
Contact the **Al Ain Hilton** (Tel: 03-686666) or the Inter-Continental (Tel: 03 686686).

FUJAIRAH:
Fujairah Hilton.Tel: 09-222411. Gym, water sports and beach.
Sandy Beach Motel and Diving Centre. Tel: 09-445050. Good beach, diving.
SHARJAH:

Sharjah Carlton. Tel: 06-283711 Gym, beach and swimming pools.

UMM AL QUWAIN:
Umm Al Quwain Tourist Centre.

Sports Clubs

ABU DHABI
Abu Dhabi Catamaran Association (ADCATS). Tel: 02-433591.
Abu Dhabi Chess Club. Tel: 02-725564
Abu Dhabi Equestrian Club. Tel: 02-455500
Abu Dhabi Golf Club. Tel: 02-463226
Abu Dhabi Rugby Club. Tel: 02-225400
PADI Scuba Diving Club. Tel: 790643 (pager)

DUBAI:
Archery. Tel: 04-442591.
Diving.Tel: 04-440389.
Dubai Creek Golf and Yacht Club.Tel: 04-821000.
Dubai Equestrian Club. Tel: 04-361 394.
Dubai Golf and Racing Club. Tel: 04-363666.
Emirates Golf Club. Tel: 04-480222.
Fishing. Tel: 04-846111.
Flying. Tel: 04-883326.
Go-karting. Tel: 04-388828.
Jebel Ali Equestrian Club. Tel: 04-845566.
Jebel Ali Shooting Club. Tel: 04-836555.
Jet Skiing. Tel: 04-342031.
Parasailing. Tel: 04-480000.
Rugby. Tel: 04-331198.
Sailing. Tel: 04-381669.
Sand Surfing. Tel: 04-666666.
Squash. Tel: 04-824122.

Shopping

Where to Shop

Goods from all over the world come to the UAE, and the choice is huge. You can go to the souqs full of small shops packed to the roof with general goods and electronics, or shop in the huge shopping malls for designer clothing or antiques from all over the world. Prices are very competitive. Bargaining is expected in the souqs, but in the shopping malls prices are usually fixed.The cities of Abu Dhabi, Dubai and Sharjah are the best for shopping malls and high-quality goods. Ajman and Ras Al Khaimah are unlikely to have anything you can't get in the major centres.

The Duty-Free complexes at the airports are some of the best in the world. The selection is huge and there are discounts, so if you cannot find a gift while in town, you will probably find something there. The largest are Dubai, Abu Dhabi and the newest shop at Al Ain (*see* Duty Free Bonanza, *page 237*).

Opening Hours

During the week (Saturday to Thursday), shops are open from 8.30/9.30am–1pm and 4/4.30–7.30/8.30pm. Some shops close for half a day on Thursday. There are often late-night shopping evenings. The shopping malls are generally open 10am–10pm/ midnight Saturday to Thursday. Most shops close on Fridays.

Export Procedures

If you want to export your purchases there are hundreds of companies who will advise on procedures and arrange for your goods to be sent anywhere in the world. It is best to seek advice from your hotel or a tour operator who will tell you a reliable company to use.

Complaints

Usually, faulty bought goods are easily exchanged at the shop of purchase, so always keep receipts and ask to see the manager if there is a problem. Shopkeepers are generally very keen to have happy customers.

Abu Dhabi

SOUQS:

Central Souq. East Street near the Central Post Office.
More than 400 shops and a floor of gold and jewellery. Will replace the old Main Souq.
Main Souq. From Hamdan Street to below Khalifa Street. Pedestrian avenues lead into squares which lead into a warren of small shops crammed with all kinds of goods ranging from gold, jewellery, electronics, household appliances and almost anything you could want to buy.
Fish and Vegetable Souq. Across from Airport Road, between Istiqlal and Al Nasr streets.
Built in traditional Islamic style, but with modern air-conditioning so the produce remains totally fresh.
Carpet Souq. Mina Road towards the port area.
Mainly machine-made copies of carpets. Also some handmade Afghani carpets. For Persian carpets go to a speciality shop.

JEWELLERY:

Many jewellers are to be found in the Main Souq on Khalifa Street,
but the main shops are actually on Khalifa Street and Hamdan Street:
Al Fardan Jewellery. Tel: 02-330330. Hamdan Street, opposite Pizza Hut.
Al Manara Jewellery. Tel: 02-275121. Hamdan Street, opposite BHS.
Al Masaood Jewellery. Tel: 02-337800. Khalid bin Waleed Street, opposite Old Fort.
Blue Sky. Tel: 02-727124. Hamdan Street next to Optical Centre.
Tiffany. Tel: 02-323717. Khalid bin Waleed Street, behind Old Fort.

ANTIQUES, CARPETS AND GIFTS:

Antiques House. Tel: 02-346633 Al Nasr Street, next to Budget Rent-a-Car. Iranian silver, antiques and old stamps.
Casablanca. Tel: 02-37885. Hamdan Street, Hamdan Centre. Brassware and antiques.
Gulf Antiques Exhibition. Tel: 02-764956. Tourist Club Area, opposite ADMA-OPCP. Artefacts, carpets, silver.
Iranian & Pakistani Carpet and Antiques. Tel: 02-328875. Hamdan Street, opposite Al Youssef Centre.
Oriental Carpet House and Antiques. Tel: 02-322459. Al Nasr Street, next to Al Masaood Travel.
Persian Carpets and Antiques Exhibition. Tel: 02-663735. Khalidia Street, Rotana Mall.
Red Sea Handmade Carpets and Artefacts. Tel: 02-776704. Hamdan Street behind Al Noor Hospital.

PERFUME:

Areej X. Tel: 02-766677. Hamdan Street, Hamdan Centre.

Dubai

Dubai is world-famous for shopping, and hosts an annual Shopping Festival when people visit from around the world to shop for bargains.

What to Buy

Carpets are brought here from all over Asia, and vary in price from reasonable to very expensive. It is wise not to buy anything too expensive without some knowledge, or without someone who understands about carpets. There are good selections in Abu Dhabi, Dubai and especially in Sharjah.
Old silver jewellery is becoming hard to find. Omani and heavy Indian Rajasthani silver is available but it isn't cheap.
Gold is good value. The selection is enormous, especially in Dubai, which has the largest gold souq. If you do want to treat yourself (or someone else), this is the place to come. The souq is very well regulated and standards are high. All gold is genuine, and not much is sold below 18 carat. The local tastes are for 22 and 24 carat gold. Old gold can be traded for new, but no consideration of workmanship is made. A cheaper rate is paid for secondhand goods.
Saffron is cheap in the spice souqs, and comes in many qualities. All sort of other spices are sold from sacks, and shops are lined with small jars of exotic ingredients.
Perfume, famous throughout Arabia, is worth buying just to visit the perfume shops, sit on cushions and smell the scents from all the decanters. A unique purchase is the scented wood or *oud* for burning in incense burners.
Dried nuts and fruits are cheap and make good presents.
Arabic coffee is sold everywhere, including cardamom-flavoured coffee, as well as the uniquely shaped coffee pots.

Souqs:

Bur Dubai Souq

There is no central Bur Dubai souq but the area of shops known as Bur Dubai Souq is across the creek from Deira Souq. It includes Al Fahidi Street (good-value electronics) and Cosmos Lane (huge array of fabrics), behind the museum, .

Deira Covered Souq

Within this area lies the Spice Market and the Gold Souq which are very close together on the Deira side of the creek near to the Saint George Hotel. From the Bur Dubai side of the creek it can be reached by taking an abra from the stand near the British Bank. Get out and walk straight ahead from the abra stand on the Deira side.

Fish Market

There are two fish markets. One is near to the British Bank in Bur Dubai, the other – older and larger – is near the Shindagha Tunnel opposite the Hyatt Hotel. This is huge and well worth a visit early in the morning. You will find a vast variety of fish and a wonderful bustling atmosphere. There are also women selling local handicrafts (baskets, incense burners and woven mats) towards the outer edge of the souq area.

Fruit and Vegetable Market

Located next to the main fish market. Piles and piles of fresh produce.

SHOPPING AREAS:

Al Diyafah Street

Satwa High Street.

Full of fast food restaurants, cafés and small boutiques. Attracts lots of young people in the evenings. Leads towards the Satwa Roundabout next to the Plaza Hotel and into a local shopping area full of interesting small shops.

Al Fahidi Street

Near Astoria Hotel, Bur Dubai. Centre of electronics and very lively in the evenings. Good prices.

Karama

Near World Trade Centre, Bur Dubai.

A huge network of shops with good-value clothing, bamboo furniture and a small fish and vegetable souq in the middle. Interesting and cheap area.

SHOPPING MALLS:

Al Ghurair Centre, Al Rigga Street, Deira.

Al Mulla Plaza, Sharjah Road.

Beach Centre, Beach Road, Jumeira.

Bur Juman Centre, Trade Centre Road, Bur Dubai.

City Centre, near Clocktower Roundabout, Deira.

Hamarain Centre, next to the J.W. Marriott Hotel, Deira.

Jumeira Plaza, pink mall on the Jumeira Beach Road.

Magrudy Shopping Mall, Beach Road, Jumeira.

Markaz Al Jumeira, Beach Road, Jumeira.

The Centre, near Dubai Cinema, Deira.

Wafi Centre, near Al Wasl Hospital.

ANTIQUES, CARPETS AND GIFTS:

Citadel Antiques. Tel: 04-389215. Service road parallel to the main Abu Dhabi Road. Turn off at Safa Roundabout and go past Pepsi. Beautiful wrought-iron furniture, mirrors and plant pots.

Heritage. Tel: 04-493568. Jumeira Plaza, Beach Road in Jumeira. Full of UAE gift items, prints and locally produced greetings cards. There is another branch upstairs in this mall selling furniture and Omani silver.

Le Sablon Antiques and Gifts. Tel: 04-389193. Al Safa Centre, Al Wasl Road near to Park and Shop Supermarket. English curios and furniture, antiques from other countries.

Red Sea Carpets. Tel: 04-443949. Upstairs at the Beach Centre, Jumeira. Ethnic carpets and artefacts.

Sharjah

A good place to buy Persian carpets. Sharjah is famous for its two main souqs.

Blue or Central Souq

Next to Sharjah Creek.

Two huge blue domed buildings full of shops, mainly selling ordinary things on the ground floor, but upstairs full of carpet shops, and curios.

Old Souq

Behind Bank Street.

Restored area near the Corniche. Old trading houses full of small antique shops selling artefacts and Indian furniture from Rajasthan. Worth visiting. Has an excellent coffee house.

East Coast

Just outside Masafi is an open-air pottery market. This makes a pleasant stopping point on the road to Fujairah and the east coast

Armchair Travel

History & Reference

From Trucial States to United Arab Emirates, Frauke Heard-Bey, published by Longmans. Covers all aspects of the UAE.
This Strange Eventful History, Edward Henderson, published by Motivate. Memoirs of a long-term resident of the UAE. A good account of how the country evolved.
A History of the Arab People, A. Hourani. Excellent general introduction to the peoples of the region. Faber and Faber
The Arabs, Peter Mansfield. Broad history of the Middle East, and look at its current politics.
The Origins of the United Arab Emirates, Rosemarie Said Zahlan. Short history of the country, now slightly dated.
Myth of Arab Piracy in the Gulf, Sultan Muhammed Al Qasimi, Ruler of Sharjah. A detailed account of how the UAE Arabs met and skirmished with the British of India in the 18th and 19th centuries.
Rashid, The Man Behind Dubai, Abbas Abdullah Makki. A very readable memoir of Dubai just before oil was found in quantity.
From Rags to Riches, A Story of Abu Dhabi, Mohammed Al Fahim. A reminiscence by one of the UAE's leading businessmen of how he started as a small boy with no education or wealth.
Inside the Arab World, Michael Field. One of the best analyses of the politics of the Arab world. A very useful read.
The Trucial States, D. Hawley. A historical perspective by a British ex-diplomat.
Arabia, The Gulf and the West, J.B. Kelly. A long history of the centuries of dealings between the West and the Gulf peoples.
Oil and Development in the Gulf, K.&A. McLachlan. A solid economic and political review.
Historical Dictionary of the Gulf Arab States, M.C. Peck. A detailed list of names, places and incidents. A reference book for the serious student of Arab affairs. Not an easy read.
The Wind of Morning, Colonel Sir Hugh Boustead. An autobiography of the extraordinary British soldier who ended his career serving in Abu Dhabi, and retired to run the ruler of Abu Dhabi's stables.
Oman: A Seafaring Nation, W. Facey, Ministry of Heritage and Culture.
Oman and Its Renaisance, D. Hawley, published by Stacey International.
Wings Over the Gulf, Shirley Kay. A history of civil aviation in the Gulf from the early 1920s.
Seafarers of the Gulf, Shirley Kay, published by Motivate. A chronicle of the importance of the sea in the history of the Gulf.
Oman and Muscat, An Early Modern History, P. Risso, published by Croom Helm.
Travels to Oman, Ronald Codrai, published by Motivate. Diary extracts and photographs of Oman at mid-century.
Forts of Oman, W. Dinteman, published by Motivate. Pictorial account of the role of the fort in Oman's history.

Business

Dubai: The City of Opportunities. A Comprehensive Manual on Investment Opportunities in Dubai.
Dubai - Rules and Procedures, Dubai Chamber of Commerce and Industry. Aimed specifically at the serious business person.
Setting Up in Dubai, Essam Al Tamimi. A very reader-friendly guide to setting up in the UAE. An important guide to the first timer, and long-term resident.
The GCC Economic Databook, Dr

The Gulf War

Guardians of the Gulf, Michael A. Palmer. Traces US and British involvement in the area back to 18th century.
An Arabian Affair, Munro. The British ambassador to Saudi Arabia at the time of the Gulf War, gives his views on the handling of the war.
Looking for Trouble, General Sir Peter de la Billière. The British commander in the Gulf campaign reviews the war.
Storm Command, General Sir Peter de la Billière. Portrait of a commander and a chronicle of the Gulf war.
Oil and Politics, the Post-War Gulf, P. Stevens. A reliable account of the post-war Gulf.
Days of Fear, John Levins. Inside story of the Iraqi invasion and occupation of Kuwait.

R. Edwards & A. Butter, published by Motivate. Invaluable statistics and analysis which are very hard to find in any other book.

People & Society

Explorers of Arabia, Z. Freeth and V. Winstone. Profiles of important early travellers.
The Merchants, Michael Field. Focusing on nine of the Gulf's prominent families, gives a good impression of how society has changed since oil.
The New Arabians, Peter Mansfield. A wide-ranging look at post-oil Gulf society by one of the most respected writers on the region. Sadly, it stops in the early 1980s.
Understanding Arabs: A Guide for Westerners, M. K. Nydell. Easy to read. General understanding.
The Bedouin, Shirley Kay. Traditions surrounding marriage and childbirth, tribal and social structures in the UAE.

Oman Before 1970, Ian Skeet. A sympathetic portrait of pre-oil Oman, giving a wealth of social detail which is still relevant today in traditional Omani society.

Culture Shock - The UAE, Gina L Crocetti. Useful guide to customs and etiquette.

Travelling the Sands, Andrew Taylor, published by Motivate. Explorers of the Arabian Peninsula.

Heart-beguiling Araby - The English Romance with Arabia, Kathryn Tidrick.

Women

Mother Without a Mask, Patricia Holton, published by Motivate. A personal account from a Western woman who lived with UAE family.

The Hidden Face of Eve, Nawal El Saadawi. Introduction to understanding women in the Muslim world by leading female Arab writer.

The Women of the United Arab Emirates, Linda U Soffan.

Women at Work, Mohammed A. Nour. Historical position of women in the Middle East.

Arab Women: Old Boundaries, New Frontiers, J.E. Tucker. Collection of women's writing.

Women of Sand and Myrrh, Hannah Al Shaykh. Collection of women's stories.

Women in Oman, Unni Wikkan. Quite academic but a good book on Gulf customs and traditions, and women's role in rural society.

Falconry

Falconry in Arabia, Mark Allen. Well-written and all-embracing.

Falconry and Birds of Prey in the Gulf, Dr David Remple and Christian Gross, published by Motivate. Good photographs and excellent insight.

Horses

Return to Our Heritage, Guide to History of Racing & Equestrianism in UAE, edited by Martin Lees.

Coffee-table Books

Images of Women - The Portrayal of Women in Photography in the Middle East 1860–1950, Sarah Graham-Brown.

A Day Above the Emirates, John Nowell, published by Motivate. Stunning aerial photography of the UAE.

A Day Above Oman, John Nowell, published by Motivate. Stunning aerial photography of Oman.

Behind the Veil in Arabia – Photography of Kamil Chadirfi 1920-1940. Social photographs.

The Seven Shaikhdoms, Ronald Codrai, published by Motivate. Collection of photographs of the UAE.

One Second in the Arab World, 50 years of Photographic Memoirs, Ronald Codrai. Photographic history.

Dubai - An Arabian Album, Ronald Codrai, published by Motivate. Diary extracts and mid-century photographs.

Abu Dhabi – An Arabian Album, Ronald Codrai, published by Motivate. Diary extracts and mid-century photographs.

Sharjah and the North East Shaikhdoms - An Arabian Album, Ronald Codrai, published by Motivate. Mid-century photographs of the area.

The Emirates, Kevin Higgins. Easy-to-read commentary with glossy photographs of the UAE.

The British in the Middle East, Sarah Searight.

The Arabian Desert, John Carter. Ecology of the desert including both plant and animal life.

Bedouin, Alan Keohane, published by Motivate. Photographs of bedouin tribes.

The Emirates by The First Photographers, William Facey and Gillian Grant.

The UAE Formative Years, 1965–75. A Collection of Historical Photographs, R Shukla.

Visions of a Nomad, W. Thesiger. Thesiger's photographs taken over 50 years.

Thirty Years in the Life of Abu Dhabi, Noor Ali Rashid. Well-known UAE photographer.

The UAE: A History in the Making, Noor Ali Rashid. Photographs from 1958 to present day.

The Oasis, Gertrude Dyck. Her life in Al Ain centred on Oasis Hospital during the last 30 years.

Sharjah – Heritage and Progress, Shirley Kay, published by Motivate. Photographic introduction.

Fujairah – An Arabian Jewel, Peter Hellyer, published by Motivate. Portrait of the east coast.

Portrait of Ras Al Khaimah, Shirley Kay, published by Motivate. Interesting account of the history and progress of this emirate.

Food

The Complete Middle East Cookbook, Tess Mallos. Contains etiquette and customs.

The Complete UAE Cookbook, Celia Ann Brock-Al Ansari. Recipes from the area, customs and traditions. Glossy with photographs.

A New Book of Middle Eastern Food, Claudia Roden. Interesting and easy to use.

Traditional Dishes of Arabian Gulf, Dr Abdul Rahman O. Musaiger. Small but useful book.

Archaeology

Looking for Dilman, Geoffrey Bibby. Useful for linking UAE with the rest of the region. Emphasis is on Bahrain.

The United Arab Emirates, Dr Muhammed Abdul Nayeem. A comprehensive study of the

earliest civilisation in the area, with many illustrations.
Atlantis of the Sands: The Search for the Lost City of Ubar, R. Fiennes, Bloomsbury. Archaeological discovery in southern Oman.

Islam

Mohammedanism - An Historical Survey, H.A.R. Gibb. A dated but still valid general introduction to Islam.
The Koran Interpreted, A.J. Arberry. For those wanting to understand the Koran.
The Koran (with parallel Arabic text), N.J. Dawood. An invaluable translation.
Islam and the West, Bernard Lewis. A view on the relationship by the Professor of Arabic at Edinburgh University.

Travel Writing/ Novels

Arabian Sands, Wilfred Thesiger. Journeys made 1945–1950 in and around the Empty Quarter of Oman, Saudi Arabia and the UAE.
The Wink of the Mona Lisa, Mohammad Al Murr. Twenty-four fictional short stories by a leading UAE writer.
The Marsh Arabs, Wilfred Thesiger. His life with the people of the south Iraqi marshes during 1951–58.
Desert Marsh and Mountain, Wilfred Thesiger, published by Motivate. Recollections and classic photographs.
Arabia Through the Looking Glass, Jonathan Raban. An excellent and amusing overview of the different Gulf and Middle Eastern countries.
Sandstorms –Days and Nights in Arabia, Jonathan Raban. Amusing observations of expatriate life.
Baghdad Without a Map, Tony Horwitz. Journalist reminiscing on travels and working in the Middle East.
Freya Stark in Persia, South

Arabia, Iraq and Kuwait, Malise Ruthyen. A biography of one the greatest British travellers in the remote parts of 20th-century Arabia.
The Southern Gates of Arabia, Freya Stark. The traveller herself telling the fascinating tale of her time in Yemen.
Dubai Tales, Muhammed Al Murr. Short stories set in Dubai and area.
The Son of a Duck is a Floater, P. Arnander and A. Skipworth. A collection of Arab proverbs and sayings and delightful lighthearted illustrations.

Art & Architecture

Omani Silver, Ruth Hawley. A great book for professional and amateur collectors of Gulf silver.
The Mosque, M. Freshman and Hassan-Uddin Khan. Glossy photographic book of the rich variety of historical and architectural styles in mosques.
Islamic Art, David Talbot Rice. The definitive general study of the subject. Rather academic.
Architectural Heritage of the Gulf, Shirley Kay and Dariush Zandi, published by Motivate. Traditional architectural styles of the UAE.

Arabic Language

Very Simple Arabic, James Peters.
Spoken Arabic Step-by-Step, John Kirkbright, published by Motivate. Language course: two books and four tapes.

Wildlife & Flora

Birds of the UAE, Colin Richardson. Pictures and descriptions.
Birds of Southern Arabia, Dave Robinson and Adrian Chapman, published by Motivate. Photographs and anecdotes.
Gulf Landscapes, Elizabeth Collins and Andrew Taylor, published by Motivate. Geology

and photographs of region.
The Living Desert, Marycke Jongbloed, published by Motivate. A year in the life of the desert.
Mammals of the Southern Gulf, Christian Gross, published by Motivate. Photographic account of the amazing variety of sea life.
The Living Seas, Frances Dipper and Tony Woodward, published by Motivate. Interesting text and brilliant underwater photographs.
Seashells of Eastern Arabia, edited by S. Peter Dance. 1,000 photographs and drawings, features over 1,270 species.
Beachcombers Guide to the Gulf, Tony Woodward, published by Motivate. Useful for anyone interested in knowing more about what they see on the beaches of the Gulf.
The Birds of Oman, Gallagher and Woodcock, published by Quartet Books.
Butterflies of Oman, Larsen, published by Bartholomew.
Arabia: Sand, Sea, Sky, M. McKinnon, published by BBC Books and Immel Publishing.
Snorkelling and Diving in Oman, Baldwin and Salm, published by Motivate. Maps and descriptions of the best places to enjoy Oman's ocean life.

Off-Road Driving

Off-Road in the Emirates 1, Dariush Zandi, published by Motivate. Fifteen detailed maps and routes, with tips. Spiral bound with photographs.
Off-Road in the Emirates 2, Dariush Zandi, published by Motivate. Twelve more routes.
Off-Road in Oman, Klein and Brickson, published by Motivate. Detailed routes and maps .

Golf

On Course in the Gulf, Adrian Flaherty. Guide to the game on grass and sand. Directory of golf courses throughout AGCC.

Language

In the UAE, local nationals make up just under 20 percent of the population, so most of the people you're likely to meet there will not be local Arabs, and may well not speak Arabic. Either Hindi or Urdu is spoken by the 60 percent of the population who are Indian or Pakistani. There are also many Arabs in the UAE who are not from the Gulf area, and the Arabic they speak is different from the local Gulf Arabic. However, you may find it helpful to know a few Arabic words and phrases, including some from the local dialect.

In Oman there is also an interesting mix of nationalities, but Gulf Arabic is spoken by a much larger proportion of the population than in the UAE

Greetings

Hello or **Welcome**/*Márhaba, ahlan*
(reply)/*áhlayn*
Greetings/*As-salám aláykum* (peace be with you)
(reply)/*Waláykum as-salám* (and to you peace)
Good morning/*Sabáh al-kháyr*
(reply)/*Sabáh an-núr* (a morning of light)
Good evening/*Misá al-kháyr*
(reply)/*Misá an núr*
Good night/*Tisbáh al-kháyr* (wake up well)
(reply)/*Wa ínta min áhlu* (and you are from His people)
Good bye/*Máa Saláma*
How are you?/*Káyf hálak?* (to a man)/*Káyf hálik?* (to a woman)
Fine, thank you/*Zayn, al-hámdu, li-la*

Please/*min fádlak* (to a man)/*min fádlik* (to a woman)
Come in. Do sit down./*Tefáddal* (to a man)/*Tefáddali* (to a woman)/*Te Afáddalu* (to more than one)
Excuse me/*Samáhli*
Sorry/*Áfwan or mutaásif or ásif* (for a man)/*Áfwan or mutaásifa or ásifa* (for a woman)
Thank you/*Shúkran*
Don't mention it/*Hafwan*
Thanks be to God/*Al-hámdu li-llá*
God willing (hopefully)/*Inshá allá*
Yes/*Náam or áiwa*
No/*La*
Congratulations!/*Mabrúck!*
(reply)/*Alláh yubárak fik*

Useful Phrases

What is your name?/*Shú ismak?* (to a man)/*Shú ismik?* (to a woman)
My name is.../*Ismi...*
Where are you from?/*Min wáyn inta?* (for a man)/*Min wáyn inti?* (for a woman)
I am from: England/*Ána min Ingíltra*
Germany/*Ána min Almánia*
the United States/*Ána min Amérika*
Australia/*Ána min Ustrália*
Do you speak English?/*Btíhki inglízi?*
I speak: English/*Bíhki inglízi*
German/*Almámi*
French/*Fransáwi*

Pronunciation

a/as in/look
í/as in/see
ya/as in/Soraya
ai/as in/eye
ay/as in/may
aw/as in/away
kh/as in the Scottish/loch
gh/as in the Parisian/r
dh/as in/the

Double consonants: try to pronounce them twice as long. An apostrophe ' indicates a glottal stop.

I do not speak Arabic/*Ma bíhki árabi*
I do not understand/*Ma báfham*
What does this mean?/*Shu al malana*
Repeat, once more/*Kamán márra*
Do you have...?/*Ándkum...?*
Is there any...?/*Fí...?*
There isn't any.../*Ma fí...*
Never mind/*Ma'alésh*
It is forbidden.../*Mamnú'a*
Is it allowed...?/*Masmúh...?*
What is this?/*Shú hádha?*
I want/*Uríd*
I do not want/*Mauríd*
Wait/*Istánn* (to a man)/*Istánni* (to a woman)
Hurry up/*Yalla/bi súra'a*
Slow down/*Shwáyya*
Finished/*Khalás*
Go away!/*Imshi!*
What time is it?/*Adáysh as-sáa?/kam as-sáa?*
How long, how many hours?/*Kam sáa?*

Vocabulary

GENERAL

embassy/*safára*
post office/*máktab al-baríd*
stamps/*tawábi'a*
bank/*bank*
hotel/*otél/fúnduq*
museum/*máthaf*
ticket/*tádhkara*
ruins/*athár*
passport/*jiwáz as-sáfar*
good/*kuwáys*
not good, bad/*mish kuways*
open/*maftúh*
closed/*musákkar/múghlik*
today/*al-yáum*
tonight/*allaylah*
tomorrow/*baachir*

EATING OUT/DRINKING

restaurant/*máta'am*
food/*ákl*
fish/*simich*
meat/*láhm*
milk/*halíb*
bread/*khúbz*
salad/*saláta*
delicious/*ladhidh*
coffee/*káhwa*
tea/*chai*

cup/*finján*
with sugar/*bi súkkar*
without sugar/*bidún súkkar*
mineral water/*mái ma'adaniya*
glass/*gelaas*
bottle/*zajaja/botel*
I am a vegetarian/*Ána nabbáti*
(for a man)/*nabbátiya* (for a
woman)
the bill/*al-hisáb*

GETTING AROUND
Where...?/*Wáyn...?*
downtown/*wást al bálad*
street/*shária*
Amir Mohammed Street/*Shária
al-amir Mohammed*
car/*sayára*
taxi/*táxi*
shared taxi/*servís*
bus/*bas*
airplane/*tayára*
airport/*matár*
to/*íla*
from/*min*
right/*yamín*
left/*yassar*
straight/*gida*
behind/*wára*
near/*aríb*
far away/*ba'id*
petrol, super/*benzín*

DAYS OF THE WEEK
Monday/*(yáum) al-itnín*

Tuesday/*at-taláta*
Wednesday/*al-árba'a*
Thursday/*al-khamís*
Friday/*al-júma'a*
Saturday/*as-sábt*
Sunday/*al-áhad*

NUMBERS
zero/*sifir*
one/*wáhad*
two/*ithnayn*
three/*taláta*
four/*árba'a*
five/*khámsa*
six/*sítta*
seven/*sába'a*
eight/*tamánia*
nine/*tísa'a*
ten/*áshara*
eleven/*hidáshar*
twelve/*itnáshar*

SHOPPING
market/*souq*
shop/*dukkán*
money/*fulús*
cheap/*rakhís*
expensive (very)/*gháli (jídan)*
receipt, invoice/*fatúra, wásl*
**How much does it
cost?**/*Adáysh?/bi-kam?*
What would you like?/*Shú
bidak?* (to a man)/*Shú bidik?* (to
a woman)/*Shú bidkum?* (to more
than one)

I like this/*Buhíbb hádha*
I do not like this/*Ma buhíbb
hádha*
Can I see this?/*Mumkin ashúf
hádha?*
Give me/*A'atíni*
How many?/*Kam?*

LOOKING FOR A ROOM
a free room/*ghúrfa fádia*
single room/*ghúrfa li-
shakhswahid*
double room/*ghúrfa li-
shakhsayn*
hot water/*mái súkhna*
bathroom, toilet/*hammám,
tuwalét*
shower/*dúsh*
towel/*footah*
**How much does the room cost
per night?**/*Adáysh al-ghúrfa al-
láyl*

EMERGENCIES
I need help/*Bidi Musáada*
doctor/*tabib*
hospital/*mustáhfa*
pharmacy/*saidalíya*
I am ill, sick/*Ana marídh* (for a
man).*Ana marídha* (for a woman)
diarrhoea/*ishál*
operation/*amalíya*
police/*shúrtee*
lawyer/*muhámmi*
I want to see/*Bidi ashúf*

ART & PHOTO CREDITS

Picture Spreads

Maps **Berndtson & Berndtson Publications**
Cartographic Editor **Zoë Goodwin**
Production **Mohammed Dar**
Design Consultants
Klaus Geisler, Graham Mitchener

The World of Insight Guides

Almost 200 companion books to the present title cover every major destination in every continent.

In addition, more than 200 Insight Pocket Guides (with fold-out maps) and Insight Compact Guides are ideal books for on-the-spot use.

Index